FREE CHOICE
A Self-Referential Argument

FREE CHOICE

A Self-Referential Argument

Joseph M. Boyle, Jr.
Germain Grisez
Olaf Tollefsen

UNIVERSITY OF NOTRE DAME PRESS

NOTRE DAME   LONDON

Library of Congress Cataloging in Publication Data

Boyle, Joseph M   1942–
    Free choice.

    Includes bibliographical references and index.
    1. Free will and determinism. I. Grisez, Germain Gabriel, 1929–
joint author. II. Tollefsen, Olaf, 1944– joint author. III. Title.
BJ1461.B684   234'.9   76–645
ISBN 0–268–00940–6

*This book is dedicated
to our teachers and our students,
and to other colleagues
with whom we have philosophized.*

v

Contents

Foreword with Acknowledgments

In this work, we clarify and examine the philosophic controversy over free choice and we attempt to present a sound, self-referential argument for the thesis that human persons can make free choices. The work is addressed primarily to professional philosophers and to serious students. Someone who is already quite familiar with the controversy can understand our own argument without reading chapters two, three, and four. At the same time, a student who wishes to gain some insight into the perennial controversy over free choice might find the first four chapters useful even if chapters five and six are not at present helpful to him. Someone who is interested in the method of self-referential argumentation will find chapter five interesting; the statement of the logic of the method in sections A through D of chapter five can be understood by itself.

Abbreviations and some rather barbarous, technical expressions are used throughout this work. The abbreviations are explained in the introduction. We apologize to our readers for the style we have adopted; we have regularly sacrificed felicity of expression to clarity and precision when we found our skill in exposition inadequate to achieve both values. We considered providing a glossary of our own technical expressions, but have not done so, since several of them are defined in quite complex contexts. However, we have taken care to include our technical expressions in the index, to assist the reader in finding passages in which they are introduced.

Stimulated by his participation in the present collaborative project, Germain Grisez wrote and published an independent work, *Beyond the New Theism: A Philosophy of Religion*. Grisez's work, although published in the spring of 1975, thus presupposes the present work, rather than vice versa. In several notes, Grisez refers to the present work. A reader who tries to follow out these references will meet some difficulty in doing so, since the chapters of this book were rearranged in the final revision, after Grisez's work was published. In one or two cases, material to which Grisez refers no longer appears in the present work, but in most cases the material can be found by checking the table of contents of this book for its new location in the text.

The present project arose out of a conversation in December, 1970. We knew of several previous attempts to apply a self-referential method of argumentation to the controversy over free choice. These attempts seemed limited and unsatisfactory in some respects. (They are discussed in chapter two, section E, of the present work.) We tried to work out a sound, self-referential argument which would be effective against any position which attempts to exclude the human capacity to make free choices.

The first published fruit of this effort was an article, "Determinism, Freedom, and Self-Referential Arguments," which appeared in *The Review of Metaphysics,* 26 (September, 1972). We received a great many reactions to this article and suggestions for important improvements in our effort. Robert Young replied to our article in the same journal, 27 (September, 1973): "A Sound Self-Referential Argument?" These critical reactions made clear to us many defects, both in substance and in presentation, in our initial attempt to articulate the argument.

The present work was planned and drafted, and several times redrafted. Many philosophers have read and commented upon at least some part of one or more of these drafts. We thank the members of the Department of Philosophy, Calvin College, Grand Rapids, Michigan, and also Thomas Flynn, Richard M. Fox, James Gallagher, Ronald Lawler, O.F.M.Cap., John Minahan, Russell Shaw, Henry Veatch, and John Ziegler for their special help. Notre Dame University Press submitted two drafts of the book to a reader whose name we do not know; his critical comments and suggestions were most helpful and significantly guided us in bringing the book to its present structure. Of course, neither he nor others who helped us should be blamed for defects which remain in the work.

Our project received support from many quarters. Aquinas College aided us with two research grants under a program generously funded by the Medora Feehan Charitable and Educational Trust. Campion College, University of Regina, provided a research grant, and the National Endowment for the Humanities a summer stipend. Mount Saint Mary's College, Emmitsburg, Maryland, provided space for work and extensive copying facilities; Capuchin College, Washington, D.C., provided space for work and received us as guests; and Campion College, University of Regina, provided working space and facilities. The library of the University of Regina, in particular the Interlibrary Loan Department, was especially helpful.

Barbara Boyle and Jeannette Grisez typed the early drafts of the work. Jeannette Grisez prepared the final manuscript and assisted with indexing and proof-reading.

We are grateful for all of this support and dedicated assistance, which alone made this collaborative project possible. We also thank our editor, John Ehmann, for his unfailing helpfulness.

September 30, 1975

Joseph M. Boyle, Jr.
College of St. Thomas
St. Paul, Minnesota

Germain Grisez
Campion College, University of Regina
Regina, Saskatchewan, Canada

Olaf Tollefsen
St. Anselm's College
Manchester, New Hampshire

Introduction

The philosophical controversy about free will and determinism is perennial. Like many perennial controversies, this one involves a tangle of distinct but closely related issues. Thus, the controversy is formulated in different ways by different philosophers. At different times in the history of thought the focus of attention has been on different issues.

The issue with which we are concerned in this work emerged most clearly in early modern philosophy. Jewish and Christian religious beliefs about man and moral obligation had shaped an interpretation of the common human experience of making choices. Within the theistic perspective, it seemed evident that whenever a person makes a choice he could equally well choose an alternative other than the one he does. Many early modern philosophers, such as Hobbes and Spinoza, replaced traditional theism with a naturalistic conception of the world and of man. This naturalistic conception became part of the worldview of science and gained increasing plausibility from the progress and fruitfulness of modern science. Within the naturalistic perspective, it seems evident that whenever anything happens, however contingent it might be, what does happen is the only possible outcome of conditions given prior to the event. The state of the world at a given time and the way the world works settles whatever is going to happen in the world at any later time.

As soon as the naturalistic view was applied to human choice the incompatibility between the modern view and the traditional one became evident. Either a person who chooses can equally well choose another alternative, or the alternative he is going to choose is settled prior to his very act of choosing. Philosophers like Hobbes faced this issue squarely and argued for the position—one unpopular at the time—that human choices are no exception to the determinacy of nature.

The heretical thesis of Hobbes is the orthodox position today. So much is this the case that most of the contemporary literature relevant to freedom and determinism is concerned with issues other than that on which Hobbes and his contemporaries concentrated their attention. However, we are as dissatisifed with the position prevalent today as Hobbes and others were with the position prevalent in their day. Thus, in this work we attempt to establish a thesis which few contemporary philosophers regard as defensible: that human persons can make free choices—choices such that only the act of choosing itself settles which alternative a person will choose.

"Freedom" has many other senses, but in this work we are not concerned except incidentally with questions about freedom in these other senses. The question whether someone can make a free choice has implications for morality and law, but in this work we are concerned only incidentally with such implications. Not only philosophers, but also scientists and theologians, have a stake in the controversy over free will and determinism. But in this work we not only concentrate on a single issue—whether someone can make a free choice—but we limit ourselves to philosophic methods of dealing with the issue. Even within the ambit of philosophical inquiry, we almost wholly avoid problems in the philosophy of science and the philosophy of religion. The present work belongs, then, in the field of philosophy of mind or philosophy of action.

In our attempt to show that someone can make a free choice, we use self-referential argumentation. We argue that any affirmation of the thesis that no one can make a free choice is self-refuting. Either the proposition that no one can make a free choice is falsified by any rational affirmation of it, or any attempt to rationally affirm it is self-defeating. The method of the argument we develop is called "self-referential" because the argument works by showing the implications of the *reference* which one who affirms that no one can make a free choice must make *to his own act* of affirming his position.

The following summary will indicate in greater detail what we are attempting in this work.

In chapter one we clarify the controversy. This clarification has two aspects. On the one hand, we define the issue with which we are dealing. There need be nothing tendentious or question-begging in defining an issue; we do not suppose that we settle any substantive question by the way we define the issue. We merely mark out the ground we claim and will defend; such a claim and defense in no way prejudices anyone else's claim to some other ground. On the other hand, we clarify the issue by stating certain facts. Some of these concern meanings of "free," some concern the experience of choice, some concern judgments which people sometimes make on the basis of this experience. None of these facts, so far as we can see, need be denied by any proponent of the thesis contradictory to that which we defend.

In chapter two we examine typical arguments proposed by previous thinkers for the position we defend. Most often arguments have been proposed on the basis of a person's sense of freedom and on the basis of moral responsibility. We find these and other arguments question-begging. Because of our own use of self-referential argumentation, we pay special attention to previous attempts to use this method to refute the thesis that no one can make a free choice. We initially thought that some of these attempts were sound, but critical examination of them forced us to the conclusion that they too are question-begging. However, we believe that self-referential argumentation is not inherently question-begging. We learned much from those who preceded us in trying to use this method.

In chapter three we examine typical arguments proposed by contemporary philosophers and earlier thinkers for the thesis that no one can make a free choice. Many philosophers who propose such arguments have called themselves or have been called "determinists." However, we are interested in all attempts to establish the thesis contradictory to our own, whether or not these attempts involve a general deterministic thesis. Like the arguments we examine in chapter two, those we criticize in chapter three seem to lack cogency. Most of them beg the question; often they do so blatantly. Those which do not beg the question are very weak.

In view of the state of the controversy revealed by our examination of arguments for both sides, we do not think there is any strong presumption, antecedent to our own effort, in favor of either side. Neither side makes a strong case for its position. The contemporary presumption in favor of the thesis that no one can make a free choice is a contingent cultural fact which has no more inherent rational force than did the presumption in favor of our position which prevailed in the time of Hobbes and Spinoza.

Today the most common approach to many of the tangled issues in the controversy over free will and determinism is some sort of attempt to reconcile human freedom with a deterministic worldview. Such attempts are often called "compatibilism." In chapter four we examine several versions of compatibilism. To some extent, compatibilists show that certain apparent issues in the controversy are not real issues. In other words, there are aspects of the complex controversy which require analytic dissolution rather than argumentative resolution. But to some extent compatibilists themselves confuse issues, and the confusion generated by their efforts must itself be dissolved. We try to show that when the fog clears the issue whether or not someone can make a free choice stands on the philosophical scene as mountainous and as solid as ever. An important reason for the irrelevance of compatibilism to the issue with which we are concerned is that compatibilism is mainly concerned with moral and legal responsibility, once it has been assumed that free choice is excluded. We are challenging the assumptions common to compatibilists and to those who maintain without compatibilist qualifications the thesis that no one can make a free choice.

In chapter five we present the method of self-referential argumentation which we use in our attempt to settle the issue whether someone can make a free choice. Although there has been some attention to problems of self-reference in recent years, this topic has been treated in scattered works on other matters. Thus, we give a rather detailed account of the logic of self-reference and of the method of self-referential argumentation. We hope this exposition of our method will forestall objections involving common mistakes and misunder-standings of self-reference and of arguments based on it. In chapter five we also provide some other preliminary clarifications essential to our argument. These concern the affirmation of the thesis that no one can make a free choice—the thesis we try in chapter six to show to be self-refuting. Proponents of this thesis must affirm it if they are to be distinguishable from proponents of our own position. In affirming this thesis, its proponents must assume what we call "rationality norms." A clarification of these norms in the final section of chapter five completes the background for our argument.

Before summarizing the argument we lay out in chapter six, we introduce the following abbreviations which we use throughout the book. "*Sfc*" will name the proposition that someone can make a free choice. "*Nfc*" will name the proposition that no one can make a free choice. These two propositions articulate states of affairs incompatible with each other. According to *Sfc*, there is nothing about the world which precludes a human capacity to make free choices, and at least some persons have this capacity. According to *Nfc*, there is something about the world—about the act of choosing, about human nature, about the natural world, or about the nature of things—which precludes a human capacity to make free choices. A proponent of *Sfc* is anyone who affirms *Sfc*, anyone who thinks the world and human persons to be such that *Sfc* is true or more reasonable to think true than its contradictory. We use "*PSfc*" to name the proponent of *Sfc*. Similarly, we use "*PNfc*" to name the proponent of *Nfc* —that is, anyone who affirms *Nfc*, anyone who thinks the world and human persons to be such that *Nfc* is true or more reasonable to think true than its contradictory. We need a name for the precise issue with which we are concerned, both to make it easy to refer to this controversy and to make it clear that the issue we are considering is distinct from all of the other issues involved in the controversy over free will and determinism. We use "*Sfc/Nfc*" to name the *controversy* between those who hold that someone can make a free choice and those who hold that no one can make a free choice.

Thus, "*Sfc*" and "*Nfc*" name the contradictory propositions which are the positions at issue; "*PSfc*" and "*PNfc*" name the persons, real or imaginary, who defend the respective positions; and "*Sfc/Nfc*" names the controversy over the precise issue with which we are concerned in this work.

We begin our argument in chapter six after having made clear in previous parts of the book that *Nfc* is neither an evident matter of fact nor a logical truth. The *PNfc* cannot rationally affirm his position without offering some grounds for it. He has opponents who are not merely ignorant of facts nor merely without insight into logical necessities. The considerations which the *PNfc* adduces in favor of his position must be relevant to the issue and must have argumentative force. The *PNfc*, then, must assume some norms by appeal to which he can, if challenged, show the relevance and the argumentative force of the grounds he adduces for the position he defends. For example, the *PNfc* might suggest his thesis as a hypothesis which *should be accepted* because *Nfc* is simpler than *Sfc*. The norm in this case is some sort of simplicity rule. Again, the *PNfc* might suggest that *Sfc ought to be rejected* because the notion of free choice is somehow unintelligible. The norm in this case is some sort of principle that whatever is real must be intelligible.

Norms demanding simplicity in explanation and intelligibility in being are not easy to classify. They are neither factual descriptions nor formal truths. Their normativity or prescriptive force is odd. They do not have the normativity of a standard of psychological normality; one cannot simply write off one's philosophical opponents as mentally ill. They do not have the normativity of technical rules which make clear what will be required to achieve some optional goal; one cannot expect one's philosophical opponents to accept the same optional goals one accepts oneself. They do not have the normativity of certain rules of logic—those which cannot be violated without falling into incoherence; one who refuses to accept a conclusion drawn in accord with a rule of simplicity or some version of a principle of intelligibility does not fall into incoherence, even if he is unreasonable. They do not have the normativity of esthetic standards; one cannot refute one's philosophical opponents by showing that they have bad taste.

A *PNfc* maintains that his position is more reasonable unconditionally, and that everyone *ought* to be reasonable enough to accept *Nfc*. Yet he cannot maintain that *Sfc* is impossible, for it is a coherent possibility. Thus the *PNfc*'s affirming of his position depends upon some prescription which directs persons interested in the issue to accept one of two coherent possibilities and which directs with unconditional normative force. Such a prescription presupposes that persons to whom it is given *can* choose the option which is prescribed although some one *might not* choose it. In other words, the norms to which the *PNfc* must at least implicitly appeal when he tries to show that one *ought* to accept his position have no force unless one *can* accept it although one *need not* accept it. Thus, the normativity the *PNfc* needs to justify his own position and to exclude *Sfc* as less reasonable presupposes that some human persons have a capacity to choose freely, for no one can accept the *PNfc*'s demand that he be reasonable—a demand which is unconditional and yet can be rejected without logical absurdity—unless he can make a free choice.

Since a *PNfc*'s very affirmation of his own position implies the demand that one be able to make a free choice, a *PNfc* cannot affirm his position without either falsifying it or asking that an impossible demand be met. If *Sfc* is true and one can meet the *PNfc's* demand, then *Nfc* is false, and the *PNfc's* position is falsified by the demand implicit in the very act of affirming it. If *Sfc* is false and one cannot meet the *PNfc's* demand, then the *PNfc's* act of affirming his position is pointless, for it is pointless to attempt what cannot succeed unless an impossible demand be met.

Since any affirmation of *Nfc* must be either false or pointless, there is in principle no way to exclude *Sfc*. If *Nfc* is false, then its contradictory is true. If any attempt to affirm *Nfc* is pointless, then no one can rationally affirm anything against *Sfc*. Yet there remains the common experience of choice, which grounds a judgment many people make: that they do choose freely. Furthermore, the normativity required to make rational affirmations is a fact, and this fact—unless it is illusory—implies *Sfc*. In this situation, *Sfc* must be affirmed to be true. To refuse to affirm it would be to dismiss the data which support it, although it is in principle impossible to have any rational ground for affirming *Nfc* and dismissing these data.

The preceding summary of this work, especially of its central argument, makes clear the main thing we are trying to accomplish. We are attempting to settle *Sfc/Nfc*, which we consider to be the core issue in one of the most interesting and important perennial philosophical controversies. A reader might wonder why we think we have a chance of success in so ambitious an attempt, when we think so many others have failed. We have several reasons for confidence.

In the first place, we focus on one well-defined issue. We do not try to deal with all the interesting, related questions; we avoid defending more ground than we must. The position we defend, *Sfc*, is modest compared with the position the *PNfc* defends. To maintain *Nfc* is to assume the burden of defending a universal negative proposition excluding in principle a certain capacity, whereas to maintain *Sfc* is only to assume the burden of defending a particular affirmative proposition that a certain capacity exists in some person or other. *Sfc* is considerably less ambitious philosophically than *Nfc*.

In the second place, there is by now a very extensive literature on the issue in which we are interested. Much of this literature has helped to clarify important points. We think that J. L. Austin's work on *ifs* and *cans*, J. R. Lucas's recent book on free will, certain articles of James N. Jordan relevant to free choice and self-reference, and other similar results of work done in the analytic tradition—liberally conceived—make important contributions to the solution of the controversy.

The vast body of work relevant to free choice is so extensive that serious work in this area would have been blocked had there not also been available to us certain comprehensive studies. Mortimer Adler's *Idea of Freedom*, for example, has gathered together and organized materials from the broader controversy. His approach to the material has made it easy to define a precise issue, and has clarified what arguments are relevant to which issues. His work in itself shows the value of the method he used. Our use of his work, we think, shows that Adler's approach also can be fruitful in the way he originally hoped it might be.

In the third place, we are using in the present work the method of self-referential argument. Philosophical controversies consist, we think, largely of question-begging arguments. One escape from question-begging arguments is to accept certain assumptions as unquestionable and to try to develop a science of metaphysics. Another escape is to stay as close as possible to empirical data and to investigate fields which have not yet been preempted by some recognized science. Still another escape is to restrict oneself to analysis and clarification, with the hope of dissolving some insoluble problems.

We regard our own approach as a form of analytic philosophy. But we do think that conclusive argumentation is possible in philosophy. The trick is to find and clarify methods of argumentation which are properly philosophical. We think self-referential argumentation is one such method, and this project is a purposeful attempt to articulate and use this method. Thus, we believe we have a tool which most of our predecessors did not have or did not know precisely how to use.

Rather than talk about the potentiality of self-referential argumentation for resolving important philosophical controversies, in this project we have attempted to discover the power of this method by experiment. The work best shows what the tool can do. However, we did not choose *Sfc/Nfc* as a controversy in which to experiment with self-referential argumentation merely to demonstrate the power of the method. We are also interested in the issue itself. Few other philosophical controversies seem to us so worthy of the effort which must be expended in an attempt to resolve them.

Our interest in *Sfc/Nfc* partly arises out of the importance of the issue to ethics. Since ethics seeks to answer questions about the moral quality of human actions, and since free choice—if it obtains—is a property of certain human acts which conditions all their other properties, one's ethical theory will be distorted if one's position on *Sfc/Nfc* is mistaken. We realize that many hold otherwise: that the truth about free choice makes little or no difference to ethics. We disagree, although we do not argue this point here.

Another motive for our interest in *Sfc/Nfc* is theological and cultural. Judaism and Christianity view the human person as a responsible agent, made in the image of God, capable of making a free choice to accept or to reject God's self-revelation. If *Nfc* is true, this theistic view of the human person makes no sense. Likewise, we believe, the contemporary concern for the autonomy and dignity of the person makes no sense unless *Sfc* is true.

1: Clarification of the Controversy

In this chapter, we clarify the issue with which the remainder of this work is concerned. "Freedom" has many meanings; we begin by distinguishing them, and then formally define "free choice." Next we describe the experience of choice, and show how this experience gives rise to a sense of freedom and leads to the judgment that one is free. We carefully analyze this judgment. Finally, we propose *Sfc/Nfc* as the formulation of the issue with which we shall deal, and explain precisely what we mean by this formulation.

A. Meanings of the word "freedom"

The word "freedom" has several distinct but related and easily confused meanings.[1] We first sort out the meanings other than the one with which we are mainly concerned.

There is no single generic meaning of "freedom." The various meanings of the word do not signify species of a genus. Rather, there is a family of meanings sharing some common elements which themselves shift in sense in various uses of the word.

What are these common elements? At least the following: something acting or behaving, the activity or behavior, and something else which could be, but is not actually, in opposition to the activity or behavior. In the uses of "freedom" applied to persons, the meaning includes someone acting, the activity, and something which in some sense could be, but is not actually, in opposition to the activity.

To distinguish various senses of "freedom," we specify these elements and describe their organization in the various uses of the word.

8

In one sense, "freedom" means physical freedom. In this sense, anything which behaves spontaneously—that is, without external constraint or restraint—can be said to be free.

In this sense of "freedom" even nonorganic entities can be called "free"; one speaks, for example, of "freely falling bodies." Animals also are called "free" in this sense; an animal in the wild is free while one in captivity is not. Similarly, a person who is drugged so that he is in a coma lacks physical freedom. A person can be called "free" in this sense if he acts spontaneously, not being constrained by someone else or restrained by prison bars and chains.

Physical freedom is subject to degree and depends on conditions. The more restrained something is by circumstances, the less room there is for its spontaneous behavior, and the less free it is. Also, the more constrained something is in its behavior, the less its behavior is its own, the less it seems active and the more it seems passive; hence the less free one takes it to be.

In a second sense, "freedom" means freedom to do as one pleases. In this sense, a person is called "free" if there is no one ordering him to do what he does not wish to do or forbidding him to do what he desires to do.

The adolescent demand for freedom from authority is often a demand for freedom in this sense. In this sense of "freedom," a slave, to the extent that he is a slave, is not free. A slave's lack of freedom need not reduce his physical freedom, although this too may be restricted. But a slave lacks freedom precisely in the sense that his action fulfills the demand of another, and only indirectly if at all any desire of his own. Historically, the quest for personal liberty from enslaving institutions also involves a quest for freedom in this sense.

Freedom to do as one pleases is subject to degree; how much of it one enjoys depends on circumstances. The more burdened one is by requirements laid upon him by others, the less scope he has to do as he pleases. The more influential one is in his relations with others, the more scope he has to do as he pleases.

"Freedom" is also used, but less commonly, to signify what we call "ideal freedom." In this sense of "freedom," individuals and societies are said to be "free" if they are not prevented from acting in accord with an ideal, whatever that ideal might be. If one is free in this sense, he has overcome or successfully avoided the obstacles to fulfilling an ideal.

With ideal freedom in mind, St. Paul considered the sinner not to be free, since the sinner is bound by his sin to fall short of the ideal of uprightness. Paul considered Christians free, because their redemption by Christ freed them for uprightness. Similarly, Freud considered the neurotic not to be free. But the cured patient, freed of his neurosis, is able to behave in accord with a psychological ideal.

One has ideal freedom if he is not blocked in efforts to do as he ought to do.

Often, what one ought to do and what one would like to do are opposed to each other. However, most ideals for human behavior are proposed with the expectation that, at some point, doing as one pleases and doing as one ought will coincide.

Ideal freedom has as many varieties as there are diverse conceptions of the ideal condition of the person and diverse views of the obstacles to be faced in fulfilling the ideal. One way of conceiving the ideal human condition is as a perfect society, such as Marx's ideal community. Ideal freedom in this case cannot be attained by isolated individuals but only by society as a whole. Yet the general concept of ideal freedom remains the same: persons have it when they *can* act as they ideally *would* act.

Another unfamiliar concept can be expressed by "freedom"—the emergence of novelty. This freedom obtains when factors which tend toward repetition are overcome.

The creative artist may be called "free" in this sense because he introduces something new and is not merely repeating previous accomplishments. Some philosophers have regarded the whole of reality as an ongoing process—rather like the creative process of art—in which novelties regularly emerge. Such philosophies admit an element of indeterminism in nature and do not reduce emerging novelties to antecedent conditions and their laws.

Freedom as emergence of novelty is distinct from physical freedom, because physical freedom is defined by the given spontaneity of the entity in question, whereas freedom as emergence of novelty can involve the emergence of a new spontaneity. Freedom to do as one pleases can be as repetitive and noncreative as one's desires happen to be, whereas freedom as emergence of novelty can involve an emergence of new desires. Ideal freedom presupposes a given principle in accord with which action should proceed; freedom as emergence of novelty can involve the creation of novel principles and the emergence of new ideals.[2]

In one sense, "political freedom" means a version of freedom to do as one pleases which applies to nations. In this sense, a country is said to be "free" when it is not subject to the rule of some other country. Nations, like individuals, can be bound in slavery or can enjoy liberty.

But there are other senses of "political freedom." In one of these, "freedom" means the participation of individuals in governing their own polity. There is political freedom of this sort in a nation to the extent that factors which would inhibit such participation are excluded. In this sense, children are not politically free. In Western liberal democracies, practically all adults are, at least to some extent. "Political freedom" can be used to refer to the social analogues of the referents of other senses of "freedom" previously distinguished.

B. "Free choice" defined

The word "freedom" also can be used to refer to freedom of choice. Since this work is concerned with *Sfc/Nfc*, we have distinguished other meanings of "freedom" mainly in order to forestall confusion. In this section, we define what we mean by "free choice" as it occurs in "Someone can make a free choice." We do not consider our definition of "free choice" arbitrary for we think that our use of the expression is the same as some uses of it in ordinary language. Moreover, the definition we propose captures the essentials of the experience on the basis of which people often think their choices are free. This experience will be articulated in sections C through F.

Someone makes a free choice if and only if he makes a choice (C) in the actual world, and there is a possible world such that he does not make C in this possible world and everything in this possible world except his making C and the consequences of his making C is the same as in the actual world.[3]

The following remarks will clarify the meaning and implications of this definition.

If a choice is free the causal conditions for that choice are such that they would also be the conditions for not making that choice except insofar as these conditions include the person's very choosing itself and the consequences of his choice. Thus, a choice's being free is consistent with its having *necessary* causal conditions other than the choice itself; such necessary causal conditions would be called "causes of the choice" provided that "cause" not be taken to mean "sufficient condition."

Normally, one chooses not merely to do an act or not to do it, but to do one act or another. Obviously, the two positive possibilities do not share all the same necessary conditions. However, one can choose either only insofar as the necessary conditions of both are given—or, at least, expected to be given. The two alternatives have a common set of conditions necessary for either of them being chosen—the person about to choose must be interested in both, must be aware of both, must regard the joint realization of the two as impossible. The person's very choosing—if choice is free—makes the difference in that all other conditions necessary for carrying out both alternatives being given—or expected—and all other necessary conditions for choosing either being given, one's very choosing is the only factor which brings it about that one alternative rather than the other is pursued.

Moreover, on our definition, a free choice would not be a chance event. Its causally sufficient condition could be specified: the necessary conditions other than the choice together with a person's very choosing. Choosing is not a wholly isolated event; it is something a person does.[4]

Partly for this reason, a number of philosophers have suggested that free choice would involve a special mode of causality: "non-occurrent causation" (C. D. Broad), "agent causality" (Richard Taylor and Roderick Chisholm), "self-determinism" (Frederick Ferré), and so forth.[5] If the proposal that free choice would involve a special mode of causality means that prior to his very choosing a person somehow determines the choice he makes—for instance, because of his unique personality—then such a proposal is incompatible with our definition. However, if the proposal is intended to mean that persons make choices and that the causality of choice-making cannot be reduced to the causality which obtains between events, then this proposal is consistent with our definition.

Some philosophers describe the freedom of free choice as "contracausal." We regard this locution as unfortunate because it suggests that choosing freely is not itself a mode of causing but rather a mysterious interference with a determinate and mechanistic course of nature. This assumption in turn suggests that if a free choice were to occur, it would be a miraculous event—a violation of what is physically necessary.

It has often been said that "free choice" means that a person who has made a certain choice "could have done otherwise." This expression can be used to mean that one would have done otherwise had conditions been different; used thus, "could have done otherwise" does not indicate free choice. But this expression sometimes is used to mean that one could have done otherwise under the very same conditions. Used in this way, "could have done otherwise" does indicate free choice, for it refers retrospectively and contrary to fact to a possibility which prospectively was as reas as the alternative in fact chosen.[6]

If the choice is free, there is in it a creative novelty such that no conjunction of relevant causal laws and any set of true propositions describing states of affairs obtaining prior to the choice entails the proposition that this choice is made. Moreover, such a choice can alter the subsequent course of events and thus introduce further unpredictability.[7]

"Free choice" as we have defined it is not synonymous with some uses of "free will." The expression "free will" is commonly used in contexts such as, "He did not do it under compulsion but of his own free will," where "free will" refers to physical liberty or to the freedom to do as one pleases rather than to free choice.

The definition of free choice, it should be noted, does not entail the possibility of the execution of one's choice. Freedom in other senses sometimes is a necessary condition for executing one's choice. Bertrand Russell once remarked that although we can do as we please, we cannot please as we please.[8] Our point here is that *if* there are free choices then we can choose as we choose even if it turns out that we cannot do as we choose.

C. Choice—what it is not

We must next describe a distinctive way in which someone is said to "make a choice."[9] The expression is used in the relevant sense in the sentence: "John made a choice to join the Peace Corps." In this experience, we think, are to be found the phenomena which give rise to the conviction that people make free choices. Of course, the mere fact that someone has an experience which leads him to judge that he makes free choices does not of itself guarantee the reality of such freedom.

The experience we are concerned with often is called "making up one's mind" or "decision." "Choice" and "decision" and "making up one's mind" have other uses. "Choice" sometimes refers to overt behavior—for example, taking a certain french pastry from a tray. Such picking of one object from an available set of objects may or may not involve the experience of choice in which we are interested. "Decision" sometimes refers to an act which is essentially cognitive—for example, a literary critic decides that Shakespeare indeed wrote "Hamlet." The experience of making such a judgment is not an experience of choosing what to do. The expression "to make up one's mind" also is sometimes used in an essentially cognitive sense. This expression, however, brings out the reflexive character of the activity we are going to describe. The same aspect of the experienced activity is emphasized by certain expressions in other languages, for example, by the French, "Je me décide."

For brevity's sake, we refer to the experience with which we are concerned simply as "choice."

Choice is not a theoretical construct, but is a phenomenon which can be described. There are, however, certain related phenomena which must be distinguished from choice. These include being interested, wishing, and behaving.

One is interested in anything of which he is aware and which makes a practical difference to him. Interest can be prior to choice. One must be interested in at least two different possibilities before any question of choice arises.

"Wishing" does not indicate an indeterminacy to be settled. It is often used in contexts in which there is some obstacle in the way of effective action. Wishing can precede deliberation and choice, and then the obstacle to action can be the need to choose how to act for that for which one wishes. Wishing also can follow choice, as when one finds a chosen course of action blocked but still wishes for the attainment of that for which he had chosen to act. Then too, one can wish for what he thinks is simply unattainable; such wishing neither precedes nor follows choice but is irrelevant to it.

Behavior which comes about by choice is obviously distinct from choice. It is possible to choose to do something and then to discover that one cannot do what one had chosen to do. For example, one can make up his mind to take an automobile trip but be prevented from doing so by lack of gasoline. The distinction between choice and behavior is clear from their separation in such cases.

Besides the experiences of interest, wishing, and behavior, there are also certain experiences of being drawn into action without deliberation. These are not experiences of choice; they must be distinguished from it. There are various such experiences.

One may feel an overwhelming need which cannot be resisted—for example, a starving man may feel an overwhelming need to eat, so that when food becomes available he eats it without hesitation. A person under torture may resist for a time, but, finally, overcome by his agony, blurt out information which is sought. In such cases, one does not choose to act; one is driven to act. No making of a choice is experienced; in fact, the experience can be one of being compelled to act contrary to what one had chosen to do.

There are also many cases in which one's behavior follows an impulse without reflection or hesitation. For example, as one is reading he becomes aware that he is thirsty, and as he comes to the end of a section goes for a drink. If someone were to ask why he behaved thus, he might reply: "I just felt like it; I felt thirsty." This reason was not a ground for choosing to drink rather than not to drink. Rather, he was aware of no alternative. Given the motive, without awareness of anything opposing, one acts without hesitation.

Experiences of acting in accord with a habitual pattern of behavior are very common. For example, one gets up in the morning, dresses, has breakfast, and sets off for work—all without hesitation, deliberation, and choice. The habitual pattern perhaps was established by choices at some more or less remote time in the past, and the habitual pattern could perhaps be altered if one reflected upon it and saw any reason to alter it. However, as the habitual behavior pattern is usually carried out, it simply does not involve any choices at all.

Acting in accord with overwhelming need, acting spontaneously, and acting habitually must be distinguished from acting upon choice. Choice follows hesitation and indecision. One must make up one's mind because it is unmade; it is in some disarray.

The preceding attempt to distinguish choice from related experiences can be challenged by two objections. On the one hand, a behaviorist might object that talk about "experiences" such as choice is misleading and question-begging in the present context. On the other hand, a phenomenologist might object that our attempt to distinguish choice from related experiences vastly oversimplifies the complexity of concrete experience.

We answer the behaviorist objection first. The distinction we have made by referring to experience could be made equally well for our purposes by referring to linguistic behavior. The distinct uses of such expressions as "choosing" and "wishing" as well as ordinary uses of such expressions as "I freely chose to do *x*" and "I made up my own mind to do *x*" are data of a sort which the behaviorist must admit.

To the phenomenologist's objection we respond that experience is indeed more complex than our brief descriptions suggest. However, despite the great richness of experience, we maintain that experience does include at least some clear-cut examples of deliberation, choice, wish, and so on, of which the descriptions we propose, so far as they go, are correct.

D. An example of choice

A young man receives a notice to report for induction into the army. He considers various possibilities. He might leave the country; he might stay in the country but not report for induction; or he might report as the notice requires. Each course of action has potential advantages and disadvantages. If he leaves the country he could live in safety and avoid reporting for induction to serve in a war which he might consider immoral. But this alternative carries the disadvantage of extended, perhaps permanent, exile. If he stays in the country and evades the draft, he avoids both exile and service, but risks imprisonment. If he reports as required, he accepts all the disadvantages of military service, including participation in a military action which he perhaps considers immoral. But if he reports, he preserves his citizenship and avoids the risk of prison. The young man considers the possibilities and makes up his mind, let us suppose, to report for induction.

There are many other examples of choice. A student considers whether to spend an evening at a beer party, or to stay in his room to study for an important test; he makes up his mind one way or the other. Someone considers whether to go out of town for a holiday weekend, or to stay and visit with a friend who will be in town that weekend; he chooses one alternative. A young person considers whether to go into law school, with the idea of entering practice in that profession, or to go on to graduate school and a career in scholarship; he decides for one or the other.

The experience of making choices occurs repeatedly throughout life; it is not unusual.

E. The beginnings of choice

The initial context for choosing is an experienced conflict of desires or interests. If the young man of our example had not felt an aversion both to reporting for induction and to the consequences of refusing to do so, he would not have had to make a choice. The situation opens incompatible possibilities, at least the two possibilities of either acting or refraining from action. Some felt emotion, interest, impulse, or inclination draws him toward each of the alternatives. The conflict leads to hesitation; immediate behavior is blocked. He stops and thinks.

The experience of choice is framed by definite alternatives, each of which presents itself as attractive in one or more ways. Yet each alternative also has its limitations; none promises complete satisfaction. The first stage of the experience of choice is being moved to consider alternatives, rather than simply being drawn by an unopposed motive to act without reflection.

It is important to notice that many factors—of which a person might or might not be aware—limit the alternatives which present themselves. If one's disposition and temperament have been formed in such a way that certain possibilities do not arouse interest, then he will not consider them as alternatives for choice. If one is ignorant of certain possibilities or mistakenly thinks courses of action impossible which in fact are possible, then such alternatives will be excluded from the very beginning. For example, a young person being brought up in unfavorable conditions of poverty and discrimination might be aware of very few possibilities, and his early formation might allow even fewer of these to become live options.

Another important point is that moral conflicts are not the only cases in which choices are called for. Situations requiring "will power" to overcome a temptation against one's moral standard can give rise to deliberation and lead to choice. But moral concerns are only one sort of motive which can give rise to choice situations, and moral conflicts are absent from many such situations.[10] A student choosing between law school and graduate school need not see his option as one between moral good and evil.

The beginnings of choice are present in any situation in which one is unsettled about his own future action. Choice does not concern the actions of others, except insofar as one is acting with them, or they are acting under one's direction. Alternatives must be open, or at least must seem to be open. Choice is concerned with the future, not with the past. The past appears settled, and choice is directly concerned with prospective action. The outcome of the situation is felt to be open only to the extent that one supposes it can be affected by what one can actually do.

The possibilities which appear to be open—the alternatives confronting the young man who has received his draft notice—seem to be live options. They are genuine possibilities *for him*; he is really interested to some extent in each of them. Of course, an apparent alternative might not be real—perhaps the border has been closed so that the alternative of going to a foreign country is no longer available. It can still appear to be an alternative and can even be chosen, so long as the young man is not aware of its impossibility. In other words, the possibility must be open so far as he knows; it need not really be open.

To one who is faced with the necessity of making a choice, it seems that the alternatives are really open and unsettled, all things considered. Normally the first thing one does is to examine the situation to see whether there are not factors already taken for granted which can settle the apparently unsettled situation, thus obviating the need for real deliberation and choice.

For example, a couple wishes to make a month-long tour of Europe. A number of factors are already settled, and they take these factors for granted when they go to the travel agency. For example, the tour must leave after the first of July and return before the end of August. The total cost cannot exceed $4,000. The tour must allow them time to visit a small town in Eastern Germany, from which the husband's family emigrated. The travel agent produces information about a number of tours, which he thinks might be of interest to the couple. Studying this information, they discover that some of the tours leave too early or return too late; some cost too much, or will not allow them time to visit the village in Eastern Germany. In fact, only one tour which they can find satisfies all of the conditions they had set in advance. They decide to take that one. They might say that they "choose" that tour.

In one sense of "choose," of course, they do choose it. However, the same choice could be made by a computer, if it were properly programmed and fed the information concerning the conditions a tour would have to meet to satisfy the couple's requirements. Given the assumptions and the actual conditions of the alternatives, there really is no open possibility except one. However, it might have seemed to the couple, when they first received the information from the travel agent, that they faced several live options, and that they would have to choose among them by criteria supplementary to those already settled.

Many choice-situations are similar to this example, and someone might argue that all choice-situations are of this sort. However, sometimes an individual feels that he has considered all available information but thinks that alternatives still remain open and does not think that anything already given will lead to a unique resolution of the question as to what is to be done.

Of course, when a person does something following a calculation which has led to the exclusion of every possibility but one, just as when he does something without needing to stop and reflect, he can proceed with a sense of "freedom"—meaning physical freedom or the freedom to do as one pleases. He need not feel constrained, compelled, restrained, or in any way forced. But he is not deliberating and choosing, and thus there is no question of free choice.

In cases of this sort, deliberation and choice perhaps occurred previously. If the couple of our example chose the conditions which settled their decision in favor of the tour which they took, then this prior choice might have seemed to them free and the later decision also might seem free. The sense of freedom might be especially strong in a person who is prepared at any time to reconsider his choice of the conditions of a decision. Thus, if the couple were not altogether committed to making the tour until they chose the particular one they accepted, then their choice of that particular tour included the final decision to make the trip. Until then, the choice was only tentative and conditional.

F. Deliberation and choice

Given alternative possible courses of action, one must settle among them if one is going to act at all. This settling among alternatives begins with active, practical reflection upon the alternatives—such reflection is called "deliberation." Deliberation forms a bridge between the opening situation, in which hesitation occurs in virtue of a conflict of desires or interests, and the closing act of making a choice.

Deliberation is active thinking; it is not merely vacillation. The opening situation does include vacillation, as motives for each alternative present themselves, and no alternative seems satisfactory in every respect. Deliberation begins when one starts to reflect on the possibilities, to consider the various motives, to seek actively for a resolution of the impasse.

The possible reasons for each choice need not all be present and clearly articulated at the beginning of deliberation. The marshalling of considerations and clarification of possible reasons are part of deliberation. As one proceeds in deliberating, one sees that certain possibilities which seemed viable at the beginning are not, while one comes to see other alternatives of which one was not initially aware. Deliberation prepares a clear reason for acting in accord with each alternative which remains under consideration. Whatever choice is eventually made, one will be in a position to say why that choice was made by recalling the considerations already adduced in deliberation in favor of the alternative finally chosen.

Deliberation begins with uncertainty. One does not know what he is going to do. But uncertainty about one's future action often carries with it a certain unsettledness about one's present self. In important choices one has the feeling that whatever one chooses, the outcome will more or less significantly alter or confirm one's identity. As a person deliberates, he considers what difference it would make to himself to carry out each of the alternatives.

One can deliberate about possible actions without knowing when the opportunity for action will arrive. For example, a person can deliberate about where he will spend his next vacation without knowing when he will next have a vacation. Such deliberation can lead to a choice based on a condition not within one's power, provided that the condition is not known to be impossible. For example, a person can make up his mind to go on a certain vacation if he is given enough time off from work or a large enough bonus to finance the trip. Such advance deliberation also can lead to a tentative decision; one can decide to take a certain trip unless some other, more interesting possiblity arises.

There is no incompatibility between carrying on deliberation and having a basis on which one can guess the outcome. Perhaps a person has a strong inclination to one alternative at the outset and on the basis of past experience with similar inclinations judges that he will most likely decide to follow it, for he has usually followed similar inclinations in similar situations before. A person in this frame of mind is still able to deliberate. However, if he knew for certain what he was going to do, there would seem to be no alternative and the possibility of deliberation would be removed.[11]

A person engaged in deliberation feels he can go on deliberating or can stop. After a time reflection no longer yields any additional considerations. One finds himself reviewing the same ground. Still, further reflection *might* turn up something new. So one can continue to reflect. If choice is not urgent, one can set aside the deliberation with a view to considering the matter later when some further factors might come into view.

It is worth noting that deliberation itself can become the subject of a second-level deliberation and choice. Thus, one can shift from deliberating about the original problem to deliberating about whether to terminate deliberation or to go on with it.

While a person is still deliberating, he sees alternative courses of action as possibilities. He sees the various choices to initiate those courses of action as all genuinely possible. He expresses this possibility: "I can make this choice, and then again I can make that one." This possibility is not mere contingency. It is not as if a person were expecting one or another set of events, all of which were beyond his control. Rather, the possible choices appear to be within his power. "It is really up to me what I am going to do," expresses this experience.

When one sees an animal vacillate between two courses of action—for example, pursuit of food and obedience to a command to stay—one might say that it "can do either one." By this one would mean that one knows of nothing constraining or restraining the animal—that it has physical freedom. One need not suppose the animal to be considering possibilities, as if it were about to choose. Rather, one supposes that the animal's impulses settle the issue, that the stronger impulse prevails. A human person, however, when he is about to choose thinks that he himself is going to settle the issue.

Thus, when the youth of our example considered that he could submit to induction, leave the country, or stay and risk going to prison, "could" did not mean mere logical possibility or causal contingency. A person supposes that he himself makes his choice and that nothing makes him make the choice he makes. In other words, he thinks that the causal conditions apart from his own choosing are not sufficient to bring his choosing about.

The act of choice involves focusing of attention on one alternative, the one chosen. But there is more to choice than focus of attention. Even in the very act of choosing, one can remain aware of what he is not choosing, as evidenced by the feeling one sometimes has of surrendering what was attractive in the rejected alternative. After choice, the choice does not come unmade when one turns his attention to other matters.[12]

As we have seen, a person deliberates with an awareness of possibilities and with a belief that he can and must settle among them. He does not experience something *happening* which he can identify as the choice itself. A person does not encounter his choices; he makes his choices. The experience of choice is an experience of doing something; it is not an experience of undergoing anything.

The connotation of passivity in the word "experience" is misleading if it makes one suppose that consciousness of choosing—at the moment of choice—is passive in the way in which having a dream, feeling dizzy, or hearing a noise is passive. A person's own choosing is not given to himself; in this sense, choice is not a datum.[13]

Even if choosing is not a datum at the moment of choice, one is directly aware of it. One can tell that he has made a choice immediately upon making it. In retrospect, of course, choice can be noted to be a datum. One is clearly aware of having moved from deliberation about possibilities to the state of having made up his mind; choice divides the two. Thus one's knowledge of his own choices is not inferential.

G. From experience to judgment

Reflecting upon the phenomena described, we distinguish three aspects of the experience. First, one experiences a state of affairs in which his desire or interest is aroused by alternative possibilities, without experiencing anything limiting the possibilities to one. Second, one feels that it is within his power to take one alternative or another, and that nothing but the exercise of this power will realize one of the alternatives. Third, one is aware of making his choice, without being aware of anything else making him make that choice. We call these three aspects taken together "a sense of freedom."

But having a sense of freedom must be distinguished from the judgments one makes on the basis of this experience. Corresponding to each aspect of the experience, there is a judgment. These judgments might be expressed as follows. Corresponding to the first aspect: "I could do this and then again I could do that; the alternatives are really open possibilities." Corresponding to the second aspect: "It is in my own power to do this or that; it is up to me alone to settle which I shall do." Corresponding to the third aspect: "I made up my own mind, and nothing made me choose as I did." If someone asserts any of these three judgments, he implies that the choice to which he refers is free.

Each of the three judgments has a positive and a negative aspect. The positive aspects of the judgments—"I could do this and then again I could do that," "it is in my own power to do this or that," and "I made up my own mind"—reflect what is present in the experience. A person is aware of possibilities as desirable but incompatible; he is aware that no possibility is attractive in every respect; and he is aware that he can make his own evaluation of the diverse respects in which various possibilities are desirable. The negative aspects of the judgments—"the possibilities are really open," "it is up to me alone," and "nothing made me choose as I did"—cannot in the same way express what is present in experience.

In a certain sense, any judgment involves more than experience. If one experiences rain falling on his head, in judging that rain is falling on his head, he makes a truth-claim which he does not make simply by having the experience. An experience can be illusory, but an experience cannot be false. Many judgments based upon experience also presuppose the truth of assumptions which are so much taken for granted that they are not noted. For example, one who experiences himself flipping a switch and seeing a light go on thinks that his flipping the switch makes the light go on, since he takes for granted assumptions about the way in which the electrical apparatus works.

Some negative judgments—for example, a judgment distinguishing two objects of perception—do not go beyond experience in ways other than affirmative judgments do. However, some negative judgments require a further step beyond experience. For example, if one looks in the refrigerator for cheese and finds none there, the judgment that there is no cheese in the refrigerator is not based upon data alone. The negative judgment can be false without the experience being illusory—for example, if the cheese is there but hidden from sight. A negative judgment based on the absence of data presupposes a framework of expectations in which the absence of those data normally grounds the negative judgment; although this framework is an epistemic condition for making the negative judgment, it is not part of the state of affairs articulated in the proposition asserted in the negative judgment.

Other examples might help to clarify the point. If someone asks me whether I have eaten breakfast and if I do not recall having done so, I judge that I have not yet eaten breakfast. One assumes that the absence of memory of an event which would have been so recent warrants the judgment that it did not occur. But this assumption is a framework of the judgment, not a premise from which the proposition affirmed is deduced. I do not infer that I have not eaten breakfast, although the judgment could be mistaken if the usual conditions set by the appropriate framework happen not to be fulfilled. Similarly, if I perceive nothing which would prevent me from doing something which I know how to do, then I judge that I can do it.

If this analysis is correct, it follows that when someone judges that he has made a free choice, his judgment is likely to seem to him self-evident, since it is not an inference but is grounded directly in his experience. At the same time, since this judgment presupposes a framework of expectations, the judgment will be false if the expectations are mistaken. Therefore, the judgment can be challenged without challenging the data as they appear to the person who makes the judgment.

For example, the judgment, "I have not yet eaten breakfast," made by someone who has just suffered a severe blow to the head, could be challenged without challenging the accuracy of the individual's description of his current experience, since in such a situation there is a plausible ground for questioning the assumption that absence of memory of an event which would have been so recent warrants the judgment that the event did not occur. Similarly, the judgment, "I freely chose x," can be challenged without challenging the accuracy of a person's description of his experience of choice. There are plausible grounds—for example, grounds suggested by modern psychology —for questioning the assumption that absence of awareness of a causal condition other than one's own choosing warrants the judgment that there is no such condition.

The phenomena summed up in the "sense of freedom" are not identical with the judgment that one is free. The sense of freedom and the judgment that one is making a free choice are to be distinguished.

The preceding point makes clear that in describing the experience of choice we have not asserted that people make free choices. One can admit the entire description of choice presented here, yet still hold that no one makes any free choice. One who holds this will challenge the framework of expectations in virtue of which many people make the judgment that they have made a free choice. For this framework, he will substitute some such assumption as the following: "Even if I am not conscious of anything which makes me choose as I do, there must be something which brings my choice about."

The significance of the experience of choice, as we have described it, is that if someone accepts it at face value, including the negative aspects, he will judge that he chooses freely; in retrospect, he will think that under the very same conditions he could have chosen otherwise than he in fact chose.

The foregoing description of the experience of choice and the analysis of the corresponding judgments show that the expression "free choice" has a reference in experience. While there are other semantic problems which must be treated prior to an attempt to resolve Sfc/Nfc, one serious obstacle to considering the controversy genuine is removed by establishing a reference for "free choice" without prejudging whether there are free choices.[14]

Should anyone challenge the foregoing formulation of the experience of choice and the corresponding judgments, our reply is that at least some people would accept this formulation as an expression of their experience and the way they talk about it.

Whether *Sfc* or *Nfc* is true remains to be settled. Some have argued that the experience of choice is sufficient to establish *Sfc*. In chapter two, section A, we show that arguments articulated along these lines are question-begging.

H. The controversy about free choice

Having defined "free choice" and having described the experience of choice, we begin an examination of *Sfc/Nfc*.

Sfc is the position we defend in this book. We think *Sfc/Nfc* formulates in a precise way a central issue in the historical debate about free will and determinism. Before beginning to examine the various arguments in this controversy, we clarify the meaning of our formulation of it and explain why we have adopted this formulation.

Sfc is not equivalent to the proposition that it is logically possible that someone make a free choice. *Sfc* presupposes the truth of the latter proposition. We shall defend this truth in chapter three, section B, by criticizing fatalism —the position that *Nfc* is logically necessary.

Sfc is not equivalent to the proposition that if someone makes a choice, then that choice is necessarily free. It has been argued that if there ever is a choice—such as we have described in sections B through F—then it is logically necessary that such a choice be free. The premises for this conclusion are that a determined choice would be in principle predictable, that it is logically possible for anyone to know what is in principle predictable, and that it is logically impossible for anyone to know what he is about to choose.[15]

These premises might seem to entail—but do not entail—that a determined choice is a contradiction in terms. The argument involves a fallacy. From the conjunction of *p* and the impossibility of *p and q*, it does not follow that *q* is impossible, but only that *q* is not the case. From the fact that it is logically impossible for a person both to know his decision beforehand and to make it, it follows only that a certain event either cannot be predicted by that person or cannot be his decision. This conclusion is compatible with someone's choice being predicted by anyone else and with the logical possibility, although not the actuality, of the individual's predicting it himself. It is logically impossible for a certain individual to be standing up and not standing up at the same time, and at a given moment—for example, when he is lying down—he is not standing up, but even at that moment it is logically possible, although not the case, that he be standing up.

Sfc is not equivalent to the proposition that someone has *actually* made a free choice. If the latter proposition is true, then so is the former; however, *Sfc* might be true even if no one ever actually makes a choice. Not all capacities are exercised.

Sfc entails the propositions that some human person has the capacity to make a free choice and that the alternative possibilities between which a person deliberates are not always foreclosed by some factor other than the person's choosing itself.

The following remarks will clarify the meaning of this formulation.

By "capacity" in this formulation we mean nothing other than what people ordinarily mean when they speak of the capacity to see, the capacity to understand, and so on. One refers to such abilities because those who see or understand have a capacity to do so even when they do not actually see or understand. A person in a dreamless sleep does not lose his sight or his intelligence—these are capacities.

In section B we defined what we mean in this formulation by "free choice." In sections C through F we described the phenomena of choice which will be given if there is a capacity to make a free choice and if that capacity is exercised. As we have already made clear, this is not to say that the mere fact that people have experiences such as we have described shows that anyone does or can make a free choice.

Those who argue that there is no capacity to make a free choice seek to show that there is some sort of impossibility in man's having such a capacity. For example, they might say that such an ability would require that something —namely, the free choice—might be without any sufficient reason for its being so rather than otherwise.

Those who argue that the alternative possibilities between which persons deliberate always are foreclosed by some factor other than the person's choosing itself seek to show that such open alternatives are causally impossible. For example, they might say that all events are covered by laws (or lawlike statements) such that anything which could be the object of a choice—this alternative or that alternative—would be determined by natural necessity. "Natural necessity" as used here need not refer only to physical necessity; it can also refer to psychological necessity, the nonlogical necessity of reasons for acting if they are considered not to be natural causes, and so on.

The terms in *Nfc* are to be understood in the same way as the terms in *Sfc*, since *Nfc* is the contradictory of *Sfc*. We formulate the controversy about free will and determinism as *Sfc/Nfc*, because *Nfc* is the least that anyone who wishes to deny the reality of free choice is likely to claim. It would not be sufficient for him to claim that while human beings can make free choices, no one ever happens to make one. It is unnecessary for him to claim—as the fatalist does—that it is logically impossible for anyone to make a free choice. He precisely claims either that no human person has the ability to make a free choice, or that no alternative possibilities ever are determinable only by a free choice, or both. In order to establish *Nfc*, the *PNfc* must proceed by excluding in principle—that is, as somehow impossible—either the ability to choose or the nondeterminateness of alternatives.

Our formulation of the issue we are examining also ought to be satisfactory to the defender of free choice. Many defenders of free choice have argued precisely for *Sfc*. Others have argued for the stronger thesis, which entails *Sfc*, that someone *does* make a free choice. The latter approach, however, usually has involved the assumption that a certain choice can be identified as free. There are special problems in the identification of free choices. Therefore, it is easier, and sufficient, for the defense of free choice, to limit the ground one attempts to defend by claiming only that someone can make a free choice.

Historically, many defenders of *Nfc* have called themselves or have been called "determinists." We avoid "determinism" as a label for the position we reject, because the *PNfc* often rejects this label. He frequently regards himself as a compatibilist and distinguishes his position from what he is willing to call "determinism." At the same time, a fatalist asserts *Nfc*, but "fatalism" and "determinism" usually are used to refer to distinct positions. Moreover, "determinism" often is used to refer to a cosmological or metaphysical thesis according to which every event has a cause, or to a state of affairs articulated by such a thesis. Universal determinism entails *Nfc,* and a *PNfc* can appeal to universal determinism to support his position. However, *Nfc* also can be and often has been asserted on grounds distinct from such a worldview.

We shall discuss various forms of compatibilism, including soft determinism, in chapter four. In chapter three we shall discuss fatalism, determinism, and other grounds for affirming *Nfc*.

Historically, many defenders of *Sfc* have called themselves or have been called by others "defenders of freedom of the will," "libertarians," "indeterminists," "self-determinists," and so on. We avoid using any of these expressions to refer to our own position, because each of them has connotations irrelevant to what we defend. Many of these connotations will become clear in chapter two, in which we review arguments which, if successful, would support *Sfc*.

2: Arguments for Free Choice

In this chapter we present a detailed review of inadequate arguments for free choice. This review makes clear why previous arguments for free choice have failed, and thus makes clear some conditions an argument must meet if it is to establish *Sfc*. Also, in the course of the review, we clarify the moves open to a *PNfc* in defending his position, and thus show what obstacles a successful argument for *Sfc* must overcome.

In general, the problem faced by a *PSfc* in arguing for *Sfc* is to reach his conclusion without begging the question at issue—that is, without making assumptions which a *PNfc* need not accept. Of all the kinds of arguments for *Sfc* which we examine, that kind proposed by those who maintain that the assertion of *Nfc* is self-refuting seems most likely to be able to avoid this fallacy. But even the examples we have found of this kind of argument do not avoid assuming what should be proved.

Our review of unsuccessful arguments begins with the simplest line of argumentation: that immediate experience demonstrates that people do make free choices.

A. Argument from immediate experience

In his *Disputationes metaphysicae,* Francisco Suarez considers the question of freedom.[1] He points out that "necessity" and "freedom" have many senses. Even animals act freely in the sense that they are not compelled or necessitated by nature to act as they do. But the debate about free choice, Suarez says, concerns necessity only in the sense that "an action is necessary which cannot fail to be or to be done, assuming always the condition that all factors required for acting are given."

26

Having set aside this kind of compatibilism, Suarez goes on to argue for free choice. His argument is based primarily on the evidence of experience. Human beings experience that they can do or omit doing something; that is why they use reason, inquiry, and consultation. The power of deliberation and counsel would be pointless if *Nfc* were true.

Suarez recognizes that it is possible to answer this line of argument by saying that it does not prove that people make free choices, since perhaps the rational processes which lead to choice are determined, and one might explain the use of rewards, punishments, exhortations, and advice as motivating principles of judgment, rather than as factors intended to elicit a free choice. To this objection, Suarez answers by admitting that the experience one has is not so clear and evident that it leaves no room for a really hard-headed opponent to wriggle out. Yet Suarez thinks that one immediately experiences the ability to sit or to stand, to turn one way or another, even while his awareness of the given situation remains constant. A person finds himself able to be moved by rewards or punishments, or to resist. And a person can take one means or another to an end, when he sees little difference between them, simply because he wills. Suarez takes these facts to show that the human manner of acting is essentially a matter of liberty or indifference, not a result of cognitional factors which, as the objection pointed out, could be determined.

Hume seems to be answering an argument similar to that of Suarez when he attacks the "false sensation, or seeming experience" which was used as "a demonstrative and even intuitive proof of human liberty."[2]

> We feel, that our actions are subject to our will, on most occasions; and imagine we feel, that the will itself is subject to nothing, because, when by a denial of it we are provoked to try, we feel, that it moves easily every way, and produces an image of itself (or a *Velleity,* as it is called in the schools) even on that side, on which it did not settle. This image, or faint motion, we persuade ourselves, could, at that time, have been compleated into the thing itself; because, should that be denied, we find, upon a second trial, that, at present, it can.

Hume's response to this argument is brief and pointed. The motive of these actions is the "fantastical desire of shewing liberty." A spectator, however, can predict someone's future actions from knowledge of that person's character and motives, and even when such an inference is impossible, the observer concludes that he might make it if he were more fully informed of the hidden springs of the person's action.

Like Hume, Descartes was acquainted with scholastic philosophy. However, Descartes accepts the position that immediate experience establishes the freedom of the will and he fails to articulate the argument as fully as Suarez, or even Hume. In Meditation IV, Descartes says that the will is a quasi-infinite capacity, which particularly shows man to be made in the image and likeness of God. The unrestrictedness of the will is used by Descartes to explain the possibility of error. He considers assent to be an act of the will and holds that men should, but need not, limit their assent to propositions within the bounds of their knowledge,[3] In objection XII of the third set of objections it is said "that the freedom of the will has been assumed without proof, and in opposition to the opinion of the Calvinists." Descartes replies: "Further I made no assumption concerning freedom which is not a matter of universal experience; our natural light makes this most evident. . . ."[4] The position is spelled out more fully in Part I of the *Principles of Philosophy,* XXXIX: "Finally it is so evident that we are possessed of a free will that can give or withhold its assent that this may be counted as one of the first and most ordinary notions that are found innately in us." And Descartes goes on to argue the point by saying that in the depth of methodic doubt he still perceived in himself a liberty to withhold assent from what is not perfectly certain and indubitable.[5]

Perhaps Descartes was moved to accept the self-evidence of freedom of the will because its reality was a supposition of his methodology. But what seemed evident to Descartes is far from evident to those who do not accept his method. Spinoza, for example, brusquely dismisses the alleged self-evidence of freedom: ". . . men think themselves free inasmuch as they are conscious of their volitions and desires, and never even dream, in their ignorance, of the causes which have disposed them so to wish and desire."[6]

Hume and Spinoza make no attempt to reinterpret or deny the experience on which the claim of the self-evidence of freedom is based. They simply refuse to accept the experience as definitive.

Other authors press their attack against the experience itself. Joseph Priestley, for example, argues that ". . . all that a man can possibly be conscious of . . . [is] that nothing hinders his choosing or taking whichsoever of the fruits appears to him more desirable, or his not making any choice at all, according as the one or the other shall appear to him preferable upon the whole."[7] Mill likewise claims that what one finds in consciousness is merely the feeling that he could choose another course of action if he preferred it, but not that he could choose contrary to his preference.[8]

McTaggart claims that one's sense of freedom is nothing else than the awareness that he can do as he chooses, without being coerced; the experience is sufficiently accounted for "by the fact that the action is determined by the will, and that there is no need to hold that the determining volition is itself undetermined."[9] Moritz Schlick says the following:

> This feeling is simply the consciousness of *freedom,* which is merely the knowledge of having acted of one's *own* desires. . . . The absence of the external power expresses itself in the well-known feeling (usually considered characteristic of the consciousness of freedom) *that one could also have acted otherwise.* . . . This feeling is not the consciousness of the absence of a cause,

but of something altogether different, namely, of *freedom,* which consists in the fact that I can act as I desire.[10]

Thus, these authors and many others propose that the experience of making a free choice is nothing more than an awareness that one can choose what one prefers, or that freedom is nothing more than an ability to do what one wills or desires.

However, the relevant data of experience, summarized in chapter one, sections C through F, show that these proposals are misleading. Keith Lehrer has pointed out, in support of the argument from introspection, that men do deliberate, that deliberation presupposes the conviction that it is within one's power to perform or not to perform an action according to one's choice, and that the only reason for doubting so universal a conviction is that it seems incompatible with determinism.[11] Moreover, various authors have said that in making choices men experience themselves as agents exercising power, as determining rather than as determined, as actively interposing the ego to settle conflicting motives.[12]

But even if the experience of deliberation includes the consciousness of alternatives each of which is possible and even if the experience of choice includes a sense of freedom, the question still remains whether these data prove that people make free choices. Brand Blanshard accurately points to the data and states that they involve something more than feeling free to do as one chooses. The feeling that is relevant is that of an open future. "After the noise of argument has died down, a sort of intuition stubbornly remains that we can not only lift our hand if we choose, but that the choice itself is open to us." Yet Blanshard thinks the data of consciousness are compatible with the reality of determinism. His explanation is that when choosing, one faces toward the future consequences which one act or the other will bring, not toward the past with its possible determining factors.[13] This distinction of Blanshard's is not unlike Hume's distinction between the perspective of the agent and that of the observer reflecting upon action.

A *PSfc* might dispute Blanshard's explanation by pointing out that if there really are factors determining choice, those factors must be effective at the time of choice itself, not merely in the past, and that the sense of openness Blanshard himself admits also can be experienced at the moment of choice, not in the future.

But the argument from immediate experience is open to other objections. R. D. Bradley, among others, develops one such objection: One might be directly aware of himself acting, but one cannot be directly conscious that his actions are uncaused, since the absence of a cause simply is not the sort of thing of which one can be directly aware.[14] Keith Lehrer, although he insists on the data of consciousness, nevertheless admits that a person's awareness of making his own choice leaves open the question whether or not his choice is caused.[15] Nicolai Hartmann, who does not himself deny free will, considers the consciousness of self-determination a subjective certainty, which clearly requires some objective ground. But he points out that the objective ground need not be the reality of free choice; the experience could be a universal illusion which has evolved in mankind because of its utility—perhaps in stimulating a sense of responsibility.[16]

Even C. A. Campbell, a strong proponent of free will, clearly states that immediate experience is not enough: "I have always explicitly recognised it to be in principle possible that the subjective assurance of contra-causal freedom which, in my view, introspection reports, may be illusory . . . and that various objections to accepting that assurance as veridical must be independently considered."[17]

Finally, Hans Kelsen points out that even if at the moment of choice one cannot escape the subjective experience of feeling free and even if one cannot consider his own future acts determined, the theoretical issue between freedom and determinism remains a quite distinct issue. On this question, Kelsen's own position is that the human will is causally determined.[18]

Thus it is clear that many who affirm freedom, many who affirm determinism, and many who take neither position agree upon the data of consciousness. These data have been used in efforts to settle Sfc/Nfc in favor of Sfc. But this use of the data can always be challenged.

Our analysis in chapter one, section G, of the common sense judgment that one has made a free choice reveals why the judgment seems self-evident to many people, but our analysis also shows that the experience of choice by itself does not justify the assertion that people make free choices. Thus, to assume that the immediate judgment that one has made a free choice is sufficient to prove Sfc is to beg the question; this assumption is precisely what is called in question by the $PNfc$.

B. Argument from moral responsibility

Christian thinkers often have argued for freedom of choice—if they considered the point in need of argument—by appealing to the fact that human beings have moral obligations and shall be rewarded or punished according to whether or not they fulfill these obligations. Bertrand Russell, while rejecting Christian morality, agrees: ". . . the conception of 'sin' is only rational on the assumption of free will."[19]

This point is of considerable importance in the evaluation of arguments for Sfc based upon moral responsibility, and also of the attempts of the $PNfc$ to meet such arguments. Such discussion is studded with references to "what *we* mean by 'responsibility'," "the *usual* meaning of 'moral responsibility'," and "what the *ordinary man* means by 'moral responsibility'." Such references, we contend, do not advance the argument. Current meanings of moral language are still, in our culture, considerably influenced by the Judeo-Christian tradition. Those who wish to argue for *Sfc* cannot simply appeal to this tradition; a *PNfc* can frankly admit, as Russell does, that he is proposing an alternative outlook.[20]

In such an alternative outlook, "free choice" and related expressions might have their uses. Of course, these expressions will not be used to refer to what we defined in chapter one, section B, as "free choice."

For example, when Hume reconciles necessity and liberty, he asserts that the universally accepted meaning of "liberty" in reference to voluntary actions is nothing more than a hypothetical liberty which belongs to everyone not a prisoner in chains—"*a power of acting or not acting according to the determinations of the will.*"[21] As we showed above, Francisco Suarez already knew about compatibilism of this sort and rejected it; he distinguished meanings of "necessity" and "freedom" and pointed out that animals also have liberty in the sense Hume here defines. As a matter of historical fact, Hume is mistaken in claiming that hypothetical liberty was the universally accepted meaning of "freedom." However, Hume does make clear that there are senses of "free" and "necessary" such that the same act can be said to be both.

Following Hume's lead, A. J. Ayer argues that the possibility of acting otherwise, which is accepted by all as necessary for moral responsibility, is not incompatible with determinism. Ayer claims that those who argue for free choice must suppose that actions chosen occur by chance and without reference to character.[22] Ayer offers a deterministic analysis of "could have acted otherwise":

> . . . to say that I could have acted otherwise is to say, first, that I should have acted otherwise if I had so chosen; secondly, that my action was voluntary in the sense in which the actions, say, of the kleptomaniac are not; and thirdly, that nobody compelled me to choose as I did: and these three conditions may very well be fulfilled. When they are fulfilled, I may be said to have acted freely.[23]

In a similar vein, Moritz Schlick defines moral freedom:

> Freedom means the opposite of compulsion; a man is *free* if he does not act under *compulsion*, and he is compelled or unfree when he is hindered from without in the realization of his natural desires.

Schlick thinks that people mistakenly argue from moral responsibility against determinism because they confuse the necessity of causal laws with compulsion.[24]

These remarks are reminiscent of Aristotle's account of "voluntariness."[25] For Aristotle, voluntariness is common to men and animals. In fact, the element of knowledge of what one is doing, which Aristotle demanded for voluntariness, goes unmentioned by Ayer and Schlick. Moreover, one can provide an analysis of "could have acted otherwise" which incorporates still further elements of ordinary uses of this phrase without thereby committing oneself to *Sfc*. In addition to the requirements for voluntariness, one might require that the action follow deliberation in which other alternatives were seriously considered and thought possible. This would not necessarily imply that the outcome of deliberation was not somehow determined—a possibility Aristotle himself seems to have left open—but that the determining conditions were effective during the process of deliberation itself, actualizing one of the initially possible alternatives and ruling out the other or others.

In discussing responsibility, those who attempt to reconcile morality with *Nfc* typically provide an analysis along the following lines. To impute responsibility is to determine who is to be praised or blamed, rewarded or punished. Praise and blame, reward and punishment need not be pointless if *Nfc* is true. Their purpose can be to provide motivation, either by their prospect or by their effectuation, either to the individual himself or to others. As Schlick says: ". . . the question regarding responsibility is the question: Who, in a given case, is to be punished?"[26] Bertrand Russell offers the following formulation:

> Praise and blame, rewards and punishments, and the whole apparatus of the criminal law, are rational on the deterministic hypothesis, but not on the hypothesis of free will, for they are all mechanisms designed to cause volitions that are in harmony with the interests of the community, or what are believed to be its interests.[27]

A number of objections have been proposed against the attempt to reconcile moral responsibility with *Nfc*. C. A. Campbell, for example, argues that Schlick's analysis does not satisfy Schlick's claim to give us what we ordinarily mean by "moral responsibility." For, Campbell says, lower animals are not regarded as morally responsible; a person no longer living is sometimes regarded as morally responsible for a present situation; allowance for unfavorable circumstances is made in censuring someone; and the morally innocent sometimes are motivated in ways which Schlick would regard as punishment.[28]

A number of points can be made in defense of the possibility of reconciling moral responsibility with the truth of *Nfc*; these points answer objections like Campbell's even if they do not save the version of the theory offered by Schlick and others.

In the first place, no *PNfc* need be embarrassed by his inability to give what "we" or the "ordinary man" mean by "moral responsibility." For one thing, some people believe that *Sfc* is true, and understand responsibility accordingly. To a great extent, current laws and customs derive from a period in which almost everyone believed *Sfc*. The *PNfc* can admit these facts. Furthermore, even if a person's experience of his own choices does not justify asserting *Sfc*, for practical purposes many people tend to take this experience at face value and to base their estimate of their own responsibility and that of others upon it. The *PNfc* can admit this too.

In the second place, the *PNfc* need not attempt to provide an explication of praise and blame, reward and punishment, solely in terms of a utilitarian justification of such activities. Feelings of anger and hatred which lead to vengeful behavior are part of human nature; perhaps such feelings are unjustified, but they might nevertheless be an important component of one's reactions to other people's actions, and therefore of what "responsibility" often means. Moreover, people also admire and despise, praise and condemn in nonmoral contexts—for example, in esthetics. Such judgments of nonmoral value might well be entangled in many uses of "moral responsibility." The *PNfc* can admit such factors in the meaning of "moral responsibility" while denying them any role in the justification of the ascription of moral responsibility.

In the third place, men do praise and blame, reward and punish animals and small children; in some sense, they are held responsible. The *PNfc* can grant this and also that there is something more to *moral* responsibility, since it requires a context of discourse, an accepted system of standards or values, and a disposition to abide by or to violate these standards or values. But to admit that moral responsibility involves more than the responsibility to which men hold animals and small children might be merely to admit the complexity of adult human psychology; it need not be to admit *Sfc*.

In the fourth place, imputing responsibility to the dead need only mean that their behavior while they were alive was such that it would receive reward or punishment if they were still alive. Making allowances for someone need only mean that one's feeling that there is responsibility is limited when one imagines oneself in his place. But this feeling that responsibility is limited might be explained partly in terms of one's awareness of the sorts of freedom compatible with *Nfc* and partly in terms of a residual belief in *Sfc*—a belief which need not be removed even if one regards *Nfc* as theoretically true. Similarly, when procedures which would usually be called "punishment" are used to motivate someone regarded as innocent of moral evil, such procedures need not be considered punishment, because punishment by definition presupposes guilt. Moreover, the distinction between guilt and innocence can be explained in a way compatible with *Nfc*.

The strategy for responding to the arguments against *Nfc* based on moral responsibility should be clear. The truth of *Nfc* demands an adequate explanation of "moral responsibility" but not a justification of moral responsibility as understood by the *PSfc*. And if a *PNfc* wishes, he can explain "moral responsibility" partly in terms of the concepts of morality which are compatible with *Nfc*, partly in terms of the residual beliefs in *Sfc* which general belief in *Nfc* has not yet eliminated, and partly by ideas and customs developed at a time when *Sfc* was generally accepted and *Nfc* generally assumed to be false.

Some *PSfc* might object to the foregoing analysis by claiming that it does less than justice to the nearly universal usage of the language of moral responsibility and to the nearly universal human experience of moral responsibility—for example, to the sense of outrage at injustices personally suffered at the hands of those whom one regards as free agents. The *PNfc* can respond by admitting the universality of such language and experience, but insisting that such language should be abandoned and such experience should be reformed, since this language and this experience depend upon an understandable but erroneous assumption—the assumption that *Sfc* is true.[29]

Moreover, the *PSfc* must contend with accounts of the language and experience of moral responsibility which are both more nuanced than those we have considered so far and compatible with *Nfc*.

W. David Ross, for example, argues:

> I am inclined to think that the only account we can give of responsibility is this: that bad acts can never be forced on anyone in spite of his character; that action is the joint product of character and circumstances and is always therefore to some extent evidence of character; that praise and blame are not (though they serve this purpose also) mere utilitarian devices for the promotion of virtue and the restraint of vice, but are the appropriate reactions to action which is good or is bad in its nature just as much if it is the necessary consequence of its antecedents as it would be if the libertarian account were true; that in blaming bad actions we are also blaming and justifiably blaming the character from which they spring; and that in remorse we are being acutely aware that, whatever our outward circumstances may have been, we have ourselves been to blame for giving way to them where a person of better character would not have done so.[30]

But does even this account of "moral responsibility" do justice to most people's experience of moral obligation? If a person ought to do x, then he can do x; if he is determined by character and circumstances to choose y at the end of his deliberation, then *he* could not choose x, and so he can have no obligation to do x.

The standard response of the *PNfc* to this line of reasoning is that there are propositions expressed by sentences such as "I ought to do x" and "x ought to be done" which are not inconsistent with *Nfc*. For our present purpose, it is not strictly necessary to sort out such uses of "ought." However, since the distinction of various uses of "ought" will be important in chapter six, section C, we shall be more expansive here than is required for our present purpose.

One use of "ought" is in sentences such as the following: "The answer to this problem in algebra ought to be: $x = 5$." This proposition entails nothing optional—it leaves no room for choice—but rather states what cannot fail to be the case if the premises are true. The normativity of "ought" in sentences of this type bears upon a reasoning process which could go wrong, not upon options among which one can deliberate and choose.

Another use of "ought" is in sentences such as the following: "If you desire x, then you ought to do y." The proposition expressed by this sentence does not entail that doing y is optional. The proposition can be true while one has no choice about doing y. If one's desire for x is an overwhelming urge, and if y is the only available means to satisfy that urge, then doing y is not optional. And even if one cannot do y, it still may be true that if one desires x he ought to do y, in the sense that y may be the only possible means for achieving x.

Another use of "ought" is in sentences such as the following: "The face of the Madonna in Michelangelo's Pieta ought not to be quite so sweet." The proposition expressed by this sentence, insofar as it expresses a criticism of the work, clearly implies no option; the work cannot be otherwise than it is. The proposition expressed by this sentence, insofar as it expresses a criticism of Michelangelo's creative activity, also leaves open the question whether Michelangelo was personally in a position to act otherwise. This proposition could be true even if it was psychologically or technically impossible for him to make the Madonna's face less sweet.

Another use of "ought" is in sentences like the following: "The baby ought to be walking soon." The proposition expressed by this sentence does not entail that the baby's walking is optional. "Ought" here points to what is regarded as normal and is expected of individuals of a given type.

C. D. Broad points out the relevance of this last use of "ought" to *Sfc/Nfc*, using the example: "A fountain pen ought not to be constantly making blots." As Broad points out, this meaning of "ought" is surely applicable to human action, and in this application enjoys a further development. For in the case of men, unlike the case of fountain pens, the individual has the power of reflexive cognition; he can be aware of the ideal. Moreover, it can be part of the ideal that one should have a desire to approximate it and not to fall short of average. Individuals can compare their own acts and the acts of others with this ideal and can criticize some such acts as falling short of what they "ought" to be. This fact does not show that the individual on the particular occasion could act otherwise than he did, nor that he could have a different ideal, nor that he could try harder to live up to his ideal—taking all of these "coulds" in a categorical sense.[31]

The sense of "ought" developed by Broad seems to fit quite well with the notion of moral responsibility outlined by Ross, and with an account of "could have chosen otherwise" compatible with *Nfc*. We think that this sense of "ought" expresses the normativity of moral goodness as Aristotle understands it. The other senses of "ought" which we have mentioned might also be proposed as providing the meaning of "obligation" in moral contexts.

Of course, the *PSfc* is likely to insist that none of these uses of "ought" expresses what he has in mind when he speaks of moral obligation. For him, the moral "ought" makes an unconditional demand, rather like a rule of logic—though perhaps modeled on a categorical divine command—but at the same time makes this demand in such a way that the person to whom it is addressed can choose either to comply with it or to disregard it. In the latter respect, the moral "ought" is somewhat like that of a conditional norm.

In summary. Anyone who argues for *Sfc* by appealing to the language and experience of morality begs the question. "Morality" can be understood in a way compatible with *Nfc*. If this understanding of morality does not reflect common opinion, this fact merely shows that common opinion in our present culture is not shaped by a coherent philosophy based on *Nfc*. Nevertheless, *Nfc* might be true. And so anyone who wishes to argue against it should avoid assuming as a starting point interpretations of moral experience incompatible with *Nfc*. If such assumptions are avoided, however, then no argument from moral responsibility for *Sfc* will succeed.

C. William James's argument

William James maintains that there can be no cogent demonstration of *Sfc*. Nevertheless, he believes in free will; he holds that there are pragmatic grounds which make it reasonable to believe in it.

In his *Principles of Psychology* James argues that the opposition between belief in free will and belief in determinism is reducible to an opposition between a moral postulate "that what ought to be can be, and that bad acts cannot be fated, but that good ones must be possible in their place"; and a scientific postulate that the world is one large, unbroken fact. The issue between the two postulates will never be settled except by choice, according to James: "Freedom's first deed should be to affirm itself."[32]

In *Pragmatism* James puts the argument briefly. Both advocates of free will and of determinism have argued for their positions on the pragmatic ground that otherwise the imputation of acts would be impossible. James dismisses this exchange as a pitiful wrangle, noting that whichever side is right, we will continue to ascribe responsibility for actions to those who perform them. Yet James himself wishes to argue pragmatically for free will, on the ground that it is a melioristic doctrine—that is, a doctrine which admits the possibility that in some respects in which things are bad the future need not resemble the past. Thus, James believes that free will is a theory of promise and a doctrine of relief.[33]

James's fullest development of his argument is in his address, "The Dilemma of Determinism." He begins his presentation by saying that he will point out two necessarily implied corollaries of determinism, which might lead his audience to join him in disbelieving in it. The most he can hope for, however, is that his argument might induce someone to assume free will to be true and to act as if it were true. The need for choice, James says, is involved in the strict logic of the situation: ". . . our first act of freedom, if we are free, ought in all inward propriety to be to affirm that we are free."[34]

Determinism, James goes on, implies a monism in which the whole universe is a solid block. If we accept as real the evil we experience—for example, the regrettable act of a brutal murderer—then the whole universe stands condemned, and a hopeless pessimism is the result. If we deny that evil is ultimately real and regard it as a good necessary for the whole, then our judgments of regret are mistaken. But, then, such mistaken judgments, paradoxically, are not what *they* ought to be. The only way to justify there being such judgments, James thinks, is to adopt a position he characterizes as "subjectivism"—a metaphysics which rationalizes and justifies everything by fitting all of it into one dramatic narrative, the significance of which is not in the objective process itself but in the observing consciousness.[35]

The position which James calls "subjectivism"—he refers to Hegel in philosophy and to the romantic movement in literature—seems to him worthy of rejection on the ground that it undercuts moral seriousness and responsibility. In practical life, James claims, this position leads either to a nerveless sentimentality or to a sensualism without bounds.[36]

It seems James's argument begs the question when he assumes that evil must be regarded with moral seriousness and that human life must be held meaningful in a way which is impossible if *Nfc* is true. Yet James might protest that it is unfair to criticize him for begging the question here; he presents his argument as a persuasive appeal, not as a demonstration.

Yet James does claim that his argument reveals necessary implications of determinism, and even this modest claim can be challenged. Surely one might be saddened by natural evils, such as the death of animals in a forest fire started by lightning, and might make a "judgment of regret" about such happenings. Even if one regards the event as wholly determined by natural causes, one can think that the suffering and death of these animals was an evil and that it ought not to have been. Yet recognition of such evils in nature need not lead to a general pessimism; one need not *impute* natural evils in parts of the universe to the whole, although one can regard parts of physical nature as deterministically bound up with the whole of nature. What is more, a worldview which includes *Nfc* need not include the proposition that the universe will remain as bad as it is or get worse; a determinist also can propose a melioristic hypothesis. He can maintain, for example, that evolution is necessarily toward what is better.

It might be objected that a deterministic account is satisfactory for natural evils, but not for the evils which James thought generated a dilemma for the determinist—the evils of human wrongdoing and error. However, unless one assumes *Sfc* to be true, the evils of human wrongdoing and error also must be regarded as natural evils, ones particularly interesting to human beings, of course, and ones having their own complexity and specific character, but evils in principle the same in kind as other evils in the universe.

Obviously, some deterministic accounts—for example, Spinoza's—are based upon a monistic metaphysics of the sort James had in mind. Yet it is coherent to maintain *Nfc* in a universe which allows chance and novelty, but confines indeterminacy to the level of subatomic particles. In such a universe, nothing will be able to generate the "character of novelty in fresh activity-situations" which James wishes to defend.[37]

James's view is not, in the end, so different from that of St. Augustine.[38] Both assume that everything in reality must either be justified or imputed to some agent as his sin. Just as Augustine was unwilling to impute evil to God, James does not wish to impute evil to the universe as a whole. Both, therefore, attribute to man a capacity in virtue of which he can be a first cause of evil. Any argument of this sort for *Sfc* fails. The *PNfc* can admit the reality of evil, deny that attempts to justify it make sense, and refuse to impute it either to man, or to God, or to the universe as a whole.

D. Thomas Aquinas's argument

In several of his works Thomas Aquinas considers questions bearing on whether *Sfc* is true.[39] Typically, he offers a version of the moral argument first, and then proceeds with an exposition of various senses in which the will is undetermined. In *De Malo*, question six, for example, he begins by stating the position that the will, while not coerced, is moved to choose by natural necessity. He rejects this position as heretical, inasmuch as it removes the ground for merit and demerit, and also as alien to philosophy, inasmuch as it subverts all the principles of moral philosophy. He then proceeds to his explanation, beginning with the words: "Ad evidentiam ergo veritatis. . . ."

One might take this phrase either as an introduction to an *explanation* (reading "evidentiam" as "clarification") of a point otherwise known to be true, or as an introduction to an attempted *proof* (reading "evidentiam" as "rational ground"). We here take what follows this introductory phrase to be an attempted proof, but we ask the reader to bear in mind that our criticism of the argument might not be fair to Aquinas if, as is possible, he intended it only as an explanation. Our present interest in Aquinas's treatment of free choice is not historical; we consider it only because it suggests a distinctive line of argument for *Sfc.*

In view of our present purpose, we summarize the argument proposed by Aquinas in *De veritate,* question twenty-two. In article five of this question, Aquinas explains that the will is not forced but is by its nature naturally and necessarily inclined to will the last end, happiness, and whatever is included in it—to be, to know, and the like. In article six, he proceeds to the further question: "Does the will necessarily will whatever it wills?"

Aquinas defines necessity as unchangeable determination which excludes alternatives. The will is not so determined except to that to which it is naturally inclined. A person also wills many other things. Therefore, he does not will of necessity everything he wills. The indetermination of the will is threefold: in respect to its object, its act, and its ordination to its end.

In respect to the object of the will—that is, to *what* one wills—the will is not determined to a particular means. While a person wills the end by natural inclination, there often is a wide choice of means for reaching the end, and some ways of reaching the end are more suitable to some people than to others. By contrast, subhuman entities have a fixed end and a fixed way of reaching it, so that for them there is no means in regard to which they are undetermined.

In respect to its act, the will is undetermined because a person can act or not act as he wishes, even in regard to a determinate object. Being animate, the will moves itself.[40] Inanimate things, by contrast, are moved by other things; a heavy body, for example, always falls unless prevented.

In respect to its orientation to its end, the will can desire what really is the end or what only seems to be. This possibility arises from the will's indetermination in respect to what can be taken as a means and from the indetermination of human apprehension. One can consider as a human good what is not really conducive to happiness, but only to pleasure, which is a sort of imitation of happiness. From indetermination in these respects, there follows the possibility of doing either good or evil.

Aquinas concludes the argument by pointing out that inasmuch as the will is free to the extent that it is not necessitated, its freedom in respect to its object and its act holds for man in any condition, while its freedom in respect to its ordination to the last end—the freedom which is the ability to do evil—holds for man in this present life, but not in heaven.

Confronted with this argument and assuming—however Aquinas intended it—that it is an attempt to establish *Sfc*, one is likely to ask a number of questions. How does one know there is a will? How does one know it is an animate, immaterial, self-moving power? How does one know that the natural necessity with which the end is willed, combined with the facts of situations in which men find themselves, do not necessitate the choice of means? How does one know that the indetermination of human apprehension of goods, true or apparent, is not settled by heredity and environment, nature and nurture?

Turning back to article four, one begins to find answers to some of these questions. The title of the article is: "In rational beings, is will a distinct power from sense appetite?"

Aquinas answers that will is a distinct power, differentiated by its more perfect way of tending. Being closer to God, who moves all things without being moved, the human will is less inclined by anything extrinsic to itself and more capable of inclining itself than is the tendency of lower beings.

A nonsentient entity has certain natural tendencies, but its inclination is completely passive. An animal has an intrinsic principle of inclination, the apprehended object of appetite, yet an animal does not have mastery over its own desires and actions, because its sense appetite has a bodily organ and so is material. Therefore, it is moved by something else and is not an active mover.

A rational creature has a natural inclination, the object of which is given from without, "but also has its inclination within its own power such that . . . it can incline or not incline." This power belongs to the will inasmuch as it requires no bodily organ; in this respect it is closer to the nature of what moves and acts and more remote from the nature of what is moved by something else. Not being determined by anything else, the will follows the apprehension of reason, for reason knows the end and the bearing of the means upon it.

In short, when Aquinas undertakes to distinguish will from sense appetite, he does so by locating it in a metaphysical hierarchy. The will's place in the hierarchy is established by the fact that it is an immaterial, self-determining power. On the other hand, when he undertakes to explain the freedom of the will, Aquinas appeals to its nature and attributes. The argument—assuming it is intended to be a proof—is circular. Any argument for *Sfc* which proceeds from the nature of the will or the nature of man will likewise beg the question.

E. The argument that determinism is self-refuting

Each of the four ways of arguing for free choice examined thus far is question-begging. The data of experience, morality and responsibility, the cosmic significance of evil, and the nature of the will yield seemingly conclusive arguments against *Nfc* only if they include the assumption that *Sfc* is true.

Attempts to resolve philosophical disputes often turn out in this way, because philosophical arguments often invoke prior principles, and any assumed theoretical framework can be called into question.

Thus, the only way to settle a philosophical issue seems to be to work from the one set of assumptions which an opponent cannot consistently deny—that is, the assumptions he makes in maintaining his own position. The simplest case is one in which it is possible to show that someone is being inconsistent, according to criteria for consistency which he accepts. A less direct approach takes the form of drawing out the implications of a position, applying these implications to the position itself, and concluding that the position is self-refuting.

The promise of this method of argumentation is that it need not be question-begging. Unfortunately, there is no guarantee that attempts to argue in this fashion will not as a matter of fact beg the question.

There have been a number of attempts to argue that the affirmation of determinism is self-refuting.[41] Those who have attempted this line of argument maintain something like the following: If determinism is true, then its affirmation, like every other human act, is a determined effect; thus determinism comes to be held on account of the same sort of factors which accounts for the holding by others of the opposite position. The conclusion drawn is that determinism itself undercuts its proponents' claim that their position ought to be preferred to its opposite. By means of this line of argument, determinism is rejected, not because it contradicts principles assumed by those who defend *Sfc*, but because it is self-refuting.

There is no consensus among philosophers that self-referential argumentation against determinism is cogent.[42] Here we examine some arguments employing this method of argumentation, and we conclude with their critics that these attempts are not cogent—in fact, that they beg the question. Later, in chapter five, we clarify the logic of self-referential argumentation; in chapter six, we propose a self-referential argument against *Nfc* which we think avoids begging the question.

In "Determinism's Dilemma," James N. Jordan articulates an argument typical of the best recent attempts to show that the assertion of determinism is self-refuting.

Jordan argues that if one accepts determinism as true, then one must admit that all theses, including the determinist's thesis, are effects of antecedent causes. It follows that whether the thesis is true or false, one's holding the thesis is wholly explicable in terms of antecedent causes. Thus the determinist and his opponent are equally determined to hold the positions which they do hold. And so one's assent to whichever position he holds has no necessary relationship to the fact that one position is true and its contradictory false.

Jordan does not deny that rational judgments have necessary causal conditions. But he argues that if someone wishes to maintain that rational judgments have sufficient conditions he

> . . . would need to produce evidence which is seen to conform to criteria of reasonable trustworthiness and which is recognized to confer, by virtue of some principle of deductive or probable inference, certainty or sufficient probability upon it. But if the proposition [of the determinist] is true, this could never happen, for it implies that whether anyone believes it and what he considers trustworthy evidence and acceptable principles of inference are determined altogether by conditions that have no assured congruence with the proposition's own merits or with criteria of sound argumentation whose validity consists of more than that we accept them.[43]

Jordan's point is that on deterministic grounds the correspondence between one's knowing the truth of a proposition and the causal factors which determine one's belief is accidental. Thus, if determinism is true, it is never possible to ascertain whether any statement—including the statement of determinism—is true.

Others who have developed an argument along the same lines have put the point in a similar way. A. E. Taylor: "If the determinist thesis is sound, then, it must follow that it is never possible to consider any issue, however purely speculative, with an 'open mind,' intending to pronounce one way or the other strictly, 'according to the worth of the evidence.' "[44] Paul Weiss: "If a determinist is willing to affirm that his theory is true, he must affirm that it is something which can be freely considered and responsibly adopted, and thus that those who know it are so far not determined by an alien power."[45] Lionel Kenner: Once the determinist "has asserted that our nervous system and physical environment are the sufficient and necessary conditions of all our thoughts and activities—that we are only very advanced electronic computers—he has relinquished the right to say that the arguments which appear cogent to us are valid arguments."[46] Malcolm Knox: "A theory claims to be true; its sponsors ask us to choose it and to reject as false a theory that contradicts it. Determinism is a theory which denies the possibility of choice, and it therefore refutes itself."[47] J. R. Lucas: "Determinism, therefore, cannot be true, because if it was, we should not take the determinists' arguments as being really arguments, but as being only conditioned reflexes. Their statements should not be regarded as really claiming to be true, but only as seeking to cause us to respond in some way desired by them."[48] A. Aaron Snyder: The inconsistency of determinism "arises out of the fact that the universal operation of physically sufficient causes would leave no room for the conceptual sufficiency of reasons."[49]

A *PNfc* certainly will object that arguments like these beg the question, because these arguments assume that certain factors cannot legitimately lead to assent if those factors are determined—factors such as "criteria of reasonable trustworthiness," "the worth of evidence," rational responsibility in considering and adopting an argument, the cogency of valid argument, the choice of a position on the basis of evidence, truth claims, and sufficient reasons. To exclude these factors betrays assumptions inherent in a point of view which the *PNfc* can consistently reject. The *PNfc* can find ways within his framework to explain the causal efficacy of factors which these arguments assume his position cannot explain.

Adolf Grünbaum, for example, claims that arguments of this sort gratuitously assume that if our beliefs are caused, they are forced upon us. Such an assumption, according to Grünbaum, confuses causation with compulsion and prevents proponents of the argument from seeing that the decisive cause of the determinist's belief might well be his consideration of the available evidence. Grünbaum goes on to argue that the causal generation of a belief in no way prevents it from being true:

> In fact, if a given belief were not produced in us by definite causes, we should have no reason to accept that belief as a correct description of the world, rather than some other belief arbitrarily selected. Far from making knowledge either adventitious or impossible, the deterministic theory about the origin of our beliefs alone provides the basis for thinking that our judgments of the world are or may be true. Knowing and judging are indeed causal processes in which the facts we judge are determining elements along with the cerebral mechanism employed in their interpretation. It follows that although the determinist's assent to his own doctrine is caused or determined, the truth of determinism is not jeopardized by this fact; if anything, it is made credible.
>
> More generally, both true beliefs and false beliefs have psychological causes. The difference between a true or warranted belief and a false or unwarranted one must therefore be sought *not* in *whether* the belief in question is caused; instead, the difference must be sought in the particular *character* of the psychological causal factors which issued in the entertaining of the belief; *a warrantedly held belief, which has the presumption of being true, is one to which a person gave assent in response to awareness of supporting evidence.*[50]

Grünbaum's point is that determinism by no means implies that the causes which determine one to hold a proposition true need exclude the factors invoked by those who try to argue that determinism is self-refuting.

In his article, Jordan responds to somewhat similar objections raised by A. J. Ayer.

Ayer contends that the hypothesis that all human behavior is governed by causal laws is not self-defeating. He holds that it is mistaken to assume that acting from reasons is incompatible with acting from causes. Believing a proposition because of certain brain processes is not incompatible with believing it because of rational grounds for it; the word "because" here is used in two senses which are not mutually destructive. Thus Ayer can hold both that he would think differently if his brain were constituted differently and that he actually thinks as he does for the reasons he gives.

Ayer points out that a calculating machine can operate both causally and according to logical laws. From this observation he draws the conclusion that the question of the adequacy of reasons for a belief is independent of the question whether there are necessary and sufficient conditions for holding that belief.[51]

Jordan responds that his argument does not assume that there is an incompatibility between acting from reasons and acting from causes. His argument only assumes the following conditional statement: If our rational assessments are causally determined, then we cannot know or rationally believe that any judgment is correct.[52] Jordan's reply, however, does not escape the point of Ayer's objection—that rational belief and causal determination are compatible. The assumption that they are incompatible is implied by Jordan's conditional statement. Moreover, Jordan's argument cannot be formulated without employing the premise that rational assent is incompatible with causal determination of that assent.

A. E. Taylor neatly sums up the view of those who have undertaken a line of argument similar to Jordan's: "To be a function of antecedent events is one thing, to be a function of logically relevant evidence is quite another," and Taylor assumes the determinist must deny this.[53] But a *PNfc* can grant this distinction, while at the same time maintaining that the evidence itself, the conviction it engenders, and even the perception of logical laws are all necessary effects of wholly determined causes. A *PNfc*, after all, does not have to maintain that the only kind of relationship is that between causes and their effects; he can, therefore, allow that there are also logical relations—being a "function of evidence"—and that these logical relations are a product not of choice but of determining conditions.

Thus, the *PNfc* can argue that when Taylor says that if determinism is correct it is impossible to consider any issue with an "open mind," he is equivocating.[54] To consider with an "open mind"—in the sense in which this is an intellectual obligation—means to reach a conclusion only after consideration of evidence and reasons, and then to be determined by them; it hardly means that one approaches a theoretical problem as if he were free to choose the position he will hold. If there is any choice involved, the *PNfc* will conclude, it might be to consider the problem with an open mind or not, and there seems to be nothing which would prevent such a choice from being determined—for example, by one's intense desire for truth.

In discussing Ayer's example of a calculating machine, Jordan states that if determinism is true then there is only a fortuitous connection between the conditions governing one's belief and the standards governing what ought to be believed. Calculating machines are built in conformity with such standards. If men are determined as calculating machines are, there is no way to tell whether human beliefs conform to such standards. Jordan says that on the determinist hypothesis, if men "make mistakes, they cannot recognize them; if they believe themselves mistaken in any instance, their belief is fortuitously correct if correct at all."[55]

As Grünbaum shows, such a response is question-begging. It assumes that a causally determined awareness of the evidence cannot be among the factors which legitimately determine and rationally alter belief. This assumption comes out even more clearly in Lionel Kenner's formulation of the argument: environment are the sufficient and necessary conditions of all our thoughts and activities—that we are only very advanced electronic computers—he has activities—that we are only very advanced electronic computers—he has relinquished the right to say that the arguments which appear cogent to us are valid arguments."[56]

Of course, no one can be certain without qualification that arguments which appear cogent to us are valid arguments. Whether *Nfc* is true or not, epistemological problems remain always with us. And a *PNfc* need not necessarily maintain that a man is nothing but an advanced computer; the analogy was only brought into service to make the point that determination by logic and by physical causality are not mutually incompatible. Most fundamentally, Kenner is assuming that there can be for the *PNfc* only one sense of "sufficient and necessary" conditions. But a *PNfc* can maintain that while a set of logical rules are the necessary and sufficient *formal* conditions of the theorems which can be deduced in a certain system, the necessary and sufficient conditions for the behavior of the mathematician are ultimately determined. The mathematician's cognitional behavior, then, would not be dependent upon any free choice on his part and would not be independent of the factors which account for natural events and processes in general.

It is fair to ask a *PNfc* how it happens that human cognitive equipment, functioning according to natural laws as he thinks it must, has a capacity for arriving at truth. The *PNfc* could plausibly answer this question in various ways—for example, by suggesting a scientific account of the survival-value of this particular capacity. C. S. Lewis tries to rule out such an answer by arguing that one cannot know such an explanation except by inference, and so unless one knows inference to be valid, one cannot even begin an argument for its validity.[57] But this objection fails. Lewis assumes what a *PNfc* can deny, namely that an account of inferential processes consistent with *Nfc* casts doubt upon the validity of such processes.

In summary, the preceding attempts to show the affirmation of *Nfc* self-refuting are unsuccessful. Even if *Nfc* is true, still the determining causes of knowledge might arise from the interaction of organism and environment—in other words, the facts might determine what we think about them. Nor would the truth of *Nfc* exclude there being criteria of adequacy logically independent of the causes of belief. The *PNfc's* admission that his own and his opponent's position are equally products of necessary and sufficient causal conditions is not self-refuting. Obviously, the concrete causes of different beliefs are in fact different, but which belief is correct is independent of how each originates.

A *PNfc* might argue that *Nfc* is true on the supposition that all relationships are cause-effect relationships. However, he also can argue for *Nfc* on the supposition that there are logical and epistemic relationships which are irreducible to causal relationships. The former argument is perhaps susceptible to the charge that it is self-refuting. The latter clearly is not. The *PSfc* himself might wish to hold (and many on this side of the controversy have held) that there are self-evident truths, evident data of experience, and necessary conclusions —and that free choice has no place in a person's cognition of any of these, except, perhaps, to the extent that he can attend to them or not.

A proof of the irreducibility of epistemic and logical relations to cause-effect relations does not establish free choice. The irreducibility of human cognition to natural mechanism is not the same as the irreducibility of choice to natural mechanism. Aristotle certainly considered the human intellect to be transcendent to natural causality, but it is by no means clear that Aristotle's voluntariness involves free choice. The preceding arguments that the assertion of *Nfc* is self-refuting do not take this distinction into account. Even if they were successful, they would prove only that human cognition is irreducible to natural mechanism.

F. J. R. Lucas's argument

In *The Freedom of the Will*, J. R. Lucas articulates an ingenious argument against determinism based on self-reference. He characterizes his argument as self-referential, but contrasts it with arguments of the sort discussed in the preceding section.[58] Lucas's characterization of his argument might suggest that he has developed a new variant of the argument that determinism is self-refuting. But the arguments discussed in the preceding section and Lucas's argument are not self-referential in the same sense.

The argument that determinism is self-refuting seeks to show that the determinist is refuted by his very act of claiming to know his position true. Such an argument is based on the reference which the determinist must make to his own act of affirming determinism; he must make reference to this act inasmuch as he is making a universal claim about human behavior. The attraction of such an argument, as we have noted, is that it seems able to avoid assuming anything which the determinist need not grant.

Lucas's argument, by contrast, is based on the fact that there is a legitimate kind of self-reference—namely, the kind of self-reference involved in Gödel's theorem. Lucas regards this type of self-reference as an expression in mathematical terms of the reflexivity of human self-consciousness.[59] He argues that no material system—which he assumes the human mind would be if determinism were true—can prove every Gödel-type theorem, while some human persons can in principle do so.[60]

It is clear, then, that Lucas's argument is not a new variant of the argument that determinism is self-refuting. His argument does not seek to "hoist the determinist on his own petard." Rather, he points to a given human ability. This fact involves the phenomenon of self-reference, which Lucas thinks no physical system can embody. Thus, Lucas's argument does not have the advantage which the argument that determinism is self-refuting would have if it were successful. Lucas's argument begins with a description which a *PNfc* can reject.

One assumption of Lucas which a *PNfc* might reject is that no physical system can embody the kind of self-reference involved in Gödel's theorem. We do not feel competent to criticize Lucas's assumption, but it seems to us that he presents little evidence for it; rather, he articulates it as if it were intuitively evident. Thus, this assumption seems to function in Lucas's argument very much as the assumption that reasons for judgment cannot be determined functions in the argument that determinism is self-refuting. Like the latter assumption, Lucas's assumption is a general thesis about the nature of the physical universe. It is unlikely that a *PNfc* would grant this limitation upon what a physical system can do, and it is not clear to us that he needs to grant it.

Even if Lucas's argument can meet the preceding objection, however, it fails to establish what Lucas sets out to prove: that man has free will. At best, Lucas demonstrates the irreducibility of human self-consciousness to physical processes. As we have explained above, this not to show that choice is irreducible to wholly determined conditions.

Thus Lucas's argument, whatever one might think of it, is not directly relevant to *Sfc/Nfc*.

3: Arguments against Free Choice

In this chapter, we examine arguments for *Nfc*. Some have proposed that people are directly aware that choices are caused; those who hold this view might challenge our description of the experience of choice and urge that a more adequate description makes any further argument for *Nfc* otiose. Others have proposed that *Nfc* follows directly from logical truths.

We take up these two proposals and argue that neither experience alone nor logic alone can settle *Sfc/Nfc* in favor of *Nfc*. Thus it becomes clear that in *Sfc/Nfc*, neither side bears a special burden of proof. In this respect, the opposing views are on an equal footing; they offer contending accounts of the initiation of those choices which people think are free. Once we have criticized the proposals that experience alone or logic alone can settle the controversy, we examine physical determinism, psychological determinism, and other arguments for *Nfc*. Finally, we criticize the theological argument that divine causality precludes human free choice.

In trying to establish his position, a *P Nfc* faces some of the same problems as a *PSfc*. Both must avoid using or assuming premises which an opponent need not admit. Our examination of arguments for *Nfc* will show that those which are not question-begging or otherwise fallacious are very weak. It is important to bear in mind that we do not claim that the weakness of arguments for *Nfc* establishes *Sfc*. This weakness shows only that our inquiry is not unnecessary. The question has not been settled.

A. Is one aware that his choices are caused?

One basis for thinking *Nfc* true, though seldom baldly stated, is to regard it as an obvious fact. This view corresponds to the argument for *Sfc* from immediate experience.

Someone who regards *Nfc* as an obvious fact would claim that the description of the experience of choice given in chapter one is incomplete and therefore seriously misleading. John Stuart Mill appears to attack a similar description of the experience of choice:

> Take any alternative: say to murder or not to murder. I am told, that if I elect to murder, I am conscious that I could have elected to abstain: but am I conscious that I could have abstained if my aversion to the crime, and my dread of its consequences, had been weaker than the temptation? If I elect to abstain: in what sense am I conscious that I could have elected to commit the crime? Only if I had desired to commit it with a desire stronger than my horror of murder; not with one less strong. When we think of ourselves hypothetically as having acted otherwise than we did, we always suppose a difference in the antecedents: we picture ourselves as having known something that we did not know, or not known something that we did know; which is a difference in the external inducements; or as having desired something, or disliked something, more or less than we did; which is a difference in the internal inducements.[1]

Thus Mill contends that in making a choice one is aware that knowledge and desire—including horror, liking, and other "internal inducements"—settle whether one elects to act or to abstain.

Mill's claim does not show that the description of the experience of choice provided in chapter one is inadequate. We do not claim to describe there an experience *everyone* has, nor do we claim that people who have this experience call it "the experience of choice." In chapter one, section C, we point out that there are acts arising spontaneously from given desires or settled dispositions, acts preceded by no deliberation and choice. The description also allows for a kind of reflection and choice which is limited to the working out of a practical application of purposes which are taken for granted; such choice need not carry with it any sense of freedom, and does provide an experience which Mill aptly describes.

A *PSfc* can point to aspects of the experience of choice described in chapter one, sections E and F, which are ignored by Mill's description. One of these aspects is the experience of conflicting motives, neither of which seems strong enough to override the other, and the subsequent experience of one's very choosing, endorsing one motive or the other and thus ending their conflict by *making* one motive effective and rendering the other ineffectual.

Thus, the *PSfc* can admit that Mill describes an authentic experience but deny that Mill describes the only relevant experience. One can claim to have had, at one time or another, both sorts of experiences. For example, a person can say that he has had the experience Mill describes when he gave in to a strong temptation to overindulgence in some way, but that he has had an experience which Mill's description does not fit when he decided to go to graduate school rather than to accept an attractive invitation to enter a large corporation's management trainee program.

Still, it should be noted that although the *PSfc* and many ordinary people have an experience of choice which the description provided in chapter one, sections E and F, fits and which Mill's description does not fit, this fact does not settle *Sfc/Nfc* in favor of the *PSfc*. What the experience does settle is that there are some data of which *Sfc* is an interpretation to be defended against the interpretation provided by the *PNfc*.

The preceding comments about the experience of choice and its relevance to *Sfc/Nfc* suggest the lines along which a *PSfc* might respond to the claim that *Nfc* is an obvious fact. The *PSfc* can maintain that an account like Mill's would be conclusive evidence for *Nfc* only if there could be no other interpretation of *any* experience of choosing. By offering his alternative for consideration, the *PSfc* shows that there can be another interpretation of some experience of choosing.

The *PSfc* also can point out that the *PNfc* asserts a universal negative proposition, a proposition which will be falsified by a single counterexample. The possibility of such a counterexample cannot be excluded by a supporting example, such as that offered by Mill, or even by any multitude of such supporting examples. Moreover, the *PSfc* will point out that his opponent not only claims that no one *does* make a free choice, but that no one *can* make one. The *PNfc* denies free choice in principle—that is, denies that anyone ever has this ability. The *PNfc* makes a claim so strong that no experience by itself could warrant it.

Thus, both a *PSfc* and a *PNfc* can appeal to experience in an effort to settle the dispute as easily and directly as possible. Neither appeal can exclude the other interpretation of the data; both appeals beg the question at issue in *Sfc/Nfc*. The appeal to the experience of choice by a *PNfc* is even less plausible than the analogous appeal by a *PSfc*, however, since *Nfc* is a universal negative proposition and it excludes an ability, while the *PSfc* makes a more modest claim—that someone at some time makes or *can* make some free choice.

Consequently, it is clear that the *PNfc* must provide some sort of reasoning or argumentation in support of his position. In fact, there already is a minimal argument in Mill's approach, for he insists upon a more complete account of the data, taking for granted an assumption—one surely correct—that a more complete account of the data is to be preferred. Only on this assumption can he even begin to draw a conclusion from the facts.

Another very simple form of argumentation, one related to Mill's, is direct generalization from instances of the sort Mill describes. Brand Blanshard summarizes such an argument:

> You may remember that Sir Francis Galton was so much impressed with this possibility that for some time he kept account in a notebook of the occasions on which he made important choices with a full measure of this feeling of freedom; then shortly after each choice he turned his eye backward in search of constraints that might have been acting on him stealthily. He found it so easy to bring such constraining factors to light that he surrendered to the determinist view.[2]

A *PSfc* can deny that a fact about Galton is representative of the experience of everyone. But Blanshard's point seems to be that the induction Galton makes is one which anyone else would make if he considered the facts as meticulously as Galton does.

The *PSfc* can reject this simple induction by saying that people who make free choices will not reach Galton's conclusion. Blanshard can only be certain that everyone must reach the same conclusion if he assumes *Nfc*—that is, if he begs the question.

Moreover, the *PSfc* need not accept Galton's description of the facts. Does Galton's ability to think of constraining factors show that they were sufficient to determine the choice? How could anyone, even Galton, be certain that he is not deceiving himself by considering his experience with a deterministic bias in order to rationalize questionable choices and thus avoid feelings of guilt or of personal failure? Just as the *PSfc* cannot rule out in principle the possibility that factors of which he is not aware determine the choices in which he experiences a sense of freedom, so the *P Nfc* cannot rule out in principle the possibility that self-deception and rationalization blind him to the data which would otherwise give rise to a sense of freedom.

Setting aside this rather personal counterattack, the *PSfc* can admit the experiential basis of the induction and concede the adequacy of the sample but still maintain that the conclusion to *Nfc* is far stronger than the conclusion warranted by any sound canons of induction. At best, Blanshard's argument shows that people *do not* make free choices, not that they *cannot* make them.

To sum up. An attempt to establish *Nfc* by appealing directly to immediate experience fails. Like the analogous argument for *Sfc*, this one is question-begging. One certainly can grant Mill's assumption that a full description of the data is to be preferred to a partial description and Blanshard's assumption that a generalization based on meticulous observation is to be accepted, but the arguments shaped by these assumptions also fail to support *Nfc*, for these arguments either are question-begging or they draw conclusions which logic does not justify, or both. The fact that a *P Nfc* rarely limits the defense of his position to such simple forms of argument also indicates his awareness that his position needs stronger support.

Thus, a *P Nfc* usually argues from a general thesis of determinism, from a theory of human behavior, from the unintelligibility of free choices, or from the fruitlessness of regarding choices as free. The strongest possible argument for *Nfc*, however, would be one showing that *Sfc* is logically impossible.

B. Is free choice logically impossible?

The view that *Nfc* follows from logical truths alone has had few serious supporters. Still, if this view were correct, *Sfc* would be absurd, and further discussion of *Sfc/Nfc* would be pointless. Therefore, we consider this line of argument with some care and attempt to make clear why it is mistaken.

The thesis that the truths of logic entail *Nfc* often is called "fatalism." However, "fatalism" also has a popular sense which must not be confused with the technical sense it has in philosophy.

Fatalism in the popular sense is the view that a certain state of affairs will inevitably obtain at a certain time in the future even though nobody can foresee with certitude when that state of affairs will obtain. It is not fatalism in this sense to hold that there are some inevitable future states of affairs which can be foreseen with certitude—for example, the next eclipse of the moon.

It is vulgar fatalism to maintain that a certain state of affairs (for example, the death of the authors of this book) will occur at a certain future time (for example, on January 1, 2000) and that this will happen regardless of what anyone does or does not do in the meanwhile. The event is inevitable since nothing can prevent its happening. Thus, vulgar fatalism amounts to picking out a particular future event, detaching it from the context of its determining conditions, asserting that the event will occur at a determinate time, and denying that the context of conditions in which one replaces the event will make any difference.

If the authors of this book were vulgar fatalists, they would see no point in trying to forestall their deaths, for they would be fated to die either on January 1, 2000, or on some other date. As a result, they might take extraordinary risks, confident that they could not die prior to the date already predetermined. It is obvious why vulgar fatalism is a soldier's favorite myth.

Vulgar fatalism often has been attacked by philosophers, especially by determinists anxious to prevent misinterpretation of their own position. So far as we know, no philosopher ever has defended vulgar fatalism. Since vulgar fatalism fails if the more sophisticated arguments for *Nfc* which we will consider fail, there is no need to consider its merits. We note it for clarificatory purposes only.

Philosophical fatalism is the position that one can deduce *Nfc* from logical truths.[3] Any conclusion which can be deduced validly from logical truths alone is logically necessary. Thus, if *Nfc* can be deduced from logical truths alone, it is logically necessary. The fatalist argument proceeds by trying to show that logically necessary truths by themselves exclude the alternative possibilities which are a necessary condition for free choice, and thus that *Sfc* is logically impossible.

Arguments for philosophical fatalism have been constructed in such a way that they involve reference to future events. This reference to future events might be useful in such arguments, but this reference is not part of the meaning of philosophical fatalism.

Since we are more interested in philosophical fatalism as a position than in the details of diverse formulations of the argument for it, we propose a formulation which we think captures the essential features of any argument for fatalism. In the argument itself—as distinct from our example—we avoid time-reference, which we consider irrelevant to the position. We also make explicit the claim that *Sfc* is logically impossible, for we consider this implication of fatalism alone to be relevant to *Sfc/Nfc*.

1) Every proposition must be either true, or if not true, then false.

2) Assume that one man affirms proposition *p* and another denies *p*, then it is logically necessary that either *p* is true or *not-p* is true. (Let "*p*" name the proposition: "The authors of this book will attend next year's meeting of the Western Division of the American Philosophical Association.")

3) Let "*R*" name the state of affairs which would be sufficient to make *p* true, and let "*not-R*" name the state of affairs which would be sufficient to make *not-p* true. It is logically impossible that both *R* and *not-R* obtain.

4) Therefore, if *p* is true, it is logically impossible that *not-R* obtain, while if *not-p* is true, it is logically impossible that *R* obtain. (If it is true that we will go to the meeting, it is logically impossible that all the conditions for our not going should obtain; if it is true that we will not go, it is logically impossible that all the conditions for our going to it should obtain.)

5) If it is logically impossible that the sufficient condition for any particular event obtain, then the occurrence of the state of affairs alternative to that event is logically necessary.

6) Therefore, if *p* is true, *p* is logically necessary; if *not-p* is true, *not-p* is logically necessary. (Whether we do go or not, whatever we actually will do is logically necessary.)

7) Therefore, it is not the case that both *p* and *not-p* are logically possible. Since one of them is logically necessary, the other must be logically impossible.

8) There can be no alternative possibilities.

9) That anyone can make a free choice is inconsistent with (8).

10) But (8) is entailed by logically necessary truths.

11) *Sfc* is logically impossible.

A *PSfc* will criticize the logic of this argument. The difficulty seems to center in step (4): "Therefore, if *p* is true, it is logically impossible that *not-R* obtain, while if *not-p* is true, it is logically impossible that *R* obtain." As it stands, this means that if any proposition is true, the conditions which would lead to its falsification are logically impossible. Taken by itself, this statement would simply beg the question in favor of fatalism, for the nonfatalist need only grant that if any proposition is true, the conditions which would falsify it cannot also be *actually fulfilled*.

What makes step (4) plausible? It is stated as a conclusion. Step (3) states that it is logically impossible for both *R* and *not-R* to obtain, where "*R*" and "*not-R*" name states of affairs which would be sufficient for the truth of the respective contradictories, *p* and *not-p*. Inasmuch as *p* and *not-p* are logically incompatible, it follows that *R* and *not-R* are necessarily incompatible. From this it seems to follow that if *p* is true, then *not-R* is impossible—and this is the conclusion stated as step (4).

To show why this conclusion does not follow, a *PSfc* need only reconstruct step (4) of the argument, being careful about the placement of the modal operators:

   4A) The following is necessary: If *p* is true, then *R* obtains.

   4B) The following is impossible: *R* and *not-R* simultaneously obtain.

   4C) The following is impossible: *p* is true, and *not-R* obtains.

The trouble is that (4C) is not equivalent to the proposition required by the fatalist argument: The following is impossible: *p* is true, and *not-R* is possible.

In other words, while it is impossible that any proposition be true and that a state of affairs which is a sufficient condition of its contradictory *also obtain*, it is by no means impossible that a proposition be true and that the state of affairs which is the sufficient condition of its contradictory *also be possible*. This assumption, unlike (4C), is not a logical truth, and if a fatalist makes it, he begs the question.

To return to our example. A fatalist would conclude that if it is true that the authors of this book will go to next year's meeting of the Western Division of the American Philosophical Association, then it is not in their power not to choose to go. The *PSfc* will admit only that if we freely choose to go to the meeting and go to it as a result of this choice, then we do not remain able to choose not to go and to stay away as a result of this choice. Free choice does not mean that one can choose both alternatives, only that one can choose either. If one could choose both, choice would be unnecessary.

Nevertheless, if it is true that as a result of a free choice we will go to the meeting, but have not yet decided to do so, then it is now possible for us to go and possible for us not to go, and the sufficient condition in virtue of which it is true that we will go, will be given only when we freely choose to go—a choice which, unless reversed, will eliminate the possibility of not going. If someone assumes that the truth of the proposition that we will go eliminates the possibility of our not going, and fails to notice that according to the *PSfc* the latter alternative will be eliminated and the former brought about by the same fact—the fact of our free choice—then he begs the question in favor of fatalism.

In formulating the controversy about free choice in chapter one, section H, we criticize a fallacious argument which is offered for the position that if there ever is a choice, it is necessary that the choice be free. This argument for free choice is an analogue of fatalism. We point out that the argument for this position involves a fallacy of modal logic: to suppose that the conjunction of *p* and the impossibility of *p and q* entails the impossibility of *q*, when it only entails that *q* is not the case. The fallacy in the fatalist argument is similar, for the fatalist argues from the impossibility of one state of affairs being given in conjunction with another state of affairs which is sufficient to bring about something incompatible with the first, to the impossibility by itself of any state of affairs which would bring about something incompatible with any given state of affairs.

Richard Taylor considers the objection that his argument for fatalism involves this fallacy. Taylor's version of the argument is expressed in terms of propositional truth and human abilities. He argues that any proposition which is true, always is true, whether the proposition is about the past or about the future. Just as a true historical statement always will be true, a true prediction always has been true. Just as no person has the ability to change the past, no one has the ability to make false a true proposition about what will be. Taylor answers the objection that his argument involves a modal fallacy as follows:

> The fatalist argument has nothing to do with impossibility in those senses familiar to logic. It has to do with unavoidability. It is, in other words, concerned with human abilities. The fact that a statement is true does not, to be sure, entail that it is necessary , nor do all false statements express impossibilities. Nonetheless, no man is able to avoid what is truly described, however contingently, in any statement, nor to bring about what is thus falsely described.[4]

The *PSfc* can agree with Taylor that no one has the ability to make true statements false, whether those statements be about the past or about the future. However, the *PSfc* can deny that *Nfc* follows from Taylor's observation. For if it is true that someone is going to make a certain choice freely, then it also is true that no one—even the individual himself—has the ability to make it false that he is going to make that choice freely. Still, according to the *PSfc*, if someone is going to make a free choice, the only thing which makes it true that he makes the choice he does is that he exercises his ability to choose thus or otherwise by choosing thus rather than otherwise. Taylor's argument, the *PSfc* will conclude, either begs the question by assuming that among past and future truths there are none about free choices, or demands a modal argument of the sort already criticized.

Some have suggested that the fatalist's conclusion can be avoided only by a drastic revision of the logical principle of excluded middle—the principle that any proposition which is not true is false.[5] The suggestion is that propositions about future events of certain kinds, including free choices, are neither true nor false until the time comes when the condition is given which will settle what will happen. If the fatalist argument does involve the modal fallacy which we have pointed out, however, this proposed revision of a logical principle is unnecessary.

A fatalist *PNfc* might urge that if his view rests on an elementary fallacy in modal logic, then the *PSfc* can hardly explain the appeal of fatalism to many intelligent people and the drastic measures opponents of the position have been prepared to take to avoid it. However, the *PSfc* can call attention to the following semantic point.[6] Often if someone calls a proposition "true," he means that someone knows it, or at least in principle *could* know it, to be true. This especially holds for propositions about particular future events. If one says that it is true that he will attend next year's meeting of the Western Division of the American Philosophical Association, his statement normally would be taken as an expression of intention or as a commitment. One seldom has occasion to talk about the truth of statements about future events unless he is considering them as known, or at least as knowable.

Of course, no proposition is known unless the conditions which would verify it are known. The *PSfc* will point out that what anyone will do in virtue of a free choice is indeterminate until the choice is made. Since free choice is one of its own necessary conditions, the conditions which verify statements about a future free choice cannot obtain until the choice is made. Therefore, in principle no one can know what someone will choose, nor can anyone know anything which depends upon a free choice yet to be made. It follows, according to the *PSfc*, that it is not possible to make categorical statements concerning future free choices or their consequences.

This semantic point renders questionable the very first step of a fatalist argument. If "true" is taken as equivalent to "in principle knowable to someone as true" and if "false" is taken as equivalent to "in principle knowable to someone as false," then the first step of the fatalist argument becomes: "Every proposition must in principle be knowable to someone as true, or if not in principle knowable to someone as true, then knowable to someone as false." In other words, the conditions sufficient to verify or falsify every proposition are always knowable, which presupposes that they are always determinate.

Some fatalists perhaps have imported an epistemic sense into "true" and "false" in the argument's first premise. An indication of such a confusion is the suggestion that there must be a middle ground between truth and falsity, if the force of the fatalist argument is to be avoided. Obviously, it is possible to suppose that there is a *tertium quid* between the extremes "in principle knowable to someone as true" and "in principle knowable to someone as false"; the *tertium quid* is: "not in principle knowable to anyone as either true or false."

A *PNfc* could suggest that fatalism might be defended as part of a wider metaphysical theory without appeal to the line of argument we have criticized. This metaphysical theory would exclude possibility from reality; whatever is actual is necessary, while whatever is not actual is impossible.

Such a metaphysical thesis has been defended by many important philosophers beginning with Parmenides. His view is that one should not think or say what is not, for what is not, is unintelligble. In modern times, philosophers such as Spinoza, Leibniz, and Hegel developed a more nuanced version of Parmenides' position. For them, all truths would be understood to be logically necessary if their connections to their ultimate grounds were known.

The *PSfc* can point out that all such rationalistic metaphysics must attempt to account for the apparent, the seemingly contingent, the moments in the Absolute which are not the Absolute. The metaphysicians distinguish between the logically necessary and the impossible, deny the intelligibility of talk about the latter, but continue to talk about it themselves.

One final point. A *PSfc*, confronted with a metaphysician who maintains fatalism, can refuse to accept the force of the rationalistic position, even if he can find no flaw in it. "I have my sense of freedom," he might say, "and no airy fabric of argument will convince me that I do not make free choices." The fatalist can reply that if fatalism is true, logic demands that *Sfc* be abandoned. Still, the *PSfc* can refuse to admit the priority of logic over experience.

In sum. A fatalist argument assumes that logical principles are to be adhered to consistently in all of one's thinking, even when doing so requires one to give up beliefs based upon experience. The fatalist maintains that logic implies *Nfc*, and so one should admit this position. The *PSfc*, however, need not grant the fatalist's claim that logical truths by themselves entail *Nfc*, for this claim is not supported by a sound argument. And even if he could find no fallacy in the argument, it would remain open to a *PSfc* to suspect that there was something wrong with logic, rather than with his belief in free choice, especially when logic is used to ground a rationalistic metaphysics.

C. Do the laws of nature exclude free choice?

Since the rise of modern science, many have regarded the thesis of universal determinism as the premise of the best argument for *Nfc*. Laplace gave this thesis its classic formulation:

> We ought then to consider the present state of the universe as the effect of its antecedent state, and as the cause of the one which is going to follow. An intelligence which knew at a given instant all the forces at work in nature and the relative positions of the entities which make it up—provided that it were great enough to submit these data to analysis—would comprehend in the same formula the movements of the largest bodies in the universe and those of the tiniest atom. For it, nothing would be uncertain; the future, like the past, would be present to its eyes.[7]

Clearly, *Sfc* is incompatible with universal determinism of the sort Laplace posits. If *Sfc* is true, there could be events—free choices—which even the intelligence Laplace imagines could not predict.

As for the thesis of universal determinism itself, many have thought that it is either presupposed or entailed—or in some way strongly supported—by the

laws of nature formulated in modern science. Thus the development of modern
science seems to provide a very strong argument for *Nfc*. This case for *Nfc*
often is called "physical determinism."

The *PSfc* can feel the force of this argument. J. R. Lucas forthrightly
expresses this feeling: ". . . physical determinism is frightening. The arguments for it are forceful." Lucas points out that the explanatory success of
modern physics strongly supports its worldview; even if the scientific account
of nature proves inadequate in some details, it remains "both well supported
and incompatible with freedom."[8]

Henry Sidgwick succinctly states physical determinism:

> On the Determinist side there is a cumulative argument of great force. The
> belief that events are determinately related to the state of things immediately
> preceding them is now held by all competent thinkers in respect of all kinds of
> occurrences except human volitions. It has steadily grown both intensively and
> extensively, both in clearness and certainty of conviction and in universality of
> application, as the human mind has developed and human experience has been
> systematised and enlarged. Step by step in successive departments of fact con-
> flicting modes of thought have receded and faded, until at length they have
> vanished everywhere, except from this mysterious citadel of Will. Everywhere
> else the belief is so firmly established that some declare its opposite to be
> inconceivable: others even maintain that it always was so. Every scientific
> procedure assumes it: each success of science confirms it. And not only are we
> finding ever new proof that events are cognisably determined, but also that the
> different modes of determination of different kinds of events are fundamentally
> identical and mutually dependent: and naturally, with the increasing conviction of
> the essential unity of the cognisable universe, increases the indisposition to allow
> the exceptional character claimed by Libertarians for the department of human
> action.[9]

As Sidgwick's lucid formulation makes clear, the physical determinist need not
claim that *Nfc* is entailed by one or several laws of nature. If there were a law
from which *Nfc* followed, the physical determinist's case would be most
powerful.

At the same time, the *PNfc* need not regard universal determinism as an a
priori truth from which *Nfc* is deduced without further argument. Rather, as
Sidgwick explains, the success of the physical sciences has grounded a cumula-
tive argument for universal determinism. The conviction grows that the deterministic thesis is universally applicable; the mysterious citadel of will is not
exempt. Proponents of physical determinism, when they argue for *Nfc*, often
offer an informal account of the mechanisms of thought and choice which
renders plausible the project of bringing this set of phenomena within the range
of the scientific method which has succeeded so well in all the rest of nature.

Paul Rée's articulation of the view that free will would violate the law of causality is typical. He mentions many hereditary and environmental factors which shape an individual's personality and character. Such factors account for differences in the feelings and emotional reactions of different persons. Then he suggests that the same model can be extended to thought and action:

> Likewise every intention, indeed, every thought that ever passes through the brain, the silliest as well as the most brilliant, the true as well as the false, exists of necessity. In that sense there is no freedom of thought. . . .
>
> Just as sensations and thoughts are necessary, so, too, is action. It is, after all, nothing other than their externalization, their objective embodiment. Action is born of sensations and thoughts. So long as the sensations are not sufficiently strong, action cannot occur, and when the sensations and thoughts are constituted so as to yield the sufficient cause for it, then it must occur; then the appropriate nerves and muscles are set to work.[10]

Physical determinism can begin as a specific deterministic hypothesis about human behavior, which then seeks some support from its conformity with the wider scientific worldview.[11] This form of physical determinism can be formulated by saying that no interpretive model in addition to the models used to account for other natural events and processes is required to account for human choice and action. Richard Brandt and Jaegwon Kim propose such a formulation of physical determinism: An explanation will be deterministic if and only if the inferential and nomological patterns found in the biological sciences are taken to be sufficient to explain human choice.[12]

Any instance of physical determinism of this type would be a hypothesis proposed to explain human choices. Such a hypothesis would be credible partly because it calls for the use in the investigation of human behavior of methods and models already successful in other fields. Thus even when *Nfc* is neither deduced from universal determinism nor from any particular law or laws of nature, but proposed as part of a hypothesis about human behavior, the physical determinist still argues for *Nfc* as the view of human behavior which best conforms to the deterministic worldview of the physical and biological sciences. To consider human behavior as the *PSfc* does is simply unscientific.

The *PSfc* can criticize physical determinism on a number of points which seem vulnerable. One possibly vulnerable point is the thesis of universal determinism.

Universal determinism, the *PSfc* might claim, lacks determinate reference. If one says that every event is determined by antecedents, "determined" serves only as a schema which must be specified in each context in a somewhat different way.[13]

However, one can propose a version of physical determinism within a restricted theoretical framework in which there is no difficulty in giving a specific meaning to "determined," and to such related notions as "cause" and "lawful account." Physical determinism can take the form of a special theory of human behavior in which the notion of cause—or some notion which functions as cause does—can be specified to fit the subject matter. For example, in behavioristic psychology the notion of cause is specified in terms of operant conditioning and genetic factors. Any special theory of the determination of human behavior would take its place in the generally deterministic worldview of science, and thus a meaning of "cause" specified to human behavior would be a legitimate member of the family of scientific meanings of the expression.[14]

The *PSfc* might object that a deterministic theory of human behavior is vacuous, for if one accepts determinism, there can be nothing which he would accept as a counterinstance to the deterministic theory of human behavior.[15]

An objection along these lines perhaps presupposes verificationism. The physical determinist need not be a verificationist, and we argue against verificationism in chapter five, section D. If a physical determinist is not a verificationist, it is not clear why the hypothesis he proposes must be disconfirmable by experience. Many truths about the world are not. For example, the truth that people learn by experience cannot be disconfirmed by experience.

Moreover, a falsifiable version of physical determinism seems possible. Jonathan Glover suggests as an analogy an imaginary computer, the inner workings of which happen to be inaccessible. One might test whether the machine was governed by causal laws by correlating inputs and outputs. One could then generalize on the data and predict future performance: "Consistently correct predictions would count as verifying the hypothesis that the machine was governed by the causal laws in question."[16]

The *PSfc* might answer that no deterministic account of human behavior, given the complexity of the subject matter, can be so simple. He will point out that a convinced *PNfc* always can account for irregularity in behavior by assuming unknown variables. However, the *PNfc* can specify some degree or type of irregularity which he would be willing to admit as evidence against his hypothesis. If the *PNfc* articulates his deterministic view of human behavior in the form of a psychology like Skinner's or Freud's, he need not reject a priori the possibility of falsification. He can admit his position to be in principle falsifiable while in practice he can account for irregularities by positing further variables.

The *PSfc* might dispute the conviction that science will vindicate determinism by pointing out that physics itself is no longer completely deterministic; the indeterminism of quantum mechanics renders obsolete the older, mechanistic view.[17]

But developments in physics do not lend support to the *PSfc* as clearly as he might wish. It is a moot question whether quantum indeterminacy is even relevant to possible scientific explanations of human behavior. Felix Mainx argues:

> Almost all biological processes take place in the macrophysical domain, so that in their case the indeterminateness of the microphysical elementary processes plays no part. This also holds for enzymatic, hormonal, and stimulus-physiological processes, for which an origin from the microphysical domain has often been incorrectly asserted on the basis of superficial estimates. . . . The idea of P. Jordan of an amplifying mechanism which could allow the processes in the microphysical domain to influence the macrophysical organic event is quite conceivable. But we know of no such phenomena in the behavior of organisms, and it would be difficult to imagine how such effects within an organism, which are only statistically predictable, can be reconciled with its existence as a highly complicated system.[18]

If Mainx is correct, a biopsychological account of human action could be entirely deterministic; such an account would not need to mention quantum indeterminacy.

Of course, one tends to think of nature as unified to such an extent that events at the microphysical level must have some causal relation with the macrophysical processes of human biology, including brain processes. But an account of those causal relations does not exist.[19] Without such an account, the claim that quantum indeterminacy makes room for free choice appears to be a speculative, not a scientific, thesis.[20]

In short, even if some scientific theory does present a picture of an indeterministic physical world, it is not clear that this indeterministic picture is relevant to human choice and action.[21]

The *PNfc* also can argue that while quantum mechanics leaves the individual event undetermined, the theory does make definite predictions about large numbers of events, and such statistical laws exclude the possibility of free choice. Erwin Schrödinger argues:

> . . . quantum laws, though they leave the single event undetermined, predict a quite definite *statistics* of events when the same situation occurs again and again. If these statistics are interfered with by any agent, this agent violates the laws of quantum mechanics just as objectionably as if it interfered—in pre-quantum physics—with a strictly causal mechanical law.[22]

Schrödinger's point is that scientific laws—statistical or otherwise—do not admit of exceptions. Hence, human actions can no more violate statistical laws than they can violate strict causal laws; indeterminism does not leave room for free choice. Schrödinger's point seems to be well taken.[23]

Thus, quantum indeterminism, far from indicating that the current scientific pucture of the world is compatible with *Sfc*, apparently remains as incompatible with it as classical physical determinism.

Nevertheless, the *PNfc* must admit that the classical deterministic view formulated by Laplace is at least oversimplified. If Sidgwick were alive today, he would observe that the forces of determinism have been diverted from their seige upon the citadel of will by a fresh challenge in the very domain which he regarded as absolutely secure. For even if quantum physics does not lend the *PSfc* the support he might wish, it does take away the clear support the *PNfc* once enjoyed from classical physics and replaces this support with a problem. If the deterministic thesis is not universal, the *PNfc* cannot deduce *Nfc* from it. Thus, the *PNfc* not only must rebut his opponent's attempt to use quantum indeterminacy to support *Sfc*, the *PNfc* also must *show* either that quantum indeterminacy is compatible with universal determinism or that quantum indeterminacy is the only possible exception to universal determinism. The former thesis has yet to be established, and we know of no attempt to establish the latter; in fact, we can think of no way in which someone might make such an attempt.

However, the physical determinist can point out that there are several formal and methodological characteristics of science which demand that any scientific understanding of any subject matter be deterministic.

For example, it can be argued that all adequately developed scientific theories involve appeals to what Hempel calls "covering laws"—laws which connect definite antecedent conditions with the consequences which necessarily follow when the antecedent conditions obtain.[24] As we pointed out above, such laws, even if statistical, seem to exclude free choices. If such laws are one of the necessary features of scientific theories, science is inherently deterministic.

A *PNfc* also can argue that scientific objectivity requires certain a priori restrictions on what will count as data which can confirm or disconfirm a proposed scientific theory. These restrictions, he might conclude, make science inherently deterministic. For example, Jacques Monod takes the rejection of all teleological explanations to be a necessary condition for scientific objectivity.[25] Thus, Monod's position excludes the possibility of free choice, for if man is free, his choices are among perceived alternatives, that is, among options which do not themselves determine the choice. Such alternatives are means to ends. Hence, any account of human actions compatible with *Sfc* will be teleological, and a teleological account seems to be unacceptable in the scientific worldview.

Again, the possibility of predictive success is essential to the confirmation of a scientific theory. To the extent that any theory admitted free choices to be among the possible conditions of the data under investigation, the possibility of predictive success would be undercut. Thus, science seems to be inherently deterministic.

Thus far in this section we have considered a number of attempts which a *PSfc* might make to find a place for free choice *within* the scientific worldview. We have seen that the *PNfc* has resources to repel such attempts. But the *PSfc* can take a more radical approach. Why *must* he accept the scientific view of human choice if science is formally and methodologically committed to determinism, as these arguments suggest? The *PNfc* leaves no room for his opponent within the scientific worldview, insisting that this worldview is thoroughly deterministic. Having argued in this way, the *PNfc* begs the question if he simply assumes, instead of independently proves, that the scientific worldview must be accepted without restrictions or qualifications.

The *PSfc* will reject the scientific worldview to the extent that it leaves no place for free choice. At the same time, he can admit that science gives a useful and accurate account of much of man's experience. The *PSfc* can even admit that some scientific knowledge is relevant to the understanding of human behavior and choice, for every free choice has many necessary conditions which can be investigated scientifically. Thus, the *PSfc* can accept the deliverances of science which are well-confirmed yet reject the speculative thesis that science eventually will provide a complete and exclusive account of everything in nature, including human choices and acts.

A *PSfc* who takes this attitude will find that many scientists themselves share it. Werner Heisenberg, for example, points out that modern science was in its beginnings modest: "It made statements about strictly limited relations that *are only valid within the framework of these limitations.*" This modesty was lost when physics wished to turn philosopher and physical knowledge was regarded as making statements about nature as a whole. But modern physics, according to Heisenberg, is returning to its former self-limitation, and this self-limitation is necessary if physics is to generate any philosophical insight.[26]

In other words, Heisenberg does not regard the laws of nature which physics now knows or can expect to know as even a start toward the knowledge which Laplace's intelligence would need. The statements which science makes about limited relations need not be regarded as part of a system of statements about all relations in the whole of nature.

The *PSfc* also can argue that the *PNfc's* belief that *Sfc* is incompatible with a scientific outlook rests on a naively realistic conception of scientific knowledge. This realistic conception often is challenged. Michael Scriven, for example, makes the challenge in blunt language:

> The examples of physical laws with which we are all familiar are distinguished by one feature of particular interest for the traditional analyses—they are virtually all known to be in error. Nor is the error trifling, nor is an amended law available which corrects for all the error. The important feature of laws cannot be their literal truth, since this rarely exists. It is not their closeness to the truth which

replaces this, since far better approximations are readily constructed. Their virtue lies in a compound out of the qualities of generality, formal simplicity, approximation to the truth, and theoretical tractability.[27]

The *PSfc* seems justified, then, in refusing to admit the unrestricted validity of a scientific worldview which systematically excludes *Sfc*.

The physical determinist can seek to explain the properties of present physical laws mentioned by Scriven by pointing to the complexity of the world. Physical determinists always have emphasized that the causal factors studied by science are complicated.[28] They can posit further unknown factors as the source of the limitations Scriven indicates.

However, the *PSfc* can reject the assumption that all the unknown factors are deterministic. One of the variables which is at present unknown could be in principle unknowable by scientific methods: free choice. If one looks at nature as a kind of mechanism and physical causality as a neat chain of events, then to suppose that free choices might occur in the world seems to posit a miraculous violation of natural laws. However, if one looks at the world as a multitude of overlapping fields, in each part of which nothing occurs except as the consequence of a great many interacting factors, then one can suppose that there are free choices occurring in the world and that such choices are a variable affecting other natural events, without regarding such choices as a violation of the laws covering other, deterministic variables. Heisenberg's conception of science does not require the hypothesis of Laplace's intelligence; the world studied by a more modest intelligence can admit the possibility of variables for which science in principle cannot account.

The *PNfc* is mistaken, then, if he thinks that science requires physical determinism and the exclusion of free choice from the world. If the scientific view of the world is thoroughly deterministic, it is reasonable to regard this view as a limited one. Moreover, the strong claims of the physical determinist are not established in the present state of scientific inquiry.

The *PNfc* can claim, however, that it is reasonable to regard the scientific view of the world as having unrestricted applicability. J. J. C. Smart, for example, has argued for a metaphysics based on the scientific view of the world. He begins by pointing out that it is the philosopher's task to seek a synoptic view of the world. Since no such view can be definitively shown to be true, the philosopher must select the most rationally plausible view—that is, the view which is most theoretically parsimonious.[29] Smart argues that scientific theory is the most plausible available synoptic view because of its economy. For Smart, "the ultimate laws of nature are those of physics."[30] And "the physicist's language gives us a *truer* picture of the world than does the language of ordinary common sense."[31] Smart goes on to argue for a deterministic view; he considers it the position most consistent with the scientific view of the world.[32]

The *PSfc* will object that "parsimony" need not have a single meaning. Smart assumes that the theory having the fewest theoretical entities is most parsimonious. "Parsimony" can be used in this sense, but in this sense parsimony is not a criterion of rationality. If two inquiries have different purposes, one cannot be rationally preferred to the other on the basis of a standard of parsimony which ignores their different purposes. For example, the explanation of the workings of an automobile engine one gives to someone learning to drive is much simpler than the explanation one gives to someone learning to repair such engines. But it would be ludicrous to claim that the former explanation is to be preferred because it is more parsimonious than the latter; the different purposes shaping each explanation call for different degrees of complexity in the explanations. In short, diverse inquiries have diverse purposes; what is a rational criterion of parsimony for one purpose need not be so for another.

To claim, then, on the basis of a rule of simplicity that the sciences together are the most plausible world-hypothesis is also to claim that the purposes of the various scientific inquiries take precedence over the purposes of other types of inquiry.

This claim cannot itself be scientific. For, given a variety of kinds of inquiry with different purposes, the claim that the purpose of one of these kinds is superior to the purpose of another cannot be justified by appealing to the results of the kind of inquiry which claims superiority. These results can exclude the results of other kinds of inquiry only on the assumption of the superiority of the purpose of the kind of inquiry which produced the results used to justify the exclusion. It is circular to say that scientific theory shows that scientific inquiry is to be preferred to other kinds of inquiry.

It follows that the preference for the values of scientific inquiry must rest on grounds other than science itself. There are two possibilities to be considered.

On the one hand, the preference for the values of scientific inquiry and for the worldview it generates might be merely arbitrary. But such an arbitrary preference cannot exclude alternative arbitrary preferences.

On the other hand, there might be a rational justification for preferring the scientific worldview. On this alternative, there must be extrascientific grounds for the preference. If so, then an adequate worldview would include not only the legitimate claims of science, but also those of this extrascientific way of thinking.[33]

If one judges what is parsimonious keeping in mind that one's purpose is to decide among world-hypotheses, then one's exclusion of the extrascientific from his world-hypothesis is not rationally parsimonious. Rather, such an exclusion is the arbitrary rejection of a datum which would falsify the hypothesis thus formed. Since, on the position we are criticizing, the scientific world-hypothesis contains all grounds for rational judgments, the fact that there must be extrascientific grounds for evaluating world-hypotheses falsifies the claim that the sciences together provide the most plausible world-hypothesis.

This conclusion does not imply that one should exclude scientific knowledge from a plausible world-hypothesis. For example, if there is a free choice, although the choice itself is one of its own necessary conditions, still there are other necessary conditions for the free choice. Some of these conditions are physical: for there to be free choices, there must be alternatives, and these depend in part upon the structure of the physical world which science investigates. Likewise, for there to be free choices, certain psychological requirements must be fulfilled—one must be aware of alternatives and interested in them. It is one of the tasks of psychology to identify and study such conditions.

In sum. The advance of modern science does provide some ground for physical determinism. Science seems to be inherently deterministic, and the scientific worldview must be taken seriously, for any view which meets the criteria of simplicity, predictive success, and explanatory power which modern science frequently meets is to be accepted. The *PSfc* can agree that anything science establishes must be accepted. But he can deny that he must accept science as a *complete* and *exhaustive* view of reality, and he can thus refuse to accept the scientific worldview. This worldview itself is not science, but is science transformed into philosophy. To the challenge that his position is unscientific, the *PSfc* can answer with many scientists that perhaps there are realities—of which free choice is an example—which in principle cannot fall within the subject matter of any genuine scientific inquiry. A *PNfc* who rejects this response is making a claim which is metaphysical rather than scientific.

D. Do purposes exclude free choice?

Even if there were no grounds for thinking that anything else is determined, there is a ground for thinking that human acts are determined. No one acts without a motive, conscious or unconscious. Purposes are conceived of differently in diverse theories of human action; they are variously called "motives," "interests," "needs," "reasons for acting," "ideals," "ends," "values," "goods," and so on. But however conceived theoretically, purposes are universally admitted to be necessary conditions for acts. The *PNfc* can argue that necessary conditions of this sort exclude free choice, for if one has an adequate purpose for acting, he cannot act otherwise than he does. This approach to *Nfc* usually is called "psychological determinism." We examine it in this section. In the next section we consider a closely related line of argument: that free choices are unintelligible.

One sign of the independence of psychological determinism from scientific determinism is the fact that while the latter has flourished primarily in modern times the former has been prevalent at least since Socrates. Only if one is ignorant or confused, Plato thinks, does he fail to choose that which is truly good. In modern times, the psychology of the unconscious lends support to this view by explaining acts in terms of unconscious motives; a person who has insight is freed to pursue his conscious purposes, while one who lacks insight is blocked by his ignorance from pursuing his conscious wishes.

Whether a psychological determinist deals with unconscious motives or not, he can point in support of his theory to the regularity and predictability of human behavior. Sidgwick argues that social life would be impossible if we could not every day make many accurate predictions of what others will do—predictions based upon experience of mankind generally, of various kinds of persons, and of particular individuals. If these predictions are mistaken, we account for the error by reference to our own imperfect knowledge of the character and motives of others, not by supposing that there is free choice.[34] P. H. Nowell-Smith likewise argues that the evidence for the predictability of human acts precludes indeterminacy in human choice:

> In calling a man "honest" or "brave" we imply that he can be relied on to act honestly or bravely, and this means that we predict such actions from him. This does not mean that we can predict human actions with the same degree of assurance as that with which we predict eclipses. Psychology and the social sciences have not yet succeeded in establishing laws as reliable as those that we have established in some of the natural sciences, and maybe they never will.[35]

Even so, the accuracy of statistical forecasts—for example, of the number of suicides which will be committed in a certain area in a coming year—leads many people to conclude that even so personal an act must arise from definite motives.

The *PSfc* can answer the argument for *Nfc* from the predictability of human acts partly by admitting that many predictable acts are not done by free choice and partly by arguing that many acts consequent upon free choice are predictable.

The *PSfc* need not hold that all, most, or even much human behavior follows from free choices. He can point out that most behavior does not follow from choice at all; people often act for a purpose, which occurs to them, without hesitation and without choice, since no alternative comes to mind. Thus one can confidently predict that on a given day most people will have something to eat and to drink; it does not occur to many people not to do so. Persons who act with normal spontaneity act freely in some sense or senses of "freely," but they certainly do not make free choices inasmuch as they do not consider any alternative to acting as they do. The *PSfc* can suggest with considerable plausibility, for example, that one reason suicide is predictable is that it is often, if not always, an instance of unfree behavior.

The *PSfc* also can point out that in many cases there are very few alternatives for choice, and in such cases specific behavior is predictable. In a primitive agricultural society, members of the society plant and harvest. For the most part, they must use the tools they have, plant the crop with which they are familiar, follow methods they know to be reliable. Behavior will be entirely intelligible and highly predictable.

A *PNfc* might object that there are a number of instances in which people suppose themselves to be free, although they act from suggestion or habit. Such acts are predictable.

For example, Smith is hypnotized, and the hypnotist tells him that when he comes out of his trance he will be extremely thirsty. He is roused, feels thirsty, and pours and drinks a glass of water. But the *PSfc* can accept this as a case of spontaneous action, initiated without prior deliberation on Smith's part. Smith might claim that he is acting freely, but he is free only in the sense that his action—as he understands it—is not coerced. He did not deliberate nor did he choose.

Someone acting from habit also feels free of compulsion. Smith habitually rises at eight, washes, dresses, breakfasts, backs his car out of the garage, and drives to work. He does not feel that any of these actions is coerced, unlike the bank manager who feels coerced when he is forced to open the bank's vault at gun-point. But neither does Smith ordinarily entertain any alternative to his habitually established pattern of behavior. Hence he might mistakenly believe that he is choosing freely when he is not.

Thus, the *PSfc* can admit that in many cases people do predictable acts which they themselves would call "free," yet nevertheless deny that such predictability has anything to do with free choice, since no choices are involved in these acts.

A *PNfc* who accepts the preceding explanation, however, need not give up his argument based upon predictability. He can point out that human conduct also is predictable in cases in which the *PSfc* is likely to wish to claim it is free. These are cases in which the agent himself thinks he is acting not only freely, but by free choice.

Smith might make this claim in respect to his habitual behavior. But the *PSfc* can account for this mistaken claim.

First, Smith's existing early morning habits were not always habits, and their formation might have been the direct result of his free choices. Smith's memory of these choices might lead him to feel that his later, habitual behavior is still done by free choice.

Second, Smith believes his behavior will continue to be controlled by habit only so long as he has no reason to act otherwise; if such a reason arises, he believes he can alter his behavior. Whether he can or not, is an empirical psychological question, depending upon how deeply ingrained Smith's habits are, what the circumstances are which call for new deliberation and choice, and so forth. Smith's expectation that he will rise to such occasions might well lead him to think himself free in his habitual behavior. But the *PSfc* can claim that Smith is mistaken to the extent that at the moment he is not actually making free choices.

A *PNfc* might concede these points but respond by pointing to cases in which Smith has the experience of choice, believes himself free, but comes to admit that he was not. The psychoanalytic literature provides many such cases. Before considering the problem they pose for the *PSfc*, however, we examine another direction in which the argument based on predictability can be pressed by any psychological determinist, whether or not he accepts the doctrine of unconscious motivation.

The point made by Sidgwick and Nowell-Smith about predictability does not primarily bear upon behavior of the sorts discussed so far. Rather, it bears upon behavior which proceeds from a person's moral character, behavior which can be called "honest," "brave," and so forth. The *PNfc* will point out that the *PSfc* is not in a position to admit that such behavior is determined. To admit this would be to maintain *Sfc* as an empty thesis, irrelevant to the moral life to which the typical *PSfc* claims free choice is essential. Yet if virtuous choices were not determined, the *PNfc* argues, they could hardly be as predictable as they are.

The *PSfc* will reply that this objection assumes that *Sfc* entails that life must be a series of unrelated choices about particular acts. But the *PSfc* can articulate an alternative view: that persons make choices not only about what they are going to do in particular situations, but also about long-range goals and very general commitments—choices which specify a life-plan or life-style. To the extent that a person's acts are consistent with such commitments, whether the commitments are morally upright or not, they shape his behavior. His future choices and actions will appear to be reaffirmations and fulfillments of his more basic choices of long-range goals and general commitments. Thus, a person's life can have considerable regularity and consistency precisely insofar as he exercises his ability to make free choices.

The *PSfc* can admit that the behavior of a person of strong and mature character—in contrast with the weak or adolescent person—is very regular, indeed, predictable, provided that one knows the life-plan according to which he makes his choices. In contrast, the weak-willed person, who is neither virtuous nor vicious, can be erratic in his behavior, to the extent that he is governed by fluctuating emotions. Likewise, the adolescent—who is such precisely because he has not yet settled his identity by determining any life-plan for himself—confuses his elders: his behavior often makes no sense to them.

The *PSfc* can contrast the adolescent's behavior and one's attitudes toward it with the behavior of small children and one's attitudes toward it. The behavior of small children is quite predictable, because one often knows what factors influence their acts. This is to be expected; one does not think small children capable of free choice. Indeed, if their behavior is erratic like that of the adolescent, one does not think that they are "finding themselves"; rather, one worries that they might be ill.

In terms of the preceding analysis, the *PSfc* can easily answer the *PNfc's* contention that moral choices are determined by character. The *PNfc*, assuming what he should prove, thinks of personality and character as products of nature and nurture, heredity and environment. But the *PSfc* thinks of personality and character as dispositions to understand alternatives and to entertain them as live options. These dispositions involve both unconscious and conscious motivational factors. They are generated by nature and nurture and free choice.

The *PSfc* can point out that in any case, character cannot be a principle of action in the sense of being its cause. Character is dispositional; honesty and bravery are like fragility and elasticity. A good man does honest and brave acts somewhat as a fragile object breaks or an elastic object stretches. Dispositions are never sufficient conditions of the acts which reveal them; dispositions are not actual in themselves but are revealed or expressed when other necessary conditions for a state of affairs are given. The *PSfc* can maintain that the dispositions which make up an individual's personality and character are actualized by free choice. Moreover, with Aristotle, he can maintain that these dispositions are acquired by actions, actions which the *PSfc* can regard as freely chosen. The idea that a disposition is acquired by acts which express it may seem mysterious, but the *PSfc* can reduce this mysteriousness to that of making basic commitments. The *PNfc*, of course, regards these as unintelligible precisely insofar as they are free choices. We consider this line of argument in the next section.

Thus, the *PSfc* can answer the objection based upon predictability by admitting that many predictable acts are not done by free choice, for they are not done by choice at all, and by claiming that acts which are in character are predictable only insofar as one understands the character which has been formed by basic choices, many of which are made in adolescence. Still, the *PNfc* can point to the material provided by the psychoanalytic literature. Unless one dogmatically dismisses this literature, one must admit that people often have the experience of choice, think they are free, yet are motivated by factors of which they are not even conscious.

Few psychiatrists accept *Sfc*. Most attribute human behavior to the interplay between normal drives and subconscious fears, defenses, and hostilities. John Hospers produces many case histories from the literature of psychoanalysis which suggest that traditional notions of responsibility and guilt are inappropriate, even though the individual himself might have made a choice and supposed himself free in making it.[36] Not only desires and aversions, feelings of anxiety and guilt, but also deliberation and choice can be explained by unconscious factors. Ernest Jones even suggests that *Sfc/Nfc* can be explained by unconscious motives. A *PSfc* either is an overly conscientious person who wants to feel that he can exercise self-control or is a rebel against an overly oppressive superego; a *P Nfc* is a person who feels insecure with the idea that natural law might allow human freedom and not keep nature completely in control or—if religious—a person afraid to claim any human independence of divine control.[37]

Hospers and Jones, like most who discuss the relevance of the findings of psychoanalysis to free choice, do not so much argue for *Nfc* in the context of this discussion as assume that other arguments for it are successful. In treating unconscious factors, their quarrel is with those who hold traditional notions of moral responsibility and guilt while admitting *Nfc* on some grounds other than a theory of unconscious motivation of undesirable behavior. Even Jones's explanation of why a *PSfc* holds *Sfc* need not trouble the *PSfc*, since one's position can be true and grounded in good reasons, regardless of one's motives for holding it. The explanation of the unconscious motives of the *P Nfc* is, of course, equally irrelevant.

Fortunately, Freud himself proposes a concise argument for *Nfc*. After explaining how unconscious factors determine apparently arbitrarily selected names, numbers, and words, he suggests that the understanding of unconscious processes in such cases might contribute to the solution of the problem of free will:

> As is known, many persons argue against the assumption of an absolute psychic determinism by referring to an intense feeling of conviction that there is a free will. This feeling of conviction exists, but is not incompatible with the belief in determinism. Like all normal feelings, it must be justified by something. But, so far as I can observe, it does not manifest itself in weighty and important decisions; on these occasions, one has much more the feeling of psychic compulsion and gladly falls back upon it. (Compare Luther's "Here I stand, I cannot do anything else.")
>
> On the other hand, it is in trivial and indifferent decisions that one feels sure that he could just as easily have acted differently, that he acted of his own free will, and without any motives. From our analyses we therefore need not contest the right of the feeling of conviction that there is a free will. If we distinguish conscious from unconscious motivation, we are then informed by the feeling of conviction that the conscious motivation does not extend over all our motor resolutions. *Minima non curat praetor.* What is thus left free from the one side receives its motive from the other side, from the unconscious, and the determinism in the psychic realm is thus carried out uninterruptedly.[38]

Thus Freud holds that the sense of freedom can be explained by the distinction between conscious and unconscious motives. Conscious motivation in cases such as Luther's is not accompanied by a sense of freedom; unconscious motivation accounts for acts which are not consciously controlled. The latter acts, in doing which one feels he is acting freely, are minimally important from the point of view of the conscious self. But they are not exceptions to psychic order.

The *PSfc* can easily answer Freud. The seemingly motiveless acts which Freud regards as free are not the ones which could be free choices, since they are not choices at all. They are like the spontaneous acts previously discussed. Freud is correct in thinking that such acts might be explained—much as the seemingly arbitrary selection of names, numbers, and words is explained—by unconscious motives. The sense of freedom which accompanies such acts is not the sense of freedom described in chapter one, for the experience of choice involves an awareness of alternatives. A weighty decision such as that which Luther expressed by saying, "Here I stand; I cannot do anything else," can be understood as a consequence of Luther's character and commitments, which arose from previous choices.

The *PSfc* can point out that Freud ignores the phenomena which make *Sfc* most plausible. These are examples such as that of the young man who must decide between reporting for induction, leaving the country, or staying and facing a prison term; and that of the young person who must decide between a business career and graduate work leading to a life of scholarship. Such choices, which have no place in Freud's scheme, combine the awareness of making a weighty decision with a sense that one must make up his own mind and could act otherwise than he does.

The *PSfc* also can point out that Luther's statement expresses determination, using "determination" to mean resoluteness, not using it to mean *Nfc*. Resoluteness is compatible with free choice; the young man who must decide whether to report for induction might decide to accept a prison term rather than to do so, and announce his decision in the same terms as Luther. Of course, he might nevertheless not be as free in choosing as he thinks he is, but the point here is that a statement like Luther's need not mean what Freud takes it to mean. It would be interesting to investigate the motives which led Luther to make this statement; perhaps he was severely tempted to betray his own convictions, and expressed himself forcefully as a way of separating himself from a course of action he clearly realized he could have chosen, but should have despised himself for choosing had he chosen it.

It also would be interesting to investigate the motives which led Freud to overlook some of the phenomena of choice. A *PSfc* might add to Jones's explanations of *Sfc/Nfc* another which Jones overlooks: Perhaps the theory of unconscious motivation is a rationalization which permits one to conceal from consciousness his moral guilt. Moralists who accept *Sfc* often talk about a form of repression, but they call it "moral blindness" or "self-deception." Thus, the *PSfc* can add to Freud's account of the phenomena of consciousness in terms of unconscious conflicts an account of certain phenomena of the unconscious in terms of conscious conflicts between one's moral standards and his free choices.

A *PNfc* might nevertheless object that the evidence in the psychoanalytic literature cannot be appreciated properly unless one studies this literature in detail. Freud's brief argument does not do justice to his own case, for he was repeatedly successful in explaining apparently free choices by unconscious determinants, and had good reason to expect continued success. A *PSfc* can point out that this argument is nothing but an example of the simple induction which we examined in section A. Freud's argument no doubt seemed strong to him, for he assumed scientific determinism. Against one who admits non-determined events, Freud says:

> Is he maintaining that there are occurrences, however small, which drop out of the universal concatenation of events—occurrences which might just as well not happen as happen? If anyone makes a breach of this kind in the determinism of natural events at a single point, it means that he has thrown overboard the whole *Weltanschauung* of science.[39]

Thus Freud himself holds determinism on grounds already considered in section C.

The *PSfc* also can admit that unconscious factors are among the determinants of some and perhaps even of all choices, yet still maintain that such choices are free. An individual may not be as free in choosing as he thinks he is, but this fact does not mean he is not free at all.

The *PNfc* will object that while the freedom signified by "free" in other senses can be subject to degree, the free choice defined in chapter one, section B, is not. Thus, if the *PSfc* admits that an individual in choosing is not as free as he thinks he is, the defense of *Sfc* becomes incompatible with the position it is intended to defend.

However, a *PSfc* can provide an analysis of "not being as free as one thinks" compatible with *Sfc* and adequate to the purpose for which this phrase is used in answering the *PNfc* who argues that choices are determined by unconscious factors. To show that the analysis is adequate for the purpose, we begin with an imaginary example similar to real examples which abound in the psychoanalytic literature.

At the end of twenty years of miserable marriage, John Smith visits a psychiatrist to see if some amelioration of his misery is possible. The psychiatrist, after some inquiry, concludes that Smith married his wife because she strongly resembled his mother, and this fact has led to a serious ambivalence on Smith's part about his role in the relationship. Smith, accepting the psychiatrist's interpretation, thinks: "I have always believed that I freely chose to marry Hildegaard, but now I know better. I was compelled to marry her because of my psychological need for a mother-figure."

But John Smith might be wrong in his belief that he was determined—that is, that he was *wholly* determined—to marry his wife. John's need for a mother-figure did not necessarily determine him to marry Hildegaard, although it clearly limited the alternatives open to him. There might have been other women who could have satisfied his need for a mother-figure, and he might also have considered not marrying but living with his mother. John Smith, in short, has taken a cause which sharply delimited his alternatives to be a cause determinative of his choice.

Such confusion between factors limiting alternatives and factors excluding free choice is common. One comes to see, in retrospect, causes which affected his choice by rendering it impossible for him to consider alternatives which would have been open were they not excluded by unconscious factors. One becomes acutely aware of the fact that he was not able to consider these alternatives at the appropriate time, and thinks that he would have chosen otherwise had he been able to consider these alternatives. He might then conclude—mistakenly—that he was not free. A *PSfc* can say that John Smith was less free than he thought, less free in the sense of having fewer alternatives open to him than he thought. But so long as there were alternatives, however limited, he did choose freely if he had the experience of doing so.

If two similar situations are compared with each other, and if there are more alternatives in one than in the other, then the situation in which there are more alternatives seems to be the freer, whether or not the individual who is making the choice is aware of the additional alternatives. Although this freedom can be very important to a person who is aware of it, it characterizes the situation of the choice, not the choice itself. The *PSfc* will hold that this freedom which characterizes a situation is one of the other types of freedom considered in chapter one, section A, and that freedom of choice is not subject to degree.

A *PNfc* can set aside arguments based on theories of unconscious motivation and instead argue for *Nfc* by referring to the conscious purposes which the *PSfc* himself holds to be necessary conditions for choice. The ethical determinism of the Greeks assumed that conscious purposes determine all of one's choices; Plato and Aristotle never question this assumption when they attempt to explain moral evil, weakness of will, and so on. Underlying their view is an argument for *Nfc* which Thomas Aquinas formulates as follows:

> If two or more things are available, of which one appears to be more desirable, it is impossible to choose any of the others. Therefore, that which appears to be best is chosen of necessity. But every act of choosing is in regard to something that seems in some way better. Therefore, every choice is made necessarily.[40]

In this argument, the purpose, which the *PSfc* admits only as a necessary condition for choice, becomes a sufficient condition for choice. A person cannot choose anything except insofar as it is or seems good; it seems to follow that he could have no reason for choosing any possibility less desirable than that which he does choose. Thus, deliberation is simply a weighing of alternative possible purposes, and choice is simply the conclusion that one of these is better than the other.

The *PSfc* might claim that this argument is merely a version of the position stated by W. D. Ross: ". . . whatever act I do, it must be because there is in me, as I am now, a stronger impulse to do that act than to do any other."[41] This is not an argument for *Nfc* but a simple assertion of it in terms of impulses rather than some other type of cause. However, the *PNfc* need not reduce the argument from conscious purposes to this form. He can regard purposes teleologically. As ideals or potential reasons for acting, the *PNfc* can argue, desirable alternatives determine choice precisely because they play the role they do in the experience of choice, as the *PSfc* himself describes it. If the *PSfc* admits, as he must, that nothing is chosen except insofar as it seems good, how can he claim that one might have chosen otherwise than one did—might have chosen something which at that very moment seemed less good than what one did choose?[42]

The *PSfc* might answer this challenge by restricting free choice to instances in which two or more alternatives seem equally good even after deliberation. But the *PNfc* can answer by pointing out that this restriction trivializes choice. A person who must choose between moral good and evil is hardly in the position of Buridan's Ass. If *Nfc* is true, immorality can be explained by the evil person's wrong inclinations. He chooses what he ought not, because it seems better to him, and this mistaken judgment is explicable by factors such as psychic abnormality, bad childhood environment, lack of acculturation, or even the original sin of traditional Christian theology. But if *Sfc* were true, the *PNfc* will conclude, then a free choice of what is morally evil would be inexplicable, for choice would be limited to cases in which the alternatives seem equally good.

The *PSfc* cannot respond that the choice of what is morally evil is simply arbitrary, that there is no reason for such a choice, that it is wholly irrational. This response is unavailable to the *PSfc* because it conflicts with a central element of the experience of choice as we described it in chapter one, sections E and F: Choice is between alternatives, each of which is interesting. Deliberation articulates reasons for choosing each alternative; in retrospect the alternative chosen ordinarily seems better. If in some cases it does not, this can be explained by the *PNfc* as a consequence of disappointment, for a person's expectations at the moment of choice sometimes are not fulfilled by subsequent events. In such cases, one who has chosen what seemed best revises his appraisal and says in retrospect that he could and should have chosen otherwise. But such revision does not alter the fact that whenever one chooses, he has a purpose in view, and he chooses what he does because at the moment this particular alternative seems good.

The *PSfc* can answer the *PNfc's* argument from conscious motivation by challenging the plausible assumption underlying this argument—the assumption that prior to the making of a choice the goods between which the choice will be made must seem definitely more or less good, if they do not seem approximately equally good. Contrary to this assumption the *PSfc* can propose another possibility: that cases in which the alternatives do seem definitely more and less good are ones in which natural dispositions and previous choices have established a definite order of priorities for one's action, and in these cases deliberation becomes clarification and free choice is unnecessary; while, by contrast, cases in which clarification of a practical situation does not eliminate the need for free choice are those in which one's natural dispositions and previous choices have established no definite order of priorities, and thus the alternatives seem good in different and incommensurable respects.[43] The *PSfc* thus can maintain that when one makes a free choice, he could choose either alternative, since neither seems unqualifiedly better. At the moment of choice, the possibility one does not choose does not seem less good than the possibility one chooses, nor do the two seem equally good. Rather, the possibility which is not chosen, the *PSfc* can argue, is attractive after its own fashion which differs in kind rather than in degree from the attractiveness of the possibility which is chosen.

A *PSfc* can illustrate this point by means of examples. A young person who is deliberating about whether to go to graduate school or to accept an invitation to enter a management trainee program finds both possibilities attractive. Each appeals to certain interests and desires, but the two do not appeal to all the same interests and desires. Perhaps he feels that an academic career would be more satisfying to his intellectual interests and his enjoyment of sharing them with others, but a career in business would be more satisfying to his interest in organizing and running things and his delight in winning clear-cut contests with keen competitors. Since these diverse aspects of his personality are not systematically integrated in any definite order, he cannot discover which of the alternatives is better, for the simple reason that neither of them is better. Each is good in its own way, but the desirability of the two has in common only that one could choose either. The *PSfc* can offer the same sort of analysis of many commonplace examples: a person's choice between different kinds of vacations, automobiles, ways of spending an evening, or meals in a good restaurant.

This explanation of the compatibility between the *PSfc's* position and the requirement—of which one is aware in the experience of choice—that one have an adequate reason for whatever choice he makes, also accounts for morally evil choices. If the young man who deliberates about whether to report for induction or not regards the former alternative as immoral, he might nevertheless be attracted by it because of his interest in avoiding the penalties for not reporting. If he chooses to violate his conscience and do what he thinks is evil, he does evil. But he has an excellent reason for his choice; it is in no sense absurd. The choice of evil is not an arbitrary preference for the less good, nor is it a mistaken judgment of what is best. It is simply the endorsement of some of one's interests at the expense of others. A person must make such choices inasmuch as his life is not completely organized; his priorities do not so completely shape his life that the moral standards he accepts make an immoral choice always seem less good than any morally upright alternative.

Finally, the *PNfc* can recall a point previously mentioned. In retrospect, it does seem that one chose the greater good. But the *PSfc* can interpret this retrospective sense of commensurability in a way compatible with his position. In retrospect, one considers both alternatives in the light of the priority established by one's choosing. In this light, one has a principle by which one alternative is definitely better than the other. This principle will remain in force unless it is altered by a subsequent free choice. Thus, according to the *PSfc*, character is formed.

In sum. The *PNfc* can point to certain facts about human action which seem to support his position. These facts include the predictability of human acts, the explicability of many such acts by depth psychology, and the requirement that one have a good reason for whatever choice he makes. The *PSfc* certainly grants that relevant facts are not to be ignored in a theoretical dispute but can claim to be able to account for the facts adduced by his opponent in a way consistent with *Sfc*. Predictable acts either are not a result of free choice or are predictable from principles established by free choice itself. Freud is not unreasonable in thinking that a method of interpretation which is successful is to be relied upon in further similar cases, but there is no evidence that the method succeeds in accounting for choices themselves, and not merely for the restriction of the alternatives for free choice. The purpose required for choosing, as revealed by the very phenomena from which the *PSfc* begins, seems to exclude *Sfc*, for on the assumption that purposes are always commensurable prior to choice, one could have no good reason for choosing other than he does. But this assumption can be denied by the *PSfc*. An account of phenomena is not to be accepted if it requires something inconsistent with the data for which it is supposed to account, but the *PSfc* can argue that possible purposes as experienced prior to choice do not appear commensurable.

E. Is free choice unintelligible?

If there can be no criteria by which particulars falling under a concept might be identified, that concept is useless. One cannot employ it to refer to anything; such a concept might be called "unintelligible" in a loose sense. Thus, if free choice is proposed by the *PSfc* as a condition for moral responsibility, the concept is useless if he does not provide criteria for identifying a choice as free or unfree. Morton White, among others, has suggested that there can be no such criteria: "But how do we find out whether a choice is not causally necessitated? I do not know and I do not think that the anti-determinist knows."[44]

This objection either assumes or does not assume that there can be no free choices. If the former, it is question-begging as an argument for *Nfc*. If the latter, the objection might amount to an argument that *Sfc* is empirically meaningless. A *PNfc* might assume some version of the verifiability criterion, and use this criterion to exclude as inadequate any criteria the *PSfc* could offer for identifying free choices. For example, the *P Nfc* might say that only public, empirical tests, not introspection, can count as evidence. The *PSfc* can refuse to accept so restrictive a criterion for the evidence by which free choices will be identified. Verificationism has its own problems, as we argue in chapter five, section D. If the objector does not rule out an account in terms of the phenomena of choice, the *PSfc* can provide criteria for identifying a choice as free or not free.

Two questions must be distinguished. How does one tell if his own choice is free? And, how does one tell whether someone else is acting by free choice? We consider these questions in sequence.

We described the experience of choice in chapter one. There are cases in which deliberation becomes clarification; one's established priorities determine which of the available alternatives one accepts. Choices of this sort are not free, although one's priorities may have been established, at least in part, by earlier free choices. There are other cases in which one has what we have called a "sense of freedom." These are the cases in which people judge themselves to be choosing freely. If *Nfc* is false, such judgments are at least prima facie credible. Thus, for an agent the criterion for telling whether his choice is free is simply that he has the experience of choosing and is not aware of anything determining his choice.

As we explained in the previous section, people sometimes think they are free although they do not have the experience of making a choice. In reflecting, an individual can confuse the experience of choice which includes a sense of freedom with the experience of selecting what he prefers when this selection is determined by already established priorities. One can even confuse the experience of choice with the experiences of acting without reflection in accord with a dominant desire and of acting from habit. But doing what comes naturally and doing as one always does do not involve any experience of choice at all.

One cannot rule out a priori the possibility that one might have an experience of choice including the sense of freedom but also have some good reason for thinking that he was not choosing freely. In many cases such reasons can be reduced to factors not under one's control which more or less severely limit the alternatives upon which one can reflect in deliberation. In such cases, one is not as free as one supposes; we discussed this kind of case—John and Hildegaard Smith—in section D. If there are sometimes other sorts of cases in which a person has an experience of choice including a sense of freedom but has good reasons for thinking himself not to be making a free choice, the criteria for telling whether or not he is choosing freely in such cases will be built into the criteria for regarding the reasons as good enough to overcome the prima facie credibility of the immediate judgment that he is choosing freely. It is hardly incumbent on the *PSfc* to produce examples of possible good reasons of this sort.

One's criteria for telling whether another's act is freely chosen are more complex than one's criteria for identifying his own choice as free. An observer lacks the introspective data available to the agent. One's experience of others is only partly the same as his experience of himself. By what criteria, then, can one tell whether the acts of another are done by free choice?

There are many cases in which an observer cannot tell whether another's act is done by free choice. A person who is doing what comes naturally or acting out of habit can be indistinguishable from one who is acting deliberately and by free choice. Since much of what a person knows about others is based on what they tell him, his belief that they act or do not act by free choice depends on his trusting them.

Keeping these limitations in mind, we state the general form of the inference a person uses in judging another's act free: "When I act in that way, I do so by free choice; therefore, he is probably acting by free choice." To support the inference, one must examine and judge reasons which would tend to show that the individual did not make a free choice. Frequently, if someone says he did not make a free choice, one tends to accept his report and judge, against appearances, that he did not. Of course, such a judgment must be tentative. A person's report is only a report; it can be false as the experience itself cannot.

This brief and general sketch of the ways in which the acts of others which are done by free choice can be identified needs to be filled out by inquiry into the reasons which would be good ones for concluding that someone is not acting freely although he initially seems to be and is acting freely although he claims not to be. A great deal of information about human psychology, the individual's culture, and his character might be brought to bear in a particular case on the question: Was this act done by free choice? The sketch provided here could guide the use of such information. To this extent, the *PSfc* can meet White's demand for criteria by which a particular choice can be identified as free.

Many determinists of various sorts argue that free choice is unintelligible in another sense. They hold the notion of free choice to be mysterious and incomprehensible, and conclude that *Sfc* is therefore false.[45] As Philippa Foot has shown, this argument has a number of distinct elements.[46]

One of these is the claim that since a free choice would lack sufficient conditions apart from the agent's choosing itself, a free choice would be a matter of chance—a random or accidental event. As Alasdair MacIntyre puts it: ". . . to say that any given event is uncaused is surely to say that such an event is random. What is random is no more free than what is caused."[47] A. J. Ayer argues similarly:

> Either human actions are entirely governed by causal laws or they are not. If they are, then they are necessary: given our heredity and environment we could not act otherwise than as we do; if they are not, then to the extent that they are not caused they must occur by chance: if they occur by chance they are indeed not necessary, but equally we have no control over them.[48]

Ayer also argues that choices are either causally determined or accidental, and that if they are the latter, then they are chance events.[49]

The *PSfc* can respond that in these arguments the words "chance," "random," and "accidental" are used in a peculiar way. "Chance" usually means "caused by unforeseen factors," not "uncaused." "Accidental" usually means "unintentional"; it is unclear how a choice could be accidental.[50] "Random" means "without regular pattern or purpose"; a *PSfc* can claim that one who freely chooses to live his life according to a certain plan will make his choices in a regular pattern.

Such analyses raise the question: What precisely is the claim of the *PNfc* who makes this sort of argument, and why is he making this claim? Does he think of chance as an epistemic or as an ontological category? If the *PNfc* regards chance as an epistemic category, the argument amounts to saying that choices are caused events whose causes are unknown. The alternatives proposed exclude *Sfc*; the argument is question-begging. If the *PNfc* regards chance as an ontological category, he must give a reason why this category could not include free choice, or why there cannot be at least three categories of events: those necessitated, those happening by chance, and free choices.

J. R. Lucas points out that such expressions as "random" and "by chance" express negative concepts. Moreover, the concepts of "explanation," "cause," and so on, are not used in wholly the same sense in diverse contexts. Thus, to say that an event is random because there is no physical explanation for it "says nothing about whether there is any human or rational explanation to be offered."[51]

Of course, the *PSfc* does hold that free choices lack sufficient conditions apart from the person's choosing itself, and that in this sense they are inexplicable. They cannot be inferred from other facts. But if a *PNfc* tries to use this sort of inexplicability as an argument against *Sfc*, he fails to go beyond stating his position, for inexplicability of this sort follows from the very definition of free choice.[52]

A *PSfc* can reply in another way to the argument that choices, if uncaused, are mere chance events. He can say that they are acts of human persons. Choices are not quasi-miraculous happenings or entities which seem to appear from nowhere, like rabbits out of a magician's empty hat. People make choices; choice is a familiar aspect of human action. The experience of choice, as the description in chapter one, sections E and F, makes clear, is not the experience of something which befalls a person, but of something a person does.

The *PNfc* will respond that when he argues that the notion of free choice is unintelligible he has a stronger sense of "unintelligibility" in mind than the ones considered thus far. He is apt to think that an act which is unintelligible in the sense that it cannot be inferred from other facts "is unintelligible in the *further* sense that we can attach no meaning to it."[53] J. J. C. Smart, for example, describes the position of some philosophers who claim that in free choices one acts from reasons rather than from causes and "that acting from reasons is neither caused nor a matter of chance. I find this unintelligible."[54]

The *PSfc* can again point out the *PNfc's* assumption that the categories of causally determined and chance are exhaustive. Since an unproved assumption of the adequacy of these categories is question-begging in the present context, the *PNfc* must attempt to rule out the possibility of an additional category—that of free choice.[55]

One explanation of the assumption that this dichotomy is satisfactory might be that a phenomenalist conception of the self is presupposed. If the self is regarded as a collection of discrete experiences bundled together only by various sorts of regularities, then any event which is not integrated into these regularities in such a way that it could be called "caused" must be regarded as a mere chance event. Of course, the *PSfc* need not accept a phenomenalist conception of the self. Thus, an argument for *Nfc* assuming such a view is question-begging.

If the *PNfc* does assume a phenomenalist conception of the self, he might propose another form of the objection that a free choice would be unintelligible. Such a *PNfc* will find it impossible to understand how a free choice could be an act of an agent, how responsibility could be ascribed to a person who acted by free choice, how the free choice could be *his*.

Moreover, even if a *PNfc* rejects the phenomenalist conception of the self, he can form an objection along these lines. He will observe that the self required by the *PSfc* is peculiar. Its choices are detached from its character and motives.[56] Hume provides a classic statement of this argument:

> Actions are by their very nature temporary and perishing; and where they proceed not from some cause in the characters and disposition of the person, who perform'd them, they infix not themselves upon him, and can neither redound to his honour, if good, nor infamy, if evil. The action itself may be blameable; it may be contrary to all the rules of morality and religion: But the person is not responsible for it; and as it proceeded from nothing in him, that is durable or constant, and leaves nothing of that nature behind it, 'tis impossible he can, upon its account, become the object of punishment or vengeance.[57]

R. E. Hobart provides a contemporary formulation of the same argument:

> *In proportion* as it is undetermined, it is just as if his legs should spring up and carry him off where he did not prefer to go. Far from constituting freedom, that would mean, in the exact measure in which it took place, the loss of freedom. It would be an interference, and an utterly uncontrollable interference, with his power of acting as he prefers. In fine, then, *just so far* as the volition is undetermined, the self can neither be praised nor blamed for it, since it is not the act of the self.[58]

Foot notes that such arguments do not conform to experience and ordinary language; we hold people responsible for past actions even when there is no likelihood they will do similar acts in the future.[59]

The *PSfc* can point out that "being one's own" does not have a single meaning. One's property and one's family are one's own, one's ideas are one's own, and one's body is one's own, but each is one's own in a distinctive way and "one's own" thus has many meanings which must not be confused. The *PSfc* can point out that several of these senses of "being one's own" do not require that what is one's own be related to an already constituted self as an effect is related to its causally sufficient conditions. One's property can be inherited; one's ideas can come from out of the blue; one's body is oneself, or in some perplexing way part of oneself. Thus, for a *PNfc* to suppose, as Hume and Hobart do, that if choices are to be one's own they must have causally sufficient conditions within the self and the situation which preexists one's very choosing is gratuitous and question-begging. The *PNfc* needs to *show*, not merely *assume*, that a person's choices could not be his own if they were free—that is, if there were not causally sufficient conditions for the choice antecedent to his choosing itself. The *PNfc* can easily show that there is some sense of "one's own" which meets the conditions his position requires, but to show this is irrelevant to the argument. He must instead show that there is no sense of "one's own" which meets the conditions his opponent's position requires. To show this would be precisely to show that no person chooses freely.

Moreover, a *PSfc* can provide an account of how the acts which a person does by free choice are his own. In the first place, a person's choice is based on *his own* deliberation. Deliberation is *his own* thinking about *his own* conflicting interests. In the second place, choice is of what is in *a person's own* power, of an act which he can perform or refrain from performing. In the third place, choice and the consequent action have many necessary conditions other than a person's choosing itself, and many of these necessary conditions are included in *his own* body, *his own* personality, *his own* skills, *his own* tools and property, and so forth. A *PSfc* can thus admit that it is not easy—if indeed it is possible—to say how a person's *choosing* is his own, yet deny that there is any difficulty in understanding how the *acts* which a person does by free choice are his own.

The *PSfc* also can point out that free choice together with nature and nurture constitute a person's character. In choosing, as we explained in the previous section, a person establishes priorities which determine which possible courses of action will seem to him better and which will seem less good. A person who freely chooses a particular lifestyle and forms his character accordingly is likely to find it incredible if he is told by the *PNfc* that acting by free choice and acting in a manner which expresses his own character are somehow incompatible with one another.

In recent years, the *PSfc* who talks about the free choices which lay down the foundation of one's character is likely to speak of "decisions of principle," "basic options," and so on. In earlier times, he might have talked of "conversion" and "mortal sin." In such basic choices, whatever they are called, a person establishes a hierarchy among the various inclinations and possibilities he finds in himself and his situation. The *PSfc* can point out that in making a basic choice a person often is aware that his whole life is at stake; a situation requiring such a choice is often called an "identity crisis." Given inclinations and possibilities are disorganized; in choosing freely, a person endorses some and gives them high priority, while consigning others to a subordinate place in his life. Thus a person organizes himself, pulls himself together, and becomes a mature person. Subsequent acts done in accord with a person's self-identity, which was established in this way, clearly are acts for which he is responsible. Thus, the *PSfc* argues that moral responsibility presupposes *Sfc*, for he thinks of responsibility as it is exemplified in acts which flow from choices which lay down the foundation of a person's character and the *PSfc* believes that such choices are free.

The *PNfc* will remain unsatisfied. The *PSfc's* account of the integration of free choice into the self still leaves totally unexplained how an individual comes to make the precise choices which he does make. Obviously, the *PNfc* will argue, if choice is one of its own *causally* necessary conditions, then all other necessary conditions and reasons together—provided that they are equally necessary conditions and reasons both for choosing and not choosing as one does—cannot explain why one makes this choice rather than not making it. This point is expressed clearly by F. H. Bradley:

> Turn it as we will, the *libertas arbitrii* is no more at last than *contingentia arbitrii*. Freedom means *chance;* you are free, because there is no reason which will account for your particular acts, because no one in the world, not even yourself, can say what you will, or will not, do next.[60]

Hobart makes the same point: "If we ask, 'Was there anything that induced the self thus to act?' we are answered in effect, 'Not definitively. The self feels motives but its act is not determined by them. It can choose between them.' "[61]

Provided that "feeling motives" means "being aware of interesting possibilities," the *PSfc* cannot disavow the answer Hobart formulates for him. Apart from the tendentious language, the *PSfc* also must admit Bradley's main point: that no reason fully accounts for a free act and no one can say what he or anyone else will choose freely to do next. However, the *PSfc* can deny that these admissions compromise his position.

The *PSfc* can point out that arguments of this sort gain much of their force from a natural and almost ineradicable tendency to think about everything on models drawn from sense experience. When one tries to think about choice, one has in mind the model of sensible changes, such as change of place. If an object is moving along a path and can go off in either of two directions at a fork in the path, then there must be causally sufficient conditions apart from its very doing so for its taking one path rather than the other when it comes to the fork. This model gains much additional force and plausibility from its analogue in reasoning; one does not assert one proposition rather than its contradictory without having some reason for preferring the one to the other.

But the *PSfc* can maintain that this model simply does not apply to free choice. His whole point is that a choice is unlike processes of natural change and processes of reasoning. This difference is a phenomenon of experience; that is why people suppose themselves to be free. The *PSfc* precisely wishes to insist that this phenomenal difference is a real one. It is no argument against him to insist that choice must conform to a model he holds to be irrelevant.

Thus, the *PSfc* admits, or better, insists, that free choice is unintelligible, if "intelligible" is taken to mean "picturable" or "reducible to a broader and more basic category." One who holds against him that there can be nothing which does not meet the conditions of physical existence assumes a position which is itself not confirmable by any possible experience; one who holds against him that there can be nothing within experience which is not reducible to a broader and more basic category assumes a monistic metaphysics. Irreducible diversity cannot be excluded a priori from reality except by a metaphysics like that of Parmenides.

The *PSfc* also can subject arguments of the sort proposed by Bradley and Hobart to a careful analysis.

If anything is intelligible, it must be intelligible either in itself or by reference to something else. The *PSfc* maintains that free choices are intelligible, up to a point, by reference to all the causally necessary conditions other than the person's very choosing itself. But the *PNfc* is not satisfied, for these necessary conditions—on the *PSfc's* account of choice—are also the necessary conditions for not choosing. The *PSfc* seems compelled either to claim that the very choosing is intelligible in itself or to admit that it is simply unintelligible.

The *PNfc* will accept the idea that something might be intelligible in itself if it is a formal truth. But whatever a choice is, it is not a formal truth. Thus, the *PSfc* seems forced to admit that free choices are unintelligible. However, the *PSfc* can resist making this admission.

The *PSfc* can claim that there is a sense in which free choices are intelligible in themselves, although they certainly are not formal truths. To understand what is involved in this claim, one must distinguish between two conceptions of explanation. One view of explanation is that in explaining anything, one relates it to something, that again to something else, and so on ad infinitum. In this view, nothing but a formal truth could be intelligible in itself. But there is another view of explanation, and whether or not it is ultimately sound, the *PSfc* can take this alternative view and claim that free choices are intelligible in the sense it makes available.

The alternative view of explanation is that in explaining anything, one relates it to something else which gives it an intelligibility it did not have in itself. In this view, what explains anything must be intelligible in a way in which what is explained is not. If this conception of explanation is correct, the explanatory process cannot go on ad infinitum. It must stop with something or many things which are intelligible yet inexplicable. Such boundaries of explanation can be called "intelligible in themselves."

Human actions and everything which depends upon them, the *PSfc* can argue, must be explained—using "explained" in accord with the second conception of explanation—at least in part by relating them to free choices. To render a person's life intelligible, one must know his basic commitments—his "life-plan," "decisions of principle." "fundamental option," or whatever one cares to call it. And one must relate everything in the individuals's life to this central reference-point. Thus, a person's free choices render what follows from them intelligible. But, according to the *PSfc*, free choices are boundaries of explanation. In this sense, they can be called "intelligible in themselves." The sun is far brighter than anything we see in its light, yet the sun is like night in that nothing illuminates it.

The *PNfc* can point out that with this argument his opponent defends the intelligibility of free choice by claiming it to be a first principle. Yet in choosing, one chooses this *rather than* that. According to the *PSfc's* own account, a moment before the choice, both alternatives are equally possible. In choosing, one possibility is realized. The *PSfc* admits many causal conditions, but denies that all of them together are sufficient to close this gap. He admits reasons in favor of both alternatives, but denies that either is definitely better than the other prior to choice. The *PNfc* insists that something must close the gap between the two possibilities and the actual choosing. Otherwise, a free choice is a fact for which there can in principle be no sufficient reason why it is so rather than otherwise.[62]

Before considering how the *PSfc* can answer this objection, it is important to see clearly what the objection is. It is an appeal to the principle of sufficient reason. Leibniz formulates this principle: ". . . there can be no fact real or existing, no statement true, unless there be a sufficient reason why it should be so and not otherwise. . . ."[63] Richard Taylor, who accepts the principle of sufficient reason, provides a contemporary formulation of it: It "is best expressed by saying that, in the case of any positive truth, there is some sufficient reason for it, something which, in this sense, makes it true—in short, that there is some sort of explanation, known or unknown, for everything."[64] What the objection means, then, is that when one says, "I freely choose this," there *must* be something which makes this statement true other than his freely choosing it. If not, there is something—this choice—which is so rather than otherwise and there can be no explanation why it is so rather than otherwise.

The principle of sufficient reason underlies many arguments for *Nfc* in which it is not expressly invoked. Laplace, in the paragraph immediately preceding that in which he gives his famous formulation of universal determinism, argues against free choice by expressly invoking the principle of sufficient reason:

> Present events have a link with preceding ones which is based on the evident principle: that a thing cannot begin to exist without a cause to produce it. This axiom, which is called "the principle of sufficient reason," extends even to the most unimportant (indifférentes) actions. The will, no matter how free, cannot without a determining motive give birth to actions; for if all the circumstances in two situations were exactly the same, yet it acted in one and abstained from acting in the other, its choice would be an effect without a cause. It would then be, as Leibniz says, the blind chance of the Epicureans. The contrary opinion is an illusion of the spirit, which loses sight of the fleeting reasons for the choice of the will in unimportant (indifférentes) matters and becomes convinced that it has determined itself by itself and without a motive.[65]

It is worth noticing that Laplace does not formulate the principle as Leibniz and Taylor do, but as a principle of causality with respect to entities which begin to be. Taylor himself formulates what he calls "the metaphysical thesis of determinism" almost exactly as Laplace formulates the principle of sufficient reason. Taylor's formulation is: ". . . in the case of everything that exists, there are antecedent conditions, known or unknown, given which that thing could not be other than it is."[66] Clearly, the principle of causality which underlies many, if not all, arguments for physical determinism is a limited form of the principle of sufficient reason.

Moreover, many of those who argue for psychological determinism make clear that they have in mind the principle of sufficient reason when they insist upon the inadequacy of any motive which is not a greater good—a good definitely more appealing than the alternative which is not chosen. And in the present section, the principle of sufficient reason emerges clearly as the assumption which underlies all the arguments against *Sfc* which charge the notion of free choice with mysteriousness and unintelligibility.

The *PSfc* can point out that many philosophers reject the principle of sufficient reason. For example, in the context of philosophy of religion, some critics of arguments for the existence of God have pointed out that one need not assume that there is a reason for everything, and that perhaps it is, in some sense, meaningless to make such an assumption. To the extent that arguments for the existence of God use the language of causes and explanations beyond the boundaries of sense experience, it is alleged, such language loses its usual sense. The *PSfc*, as we have shown, will reject the reduction of choice to the categories of sense experience. Thus, for the *PNfc* to insist that the *PSfc* accept the principle of sufficient reason, is question-begging.

Moreover, the *PSfc* can point out that there seems to be no sufficient epistemic reason why he should accept the principle of sufficient reason. It is not a fact. It is not a generalization from facts. It is not a logical truth. This, of course, does not show that the principle of sufficient reason is false. But it shows that it is a very peculiar sort of statement, if it is a statement at all, rather than some sort of prescription, or something else.

The *PSfc* can admit a restricted version of the principle of sufficient reason as a rule of thumb: There is a sufficient reason for everything except for those things in terms of which other things are finally explained. The *PSfc* has a good reason for making this restriction. If there are boundaries of explanation—a supposition which must be admitted by anyone who uses the principle of sufficient reason—then at these boundaries either everything would' be explained in terms of some one thing or there would remain an irreducible multiplicity of explanatory principles. Anyone who rejects monistic metaphysics will prefer the latter alternative to the former, and thus will maintain that there are many ultimate principles and no sufficient reason why this fundamental multiplicity is as it is, and not otherwise.

If the *PNfc* insists upon an unrestricted version of the principle of sufficient reason, a version incompatible with free choice, he begs the question unless he *shows*, not *assumes,* that the *PSfc* must accept the principle in its unrestricted form.

Hobart argues that the *PSfc* requires that when a person makes a free choice, he should be an "absolute source"—"a source that has in turn no source; a source, he thinks, cannot in the fullest and truest sense be such if it derives what it emits."[67] Again, Hobart rejects *Sfc* on the ground that the "moral self cannot be *causa sui.*"[68] Roderick Chisholm, who argues for *Sfc*, makes a similar statement:

> If we are responsible, and if what I have been trying to say is true, then we have a prerogative which some would attribute only to God: each of us, when we act, is

a prime mover unmoved. In doing what we do, we cause certain events to happen, and nothing—or no one—causes us to cause those events to happen.[69]

The *PSfc* is not in as absurd a position as Hobart suggests and he need not go quite so far as Chisholm goes.

The *PSfc* does not claim that the moral self is *causa sui* as if he did not admit necessary conditions antecedent to choice. One does not make himself out of nothing; he is, is able to make free choices, and faces alternatives not of his own making. Moreover, the typical *PSfc*, unlike Sartre, maintains that there are moral standards antecedent to free choice, and that one's choices can be judged by such standards to be good or bad. What the *PSfc* does claim, as we have seen, is that in choosing a person establishes his own dispositions for choosing, sets his own priorities, forms his own character.

When Hobart demands that a person not emit anything which he does not derive, he simply rejects the *PSfc's* claim that a man—given all other necessary conditions—does make himself be an honest man or a dishonest one, a saint or a sinner, by doing what lies in him alone: making a commitment one way or the other. The typical *PSfc* is acutely aware that at the moment of a basic commitment which determines the course of a person's life he has a sense of ultimate responsibility. The *PSfc* thinks that if the sense of freedom one has at the moment of such a choice is illusory, if one is only emitting what he is receiving, then the sense of responsibility also is illusory, and a dishonest man or a sinner only differs from an honest man or a saint by a difference in luck, by what happens to befall each at this critical moment.

The *PSfc* admits that if he is correct, there is no sufficient reason at this critical moment why a person chooses this rather than that; this lack of a sufficient reason is necessary if this choice and the life it shapes is to be the person's own noble or ignoble existence, his own sealing of his own destiny. If the principle of sufficient reason is true, then according to Leibniz, at least, the principle of the identity of indiscernibles follows from it.[70] Some philosophers have rejected the latter principle simply in order to maintain that the givenness of the empirical world is not in principle reducible to a complex of properties. If the individuality of each particular entity in the world—each drop of rain, each grain of sand—is sufficient reason to reject the principle of sufficient reason, the *PSfc* will argue, then surely the existential personhood of each man and woman is sufficient reason to reject it.

But there is still another aspect to the objections of Hobart and the observations of Chisholm. If one's choice really is free, then prior to it there is not anything from which it emerges by a continuous process of development. Even if one allows that there can be a choice *of this rather than of that* with no sufficient reason, how does one account for there being at one moment something merely possible, and at the next moment something actual—at one moment a person's *being able to choose this,* and at the next, one's *actually choosing this.* Here, it seems, the person who makes a free choice would have to bring something out of nothing, for if that choice which is about to be were somehow already present in the being and the ability of the one who chooses, then there would be no real initiative; the individual would merely unfold the identity which is latent within him.

The *PSfc* can admit that the coming into being of the free choice also is mysterious. But if one can make the choice he makes without a sufficient reason for choosing this rather than that, the emergence of this choosing into reality is not a mystery peculiar to choice. Many philosophers have held that there is emergent or creative evolution. Some of these, like John Dewey, reject *Sfc*; others, like Bergson, affirm it.

Thus, the *PSfc* can claim that the new reality which is present in the universe each time a free choice is made presents no special problem. Those who have defended the emergence of real novelty have answered critics by pointing out that there is nothing more mysterious about the emergence of new reality than there is about the presence of existing reality. There is something mysterious about both.

J. J. C. Smart criticizes various versions of the cosmological argument for the existence of God and finds them all wanting. Yet he expresses a respect for the question, "Why should anything exist at all?" Smart says that he feels he wishes to go on asking the question:

> Indeed, though logic has taught me to look at such a question with the gravest suspicion, my mind often seems to reel under the immense significance it seems to have for me. That anything should exist at all does seem to me a matter for the deepest awe. But whether other people feel this sort of awe, and whether they or I ought to is another question. I think we ought to.[71]

Whatever one thinks of Smart's attitude toward this question, there are only two possible stands on the question itself. Either one must say that the world simply exists because it exists, and there can in principle be no reason why it exists, or one says that the world exists because it is created by an entity which exists of itself. The world either simply happens to be or it is the creature of a first being who has to be. Similarly, one who accepts as real the emergence of novelty in the existing world can regard such novelty as the constant wonder of something coming from nothing at all, or he can accept it as the constant wonder of something coming from God's "Let there be. . . ."

The *PSfc*, compelled by his opponents to face all the wonder of the reality he tries to defend, has the same two options. He can think that man has a "prerogative which some would attribute only to God": that of bringing forth from nothing in the act of choosing, in man's own "Let there be. . . ." Or he can think that although man shares the divine prerogative of choosing this or that, he does not share the divine prerogative of bringing what he wills out of nothing into the newness of being. In the latter case, the *PSfc* will accept the difficult position which has been held by many theists: that divine providence and creative causality extend to all things, even to man's free choices. This position is paradoxical; some who have accepted God's providence and causality have argued that *Nfc* is true precisely on this ground. We shall consider this argument in section G.

In sum. The *PNfc* argues from the assumption that nothing inexplicable is to be admitted as possible, and from the definition of free choice which includes having itself as one of its own causally necessary conditions, to the conclusion that a free choice would be unintelligible, and thus that *Nfc* should be accepted. The *PSfc* admits that a free choice is not intelligible in some senses of "intelligible," but denies that it is "unintelligible." He rejects the principle of sufficient reason to the extent that it would require a factor other than a person's choosing to determine which alternative he chooses, for this requirement is simply incompatible with *Sfc*. As for the emergent novelty of the choice, the *PSfc* can regard the wonder of this in the same way as he regards the wonder of being in general: either it is to be accepted as an insoluble mystery or it is to be reduced to the mystery of the creative causality of God.

F. Is free choice useless?

All the grounds for asserting *Nfc* considered thus far seem to involve rationalistic assumptions. But a *PNfc* can assert his position on nonrationalistic grounds. He can assert *Nfc* on pragmatic grounds—using "pragmatic grounds" in a wide sense to mean any sort of operational or existential grounds—as a belief warranted by its utility or fruitfulness.

The physical determinist as described thus far has moved within the arena of speculative argumentation. In this arena, the *PSfc*, as we have shown, cannot be compelled to accept physical determinism. But a *PNfc* who adopts a pragmatic approach can argue that the scientific worldview is to be accepted inasmuch as it is more useful. It alone enables us to organize our experience, control the environment, and thus solve real problems.

W. V. O. Quine uses a pragmatic criterion to distinguish myth from science: theories which are scientific better enable men to organize and control their future experience.[72] On such a criterion, one might assert *Nfc* without assuming any suspect principle from speculative philosophy.

A more radical operational view also is possible. One not only can appeal to an operational criterion in asserting the preferability of one thesis over another, one also can adopt an operational logic and theory of knowledge, in which meaning and truth themselves are defined in operational terms. *Nfc* also might be asserted within such a radical operational framework.

John Dewey, for example, argues against free choice and in favor of a mode of freedom consistent with *Nfc*. He argues that free choice is incompatible with individual responsibility.[73] He also argues that the traditional doctrine of free choice is a vague notion, that it is a caricature of genuine contingency, and that if it obtained it would be "the mark of a person who has acquired imbecility of character through permanent weakening of his springs of action."[74]

One might take Dewey's argument to be a version of the argument that *Sfc* is unintelligible. However, it should not be assumed that there is anything like the rationalistic assumption of the principle of sufficient reason underlying Dewey's argument. Dewey eschews metaphysics. He calls free choice "the metaphysical doctrine of free-will," and attacks its proponents for failing to consider the facts rather than for being unintelligible in a rationalistic sense.[75]

Dewey's treatment of responsibility makes clear in what sense he regards free choice as meaningless. His question is: How are men responsible for their acts if these acts result from nature and character?

> Holding men to responsibility may make a decided difference in their *future* behavior; holding a stone or tree to responsiblity is a meaningless performance; it has no consequence; it makes no difference. If we locate the ground of liability in future consequences rather than in antecedent causal conditions, we moreover find ourselves in accord with actual practice. Infants, idiots, the insane, those completely upset, are not held to liability; the reason is that it is absurd—meaningless—to do so, for it has no effect on their further actions. A child as he grows older finds responsibilities thrust upon him. This is surely not because freedom of the will has suddenly been inserted in him, but because his assumption of them is a necessary factor in his *further* growth and movement.[76]

As Dewey sees it, free choice at best makes no practical difference at all; at worst it is harmful.

Dewey assumes that such considerations settle *Sfc/Nfc* in favor of *Nfc*. On Dewey's instrumentalist theory of meaning and truth, a notion such as free choice, which either makes no difference or makes only a deleterious difference to future behavior, is meaningless.

Like Dewey, many social scientists—whether or not they subscribe to Dewey's radically operational theory of meaning and truth—assert *Nfc* on operational principles. Edward Tylor argued in a work published in 1871 that the study of human life should adopt the model of the natural sciences. Tylor rejects free will because of its incompatibility with this project. He justifies the project of making the study of man and culture an extension of the natural sciences, not by speculative arguments about metaphysical issues such as free will, but by pointing out the practical advantages to be expected from the project.[77]

B. F. Skinner is among the contemporary social scientists who take a similar view. Resistance to a science of human behavior—a science in which free choice has no place—blocks the scientific progress which is necessary for the evolution and survival of man. Therefore, behaviorism must be accepted and

Sfc rejected.[78] For Skinner, the notions of freedom and responsibility serve some purpose, but they are ill-adapted to the purpose they serve. If people realize that there are always variables determining their acts, they will discard such notions and adopt methods of reinforcement more efficient than the quite inefficient methods of traditional morality and law, which make use of the notions of freedom and responsibility.[79] Skinner's argument for *Nfc* is an operational one.

The *PSfc* can answer such operational arguments by pointing out that utility presupposes a goal in relation to which diverse means can be evaluated and found to be more or less fruitful. The *PSfc* can reject any account of goals and any particular goals which are incompatible with *Sfc*.

The *PSfc* can grant that science is useful for some goals, inasmuch as science enables men better than myth does to organize and control their future experience. But whatever rational credibility science has from its usefulness for certain purposes, science cannot show that every extrascientific statement is mythical or even that every myth is false.

The *PSfc* makes an admittedly extrascientific claim that there is something which in principle cannot be controlled: the free choice of a human person. Against this claim it is question-begging to argue that since control of experience is important for some purposes and since science is good at controlling experience, nothing which in principle cannot be controlled is to be admitted. The argument assumes that the project of control *can* succeed, and that what would block it or be a serious obstacle to it is to be denied. But the *PSfc* thinks the ability to make free choices is a reality which cannot be eliminated without eliminating human persons; to the *PSfc*, his opponent's view seems utterly unrealistic—seems more a myth expressing a wish for technological omnicompetence than an understanding of the nobility of man's limited but real freedom and power.

The *PNfc* can answer that the preceding argument takes for granted a nonoperational conception of meaning and truth. If a more radical approach is taken, one using operational criteria of meaning and truth, the *PSfc* will be prohibited from speculating about the truth of his position in terms of some conception of an antecedent "reality." The issue will be decided strictly on the grounds of utility.

However, even without attacking the radical operationalism of his opponent's approach, the *PSfc* can reject this version of the thesis that *Nfc* is true because useful. The *PSfc* can accept the criterion of fruitfulness—at least for the sake of argument—and argue that *Sfc* is more fruitful for the purposes he has in mind.

Clearly, the purposes which a view such as Skinner's is intended to serve are not the only purposes people wish to have served. Skinner's project—and even more appealing projects such as the educational reforms promoted by Dewey—would not meet the resistance they do if everyone shared the same purposes. Those who oppose reform, revolution, and projects of control can be labeled "reactionary" and "obscurantist," but such expressions lose their hard cutting edge if one consistently holds a radical operational conception of meaning and truth. The makers and upholders of myths have their own purposes, and in terms of these purposes their beliefs might be warranted as true or more reasonable than any alternate set of beliefs.

The *PNfc* who assumes a radical operationalism when he asserts and defends his own position seems to assume a different view when he criticizes and denies *Sfc*, for he treats this position as if it were *theoretically* false. If he did not treat it so, he would have to face the fact that some people cling to the myth that groups of human persons can make common commitments to goods which they love and can freely cooperate in faithful service to such shared goals. On a radically operational theory of meaning and truth, such people can assert *Sfc* as a thesis for which one ought to opt. William James's argument, discussed in chapter two, section C, shows how a pragmatist who opts for *Sfc* can proceed. A radical operationalist is in no position to reject on theoretical grounds an argument like that of James.[80]

The *PNfc* might argue that there is one purpose—survival—which all men share. The control of human behavior is necessary for this purpose, and so the usefulness of a view of man including *Nfc* is not merely an optional means to an optional end.[81]

The *PSfc* can reply that this view assumes what his opponent should prove: that *Nfc* is true. The thesis is assumed implicitly in the assumption that there is only a single goal, naturally given; if this assumption were true, deliberation would be reduced to clarification, and in any practical situation one possible alternative would be definitely better than others. The *PSfc* can deny this assumption, as we explained in the discussion of psychological determinism.

The *PSfc* can point out that many people are interested in many things other than survival: play and art, esthetic experience and theoretical knowledge, finding themselves and being true to themselves, justice and friendship, redemption from sin and the hope of heaven. Many people are prepared to die for some one or several of these purposes, no matter how many other people regard such beliefs as foolish and such hopes as vain. There are other people who care far more about personal interests than they do about the survival of mankind. The ecological problem makes all too clear how widespread is the attitude: After us—desert, rubble, garbage. People who are willing to die for what they believe in—if they were willing to live without freedom and dignity—would submit to a technology for controlling human behavior if it were necessary for the survival of mankind. People who do not care whether the world will be habitable when they are no longer in it are unlikely to grant even conditionally the usefulness of a technology for controlling human behavior—a technology which might curb their self-indulgence.

Finally, the *PSfc* can argue that by the very nature of operational approaches, no *PNfc* who adopts such a theory of meaning and truth can establish the strong claim he wishes to make. The method is inherently relativistic: problems shift from person to person, from place to place, from time to time. Each situation is new. But *Nfc* means that no person anywhere ever has the ability to make a single free choice. If meaning and truth are defined by fruitfulness in solving problems, then no claim as universal as *Nfc* can be justified. If *Nfc* were to be maintained on operational grounds, then it would have to contribute to the solution of one big problem which is to be faced by everyone, always, and everywhere. However, there can be no universal problem if there is no universal, comprehensive, overriding human purpose, and there is no such purpose. If the *PNfc* assumes that there is, he begs the question.

Thus, no matter how useful *Nfc* might be in some contexts, the *PNfc* who holds his position on operational grounds cannot exclude the possibility that in another context *Sfc* might be true, and that in that context someone might even make a free choice. It should be noted that the *PSfc* who holds his position on nonoperational principles can admit that in some contexts it is useful to proceed on the assumption that free choice is excluded, but he will wish to claim more than that *Sfc* is operationally true. A *PSfc* who is not an operationalist can more radically attack an opponent who is one by pointing out that operationalism itself is a *general* theory—a theory of a sort excluded by its own principles.

Operational arguments for *Nfc* have been closely related to the development of the social sciences. The desire to use scientific method in the study of man and to open the way to some form of social engineering in dealing with human problems has seemed to require that belief in *Sfc* be set aside. However, the *PSfc* can articulate a view in which the legitimate claims of the social sciences are vindicated and he can project an important role for social scientists in building up the body of human knowledge and in carrying on the pursuit of human happiness.

The *PSfc* can adopt a view of the social sciences similar to that articulated by Karl Popper. Popper rejects the view that the social sciences can ground "unconditional historical predictions." Although science inasmuch as it is theoretical must predict, the nature of historical subject matter precludes the sort of prediction which Popper calls "prophecy." In human affairs, the conditions for scientific prediction do not obtain. No modern society is a well-isolated, stationary, and recurrent system.[82]

In view of these limitations set by the subject matter of the social sciences, Popper proposes a view of them more modest than that proposed by those who think that the study of man can model itself closely on the study of physics, chemistry, and biology. Yet the view of the social sciences Popper proposes leaves them with some power to predict and with some purpose to serve. The purpose of the social sciences, according to Popper, is *"to trace the unintended social consequences of intentional human actions."* Thus the social sciences, like the natural sciences, lead "to the formulation of practical technological rules stating *what we cannot do.*" The social sciences thus can serve the practical purpose of promoting wise decisions by predicting remote, unintended consequences which are likely to follow if certain courses of action are adopted.[83]

Social sciences of the sort Popper projects are compatible with *Sfc* and with the *PSfc's* conception of free choice as a central reference-point for making sense of human life and history. A social science of this sort makes conditional predictions; it tells what will follow if one choice or another is made. Moreover, there is nothing in Popper's conception of social science which would require the discarding of anything in the social sciences which can plausibly claim to be scientific—that is, of anything about which competent social scientists working within a given discipline have reached consensus.

Of course, any coherent theory of the social sciences must exclude much of what is regarded as scientific by many social scientists, for there are many substantive issues about which there is little consensus among social scientists and there are many problems of method about which they are in sharp conflict. To an outsider, at least, the lack of consensus on many things among social scientists seems to be a function of diverse and competing ideologies—that is, of different sets of unexamined assumptions which are organized by different purposes to which different schools within each discipline of the social sciences direct their effort. A *PSfc* would expect such a situation; he can explain it as a result of different basic options, freely chosen, each shaping a different community, whose members easily speak one another's language but find it necessary to translate the rather strange and inadequate languages of others, if, indeed, the efforts of others to speak can be heard as anything but babel.

However, despite their limitations, the social sciences do include some propositions about which there is consensus; these propositions can be called "scientific" in a sense which will not be disputed by any competent social scientist in the relevant discipline. As in other sciences, the truth of such propositions will be challenged within the discipline, but their legitimacy as scientific propositions will not be denied. In other words, there are some general propositions within the domain of the social sciences which are regarded as true or as probable or at least as appropriate to entertain. A *PSfc* cannot deny such propositions without challenging the competence of those most likely to know what they are talking about.

The *PSfc* can admit such propositions and the elements of method essential to the inquiries necessarily connected to these propositions. Some such propositions can be accounted for in terms of factors which are not subject to human free choice: man's natural environment and human nature. Others can be accounted for in terms of factors of the preceding sort together with human free choices. The *PSfc* can maintain that free choice has contributed in the past to the now unalterable facts of history and to the present state of culture. He can also maintain that present cultural and social conditions are in many respects similar to individual character, for these conditions derive in part from free choices, and they are maintained at least by the continuing acquiescence of people who might freely choose to change them, if not by the continuing endorsement of people who make free choices in accord with them.

The *PSfc's* attitude toward the social sciences need not be altogether negative and critical. He also can project a positive role for the social scientist and encourage him to adopt this role. As Popper points out, knowing one's limits is useful. But beyond this, the social sciences can articulate various options which are open to a given society. If legislators and other leaders of society are to make sound choices, someone must help them to deliberate intelligently, for the problems are extremely complex, and although there are usually many possible courses of action there are seldom many promising options.

To some extent, social scientists already play this role. During the present century social scientists have suggested courses of action—which otherwise would have been ignored or brushed aside—in the fields of race relations, population control, prison reform, ecology, economic policy, international politics, and so on. This work has had a broad transforming affect on society and has helped to shape the state of affairs in which we now find ourselves. A *PSfc* would say that this shaping has not occurred because of determining causes alone, but also because social scientists whose work has been guided by their personal, freely chosen hierarchy of values have communicated their practical judgments to other members of the society, and gained some degree of general acceptance for the personal commitments in which these practical judgments are grounded.

No doubt, many social scientists would regard the role which the *PSfc* can project for them as one inappropriate to them precisely insofar as they are scientists. But the *PSfc* can point out that there is nothing ignoble in the role he encourages social scientists to accept. Modern science in general has won universal respect because of its contributions to human well-being. If the social sciences can contribute to wise deliberation, then they will fulfill an even more important role than the natural sciences have fulfilled.

In sum. The *PNfc* is correct in pointing out that belief in *Nfc* can be useful for certain purposes. He also is correct in assuming that if one accepts a certain goal, a view of things helpful for achieving that goal is to be preferred—other things being equal—to a view of things which blocks effective pursuit of it. The *PSfc*, however, need not agree that belief in *Sfc* is useless for all purposes. The

PNfc, arguing on operational assumptions, cannot ask the *PSfc* to grant that there is a single, permanent, universal, overriding human purpose. The desire of many thoughtful people to promote rational inquiry into human life and society can be satisfied in a way consonant with *Sfc*, for *Sfc* does not preclude the possibility of predictions relevant to human affairs. Finally, the *PSfc* can project a role for social science in the process of social deliberation, for if *Sfc* is true, then a man who is about to choose needs to know the options which are available to him and the limitations within which his capacity for free choice must be exercised.

G. Does divine causality exclude free choice?

Some who have held—either on grounds of faith or of reason—that God causes everything have believed that his universal causality is incompatible with *Sfc*. For this reason they have maintained *Nfc*. We call this ground for affirming *Nfc* "theological determinism."

John Stuart Mill still used this argument, but more recently it has been discarded from the *PNfc's* standard repertoire. Hobbes's formulation of the argument is classic:

> . . . whatsoever God hath purposed to bring to pass by man as an instrument, or foreseeth shall come to pass, a man, if he have liberty, such as he [Bramhall] affirmeth from necessitation, might frustrate and make not to come to pass: and God should either not foreknow it and not decree it, or he should foreknow such things shall be as shall never be, and decree that which shall never come to pass.[84]

In this formulation, the argument is a dilemma which the *PNfc*—whether himself a believer or not—can press upon anyone who wishes to hold both that *Sfc* is true and that God causes everything. In recent years, this alleged inconsistency has occasionally been pressed against a theistic *PSfc* by his nontheistic opponents, and has less often been used by theists themselves as an argument for *Nfc*.

The traditional theist not only claims that God causes everything, but also that God knows everything. The latter claim by itself seems incompatible with human free choice, but we think this problem is merely part of the problem of divine causality. To make clear why we think this, we begin with a version of the position that divine omniscience is incompatible with *Sfc*.

Our criticism of fatalism in section B makes clear that a typical fatalist argument gains much of its plausibility from a confusion between "true" and "knowable in principle to be true." If one supposes that God knows everything—past, present, and future—fatalism returns with renewed force. For on this supposition, any proposition which is ever true is always known by God to be true. God knew from all eternity what each person's free choices would be, and according to traditional theism it is impossible that God's foreknowledge be falsified.

Of course, one can argue that the necessary truth of God's knowledge ought not to be projected upon the realities he knows. A human knower knows things in advance—using "knows" in a strong sense—only if he knows that the sufficient conditions for those things will obtain. But, presumably, God's knowledge does not work in the same way. If God is believed to be extratemporal, then he is believed to have no future, and it is inconsistent to try to relate God's knowledge to what is future for us as if his knowledge and our lives were subject to the same temporal conditions.

But the incompleteness of this solution to the problem becomes clear as soon as one asks how God can know things infallibly. A traditional theistic answer has been that God knows all things insofar as he creates or could create them. This answer has been given to avoid saying that God's knowledge depends upon creatures, for this would seem to make God contingent upon and somehow in need of the things he has made.

On the view that God knows all things insofar as he creates or could create them, God's omniscience is somewhat like human practical knowledge. God knows existing things inasmuch as he causes them to be. He knows infallibly because his causality is omnipotent. His knowledge is without change and is not subject to temporal conditions, because his creative act is identical with his eternal reality.

If this position is accepted, then the difficulty of reconciling human free choice with divine knowledge merges into the difficulty of reconciling human free choice with a universal and perfectly efficacious divine causality.

Today, many who regard themselves as theists do not claim that God is omniscient or that he exercises universal causality.[85] If this claim is not made, there is no ground for theological determinism. Moreover, anyone who simply does not believe in God obviously will have no theological reason for asserting *Nfc*. Thus, the following arguments and analyses are addressed to theists who take a traditional view of divine knowledge and causality and who affirm *Nfc* on that ground, and to theists who affirm *Sfc* and make some concessions with respect to divine knowledge and causality only because they do not see how the traditional view can be reconciled with *Sfc*.

"Reconcile" has two senses. In one sense, one can reconcile divine causality with human freedom by redefining human freedom in such a way that man's choices are determined by God. *Sfc* is denied, but man is held to be free and responsible although he cannot choose otherwise than he does. In another sense, one can try to reconcile divine causality with *Sfc* by showing the logical consistency of *Sfc* with the proposition that God causes all human choices. The first sort of reconciliation is a form of compatibilism. Various theists have attempted it.[86] We do not think their attempts differ in any important way from the forms of compatibilism we discuss in chapter four, and so we do not treat these attempts here. The second sort of reconciliation is a defense of *Sfc* against arguments for *Nfc* based upon a traditional view of divine knowledge and causality. This defense succeeds only if neither *Sfc* nor the traditional view of divine knowledge and causality is given up. We attempt such a defense of *Sfc*.

The *PSfc* can begin by pointing out that although it is difficult to see how *Sfc* can be true if God knows and causes everything—including all free choices —both propositions are firmly rooted in traditional Jewish and Christian faith.

On the one hand, God makes man in his own image. Man is wholly dependent upon God, yet God confronts man with a choice: Accept the Covenant or reject it, accept the Gospel or reject it. The paradigm for the Judeo-Christian conception of human free choice is the free choice of God in creating; the paradigmatic act of human free choice is the choice by which man accepts or rejects God as he reveals himself in the Covenant or in the Gospel.

On the other hand, the universality of God's knowledge and causality also is stressed in the Bible. The universality of God's providence is asserted, and it is said to extend to details such as the fall of a sparrow. The universality of God's causality also is asserted: In the beginning, God made heaven and earth, and all things; in the beginning was the Word, through whom all things were made.

Thus, a puzzling conjunction of divine causality and human free choice is fundamental Judeo-Christian doctrine. God knows and causes all things. Yet freedom—for most traditional theists—is common in some way to the creative act of God and to the choices of human persons made in his image, to God's self-revelation and to the human person's response of belief or unbelief.[87]

The fact that both divine causality and human free choice are rooted in Judeo-Christian faith explains why many of the strongest proponents of *Sfc* have been thinkers within this religious tradition. A *PSfc* of this sort could hardly have overlooked the apparent inconsistency of his view, but he would have thought that behind the apparent inconsistency lay a mystery beyond human understanding. Where God and his causality are involved, the most rigorously critical Jews and Christians proceeded with a sense of mystery—a sense of God's majesty and of the human mind's limitations.

Henry Mansel seems to take this approach in responding to Mill's theological determinism: "This question is insoluble, because we have nothing but negative notions to apply to it. . . . In this, as in all other revelations of God's relation to man, we must be content to believe without aspiring to comprehend."[88]

Mansel's statement—which would be accepted by many traditional theists—suggests that the conclusion that divine causality entails *Nfc* is not an obvious one. Probably most traditional theists would regard the conclusion as not obvious precisely because they would consider it to be incompatible with their faith. Theological determinism, consequently, is a controversial thesis

among believers; most of them regard it as a concession of one essential
doctrine to preserve another. Unless a particular believer has independent
grounds for holding one of the two apparently conflicting doctrines, he has no
better reason to give up one than the other; assuming his faith as such is not
irrational, he has an equal reason for holding all its doctrines true, and for
refusing to yield one of them to a theological *P Nfc*. Under these conditions,
Mansel's attitude is understandable and is not as absurd as might at first appear.

The theological *P Nfc* can counter a move such as Mansel makes. He can call
it a mere evasion of contradiction. But to make good this charge, the *P Nfc* has a
difficult burden of proof: he must show that there is no sense of "cause" such
that one can consistently assert that God causes all human choices and that at
least some of them can be free.

Mansel's answer to Mill suggests what many believers have claimed: there is
a sense of "cause" which permits one to make both assertions without inconsistency. A classic statement of this thesis is that of Thomas Aquinas. After
quoting a theological authority to the effect that it is characteristic of divine
providence to preserve rather than to destroy things, Aquinas states:

> Therefore, God causes all things in line with their own character. Thus by God's
> causing, effects follow with necessity from necessary causes, yet effects follow
> contingently from contingent causes. Since, then, the will is a principle of acting
> which is not determined to a single act, but is equally capable of alternative acts,
> God so causes it to act that he does not determine it of necessity to one of the acts
> open to it, but rather leaves its action contingent and not necessary, except in
> respect to those ends to which it is naturally drawn.[89]

The last phrase in this statement refers to acts of the will by which it naturally is
interested in various goods; for Aquinas, such acts are a presupposition of free
choice, since no one can choose what will in the first instance appeal to him as a
possible object of choice.

The theological *P Nfc* cannot simply say that Aquinas's use of "causes" is
meaningless. Such language might be suspect, but in this context a simple
assertion that it is meaningless would be question-begging. The theological
P Nfc must *show*, not merely *say*, that such language cannot be meaningful.
Only by excluding the possibility of such a meaningful use of "causes" can the
theological *P Nfc* show that the belief in universal divine causality entails *Nfc*.

It is difficult to see how the theological *P Nfc* can accomplish this task. We
know of no attempt to accomplish it. If the *PSfc* can articulate a meaning of
"cause" which will meet the requirements of the traditional theist, the theological *P Nfc's* task will be shown to be virtually impossible. We think such a
meaning of "cause" can be articulated.

The *PSfc* can begin by noting that according to traditional theism, God is the
creator. This means that everything but God is related to him as his creature.

The notion of creature implies total dependence on God; without God's creative act, no creature would be at all. In short, traditional religious belief is that nothing with which man is directly acquainted would exist but for God's creative act.

Believers often have set out to prove the existence of God bearing clearly in mind their belief in the creatureliness of the whole world of experience. In this context, a believer tries to formulate such an argument not only for apologetic use, but also to clarify for himself and other believers the relationship he believes to hold between creator and creatures. Thomas Aquinas's famous Five Ways, for example, were sketched by him in a work intended for use as a textbook in theology. It is fair to assume that if he had intended to present a tight proof for the existence of God, he would not have limited himself to so brief a sketch. In context, the Five Ways serve a different function: They are used as a basis for the explication of the creator-creature relationship.

Arguments similar to Thomas's can help show what it means to say that creatures wholly depend upon God, and thus clarify the *unique* character of this relationship. Ordinarily, effects are independent in some respects of any of the particular causes upon which they depend, and so ordinarily effects can be understood in many respects without reference to their causes. Ordinarily, also, causes are known in other contexts than the one in which they are understood as causes of their effects. But creatures are effects which depend upon God in every respect. They depend upon him for their very being; without him they are nothing at all. Thus the very being of creatures can be understood only by considering their relationship to God. Moreover, God is not part of the universe which we might experience and know apart from our knowledge of the relations of creatures to him. Thus the creator-creature relationship is *unique;* no other cause-effect relationship could be like it.

It follows that if choices are created entities, as the theist holds, they depend upon God's creative causality. Yet if choices are free, they must exist as what they are: free choices. To suppose that a choice's dependence upon creative causality *must* exclude that choice's being free is to assume that the relationship between creative causality and the being of creatures is like the relationship between other causes and their effects—causes and effects with which we are acquainted, where both terms of the relation are created entities involved in states of affairs which obtain within the world. However, the arguments for the existence of God make clear that the mode of causality in God's creating is unique; it utterly transcends the matrix of experience in which other senses of "cause" are grounded.[90] If creative causality were not unique, arguments which begin from the world could not point beyond it to God; all arguments which begin in the world would point to something within the world.

As we explained in section E, a *PSfc* must reject the principle of sufficient reason insofar as that principle would demand an explanation why a person makes the choice he makes rather than not making it. It is worth noticing in the present context that the believer who accepts both divine causality and human free choice does not invoke divine causality to explain why a person makes the choice he does. If a believer invoked divine causality to explain this, he would only push the problem back a step, for a traditional theist believes as firmly in the freedom of God's choices as in the freedom of man's.

We also considered previously another aspect of the mysteriousness of choice: that it comes to be, not by a continuous process of development from what was, but as a new beginning. The believer who invokes divine causality to account for the existence of things is concerned with this aspect of the mysteriousness of the world. The doctrine of universal divine causality primarily means that the world and everything in it—emergent novelties and human free choices as well as the world's older and more enduring constituents—does not just happen to be, but is because God says: "Let it be." The believer is aware of the strangeness of his saying that God makes all things from nothing, but he feels even more keenly the strangeness of saying either that there is never any newness in being or that some things come of themselves from nothing.

Thus, the paradox of "God causes free choices" is dissolved by the uniqueness of the meaning of "cause" said of God. To hold that God causes free choices is not to claim both that God determines one to choose this alternative rather than another, and also that such choosing, determined by an omnipotent cause, somehow is free. Rather, to hold that God causes free choices is to claim that God brings into being the whole reality of *a human person's freely choosing this alternative rather than another*.

The primary mystery of divine causality is not in particular instances of it—for example, in God's causing free choices—but in the very idea of the creature as creature. How can the creature be other than the creator, yet wholly dependent upon the creator? How can a creature be what it is in any respect if what it is in every respect wholly depends upon the creative act of God?

The theological *PNfc* cannot respond by setting aside creation itself as absurd. For him to do this is to give up all theological ground for asserting *Nfc*. But remaining within the context of the theistic position, he can object to the foregoing explanation along the following lines. Free choice is only free inasmuch as it is one of its own necessary conditions. If God causes free choices, his causality is a necessary condition of this necessary condition; the choice would be different if God caused it to be so. Thus, choice cannot be free.

The *PSfc* can answer that the objection assumes that "necessary condition" has the same meaning applied to God as it does applied to one's choosing itself. This cannot be, for in the sense in which God is called a "necessary condition," the whole truth about anything other than God always includes the fact that God is a necessary condition of all the conditions usually considered sufficient to account for the thing. The problem, once again, is not peculiar to free choice.

The *PSfc* also can point out that the objection is ambiguous in saying "the choice would be different if God caused it to be so." This might mean that the choice which God causes to be, need not be, for it is a created entity wholly dependent upon God's creative causality, which he exercises freely. Or it might mean that God could cause this very same choice to be of the other alternative. In the first sense, the alternative to the choice's being as it is, is not its being different; the alternative is the choice's not being at all. In the second sense, also, the alternative to the choice's being as it is, is not its being different, for if the choice were different—that is, if it were of the other alternative—it would not be the choice it is; God would cause the alternative choice to be.

The *PSfc* also can point out that if God is the ultimate necessary condition for free choices, this cannot mean that he intrudes upon them from without. According to traditional theistic beliefs, God can no more be considered outside things than within them, no more as imposing on things than as absorbing them. And it certainly does not make sense to imagine that God can create the whole reality of a person making the free choice which he makes, yet at the same time determine the person to choose this rather than that.

The preceding considerations mitigate the paradox of saying that God causes free choices. "Cause" here clearly is used in a unique sense. What such creative causality might be like in itself, according to the entire tradition of Jewish and Christian faith, is incomprehensible to man. Thus, to say "God causes free choices" is not to say that one comprehends how he brings such choices about. Rather, it is to claim that there are free choices, that they are not uncreated, and that God is what he must be to account for one aspect of their mysteriousness: their being as new initiatives in the world, their emergence from nothing into the newness of being, their standing, together with the entire world, as entities which might never have been.

In sum. A *PNfc* can argue from suppositions concerning divine knowledge and causality. On the approach followed here, the problem reduces to the apparent inconsistency between God's universal creative causality and the freedom of human choices. Theological premises do not lead to the assertion of *Nfc* unless one takes seriously a traditional conception of the creator-creature relationship. But on a traditional conception of this relationship, there is a *unique* sense in which God must be said to cause whatever he causes. A *PSfc* can admit that if one is reasonable in accepting traditional faith, then all its doctrines, without qualification, are to be accepted as meaningful and as true. A *PSfc* also can think it reasonable to accept traditional faith, and consequently accept the doctrine of universal divine causality, without conceding anything to theological determinism. Theological determinism fails to show that the proposition that God causes all human choices entails *Nfc*.

4: Compatibilism

In chapters two and three, we have examined arguments for and against *Sfc*. Neither side has succeeded in establishing its position. This situation naturally raises the question whether the controversy is at all soluble. One possible answer to this question is that the point at issue in the controversy has been misconceived.

We have claimed that *Sfc*/*Nfc* formulates a central issue in the historical debate about free will and determinism. There are many philosophers, however, who would object that our formulation oversimplifies the debate by allowing no voice to the proponents of the most plausible position: some form of compatibilism. Compatibilists regard their approach as a nuanced solution to the controversy over free will, a solution which avoids confusions or mistaken assumptions common to the *PSfc* and to the extreme—or so-called "hard"—determinist.

In this chapter we discuss the diverse forms of compatibilism and show that they provide no solid ground for formulating the issue otherwise than we do. We argue that soft determinism or reconciliationism—the position often simply referred to as "compatibilism"—either includes *Nfc* or is relevant to the controversy over free will and determinism only to the extent it includes *Nfc*. We also argue against various versions of the thesis that freedom and determinism can be rendered compatible by limiting each to a distinct domain, or by carefully observing the difference between the languages or viewpoints proper to each. We show that all versions of the latter thesis fail on semantical or on formal grounds.

A. Soft determinism

Soft determinism is the position that free will and determinism are compatible inasmuch as "free" means "uncoerced," not "uncaused." This position on the controversy is the one most widely held by English-speaking philosophers. Among those who have articulated and defended it are Hobbes, Locke, Hume, Mill, Moore, Ayer, and Nowell-Smith.[1] Compatibilists in the present century often have defended their position by proposing an analysis of "could have done otherwise" which is consistent with saying it of someone whose act is imputable to him although it is caused.

Most members of this tradition have taken for granted the truth of the scientific worldview and have considered it to involve universal determinism. For example, as Richard Taylor points out, Locke's whole consideration of the free will issue assumed "that determinism is true and that indeterminism is irrational and unintelligible. The philosophical problem, as he understood it, is simply that of showing that determinism is compatible with what all men believe concerning human liberty."[2] Even if some soft determinists do not assume the truth of universal determinism, it is clear that they wish to exclude *Sfc*. This is shown by the defenses which philosophers in this tradition make against arguments from immediate experience and moral responsibility for *Sfc*. In chapter two, sections A and B, we described these defenses.

Some reconciliationists reject the characterization of their position as "determinism" or even as "soft determinism." Perhaps they regard the thesis of universal determinism as false or perhaps they regard it as irrelevant to the initiation of human acts. Nevertheless, reconciliationists hold *Nfc*. If they did not, they would hold nothing which needed to be reconciled with that freedom which they do admit and defend.

It should be noted that when we say that reconciliationists hold *Nfc*, we mean that they reject free choice as we have defined "free choice" in chapter one, section B. Of course, "free choice" as we have defined it signifies a mode of freedom which is rejected by some proponents of free will. For example, anyone who accepts the principle of sufficient reason—as many proponents of free will do—is likely to reject the position that a person's very choosing is one of its own necessary conditions. Such a proponent of free will might regard himself as a soft determinist of the sort classically described by William James—that is, as one who holds both that determinism obtains and that moral responsibility is real.

Apart from their rejection of *Sfc*, compatibilists of this sort seem to us to affirm what is true. There are senses of "freedom," "responsibility," "imputability," "voluntariness," and so on, compatible with *Nfc*. Moreover, these words often are used in such senses, especially in legal and social contexts. It is not clear that law requires any mode of imputability other than that which a sophisticated compatibilist can admit. Aristotle's concept of voluntariness, for example, seems both consistent with *Nfc* and adequate for legal purposes.

Thus, in our view, "freedom" does have a sense compatible with *Nfc*. In fact, as we make clear in chapter one, section A, "freedom" has many such senses, for it can signify physical freedom, freedom to do as one pleases, ideal freedom, political freedom, and creative freedom.[3] But in chapter one, section B, we also define another mode of freedom: free choice. Clearly, no compatibilism which includes *Nfc* can allow that "freedom" used in this sense refers to anything real. Yet "freedom" can be used in this sense, even if mistakenly, to refer to a supposed property of choice, the data of which we also describe in chapter one, sections C through F. As we show in chapter two, section A, these data can be interpreted in a way consistent with *Nfc*, but as arguments for free choice based upon immediate experience make clear, these data also can be interpreted in a way inconsistent with *Nfc*.[4]

The fact that the data of choice can be interpreted in a way consistent either with *Sfc* or with *Nfc* establishes *Sfc*/*Nfc* as a genuine controversy. The issue in this controversy cannot be evaded by pointing to other senses of "freedom" in which the assertion that one is free is consistent with *Nfc*, any more than the demand for political freedom can be evaded by pointing out that oppressed people can be called "free" in other, irrelevant senses.

If someone straightforwardly asserts soft determinism as a position which excludes *Sfc*, then, no matter what other modes of freedom he asserts to be real, he asserts *Nfc*, that is, he denies to be real the very freedom at issue in *Sfc*/*Nfc*. Therefore, if this is a soft determinist's position, the compatibility he defends is not relevant here; his position does not state that *Sfc* and *Nfc* are compatible.

As the exposition in chapter two, sections A and B, makes clear, an important element of the soft determinist's position, as it developed historically, is the contention that "freedom" means *only* physical freedom and freedom to do as one pleases. Hume's statement of the position is classic. Anyone not a prisoner and in chains is free. For Hume and those who follow him, "free" does not mean anything more than "not compelled" or "not coerced."

Despite its plausibility to many philosophers even today, this line of argument is fallacious. It is not fallacious in indicating that physical freedom and freedom to do as one pleases are compatible with *Nfc*; they are. It is not fallacious simply because it implies that no one can make a free choice; this is a position for which one can argue. But it is fallacious in arguing that the controversy over free choice is dissolved by pointing out the compatibility of determinism with physical freedom and freedom to do as one pleases. There remains another *possible* sort of freedom—free choice.

"Freedom," however, is not the only relevant expression which has several distinct meanings. "Responsibility" likewise has a number of meanings, and the various senses of "responsibility" correspond to various senses of "freedom." Language used in evaluative statements also has multiple senses, and in at least some cases these senses correspond to distinct senses of "free" and "responsible." If one uses any one of these expressions in a given context in a certain sense, he is likely to use the related expressions in a corresponding and appropriate way. Thus, if a three-year-old child has a tantrum and purposely breaks something, one might say that the child is "acting freely," is "responsible," is "naughty," and deserves "punishment." One might use the same expressions in referring to a president who obstructs justice, except that one probably would say "did wrong" rather than "was naughty." Many people using these expressions in such different contexts would use them with different senses, believing that the president was free and responsible in a sense in which a three-year-old child could not be. In each context, all of the relevant expressions would systematically shift in meaning.

Therefore, since there is a *possible* mode of freedom—free choice—in addition to those for which the soft determinist can account, there will be corresponding senses of the other relevant expressions for which he cannot account. Thus, although the soft determinist shows that "free," "responsible," and related expressions can be correctly used in talking about human action in senses compatible with *Nfc*, he does not succeed in dissolving *Sfc/Nfc*. *Sfc* remains incompatible with the theory of universal determinism and with any other theory which excludes free choice as impossible.

One of the common arguments in favor of *Sfc* has been that a person cannot be morally responsible for his acts unless it is possible for him either to conform to a norm or to violate it. This is the meaning of the assertion: " 'Ought' implies 'can.' " To defend their position against this argument, compatibilists in recent years have tried to provide an adequate analysis of "I could have done otherwise" compatible with *Nfc*. Candidates for such an analysis include "I would have done otherwise had I so chosen," or "had I tried," or "had circumstances been slightly different." These are possible meanings of "I could have done otherwise." They express what people sometimes mean when they utter these words. These expressions can be used to refer to physical freedom, to freedom to do as one pleases, or to both.

But these are not the only possible meanings of "I could have done otherwise." "Could" also can correspond to the "can" in "I can choose either *A* or *B*." As we make clear in chapter one, section G, "can" might be used by a person to express the belief—true or false—that there are alternatives to be settled by his choice alone. In other words, the description of the experience of choice in chapter one, sections C through F, exhibits a foundation for a meaningful use of "can" incompatible with *Nfc*.

This particular use of "can" cannot be analyzed in a way inconsistent with

Sfc. To refuse to admit that "can" might sometimes be correctly used in a way inconsistent with *Nfc*—that is, to affirm *Sfc*, even if this affirmation is false—is to maintain that stipulation can resolve a substantive question.[5]

However, because of the impressive array of philosophers who have espoused soft determinism, it seems unlikely that there is nothing more in the case for this position than a stipulation that expressions such as "freedom" and "responsibility" be defined in a way consistent with *Nfc*. Thus, it is worth asking why a soft determinist would suppose that he has disposed of the sense of "freedom" required to affirm *Sfc* merely by showing that "free" and certain related expressions have at least one meaning compatible with *Nfc*.

One possible answer to this question is suggested by our discussion in chapter two, sections A and B, of the arguments for *Sfc* from immediate experience and from moral responsibility. The argument from immediate experience fails because there are senses of "freedom" compatible with the phenomena of choice and with the ordinary language required to describe these phenomena, as well as with the denial of *Sfc*. The argument from moral responsibility fails because there is a sense of "moral responsibility" compatible with *Nfc*. In criticizing these arguments, a *PNfc* need only show that there are in fact distinct senses of "free" and "responsible." He need not show that no one ever uses these expressions in propositions inconsistent with *Nfc*.

The experience of choice does not by itself demonstrate the reality of free choice, since—as we have made clear—an interpretation of the phenomena of choice compatible with *Nfc* remains a logical possibility. To point to this logical possibility is sufficient to show the invalidity of the argument: "Since one makes choices, one makes free choices." Likewise, moral responsibility is not conclusive evidence for *Sfc*, because there is a plausible *sense* of "responsible" compatible with *Nfc*.

Nevertheless, the soft determinist calls attention to the possible use of "free," "can," and so on, in a sense compatible with *Nfc* in contexts other than that of answering unsound arguments for *Sfc*. The soft determinist characteristically argues as if to note meanings of the relevant expressions compatible with *Nfc* were sufficient to rule out the notion of free choice as in some way confused or suspect. But, clearly, more must be involved in such arguments than the mere observation that these words sometimes have meanings compatible with *Nfc*.

To make clear what might be involved in such a claim, we note that all the key terms in the discussion have parallel shifts in their meanings. If a soft determinist ignores this point, he might suppose, for example, that an account of moral responsibility which involves *Nfc* renders superfluous the sense of "responsibility" which includes "free choice" in its definition. Moreover, assuming that "responsibility" has only one meaning, the soft determinist might think that given his deterministic account of moral responsibility, an analysis of "responsibility" involving "free choice" is necessarily mistaken.

In fact, however, the soft determinist accounts not for every *possible* mode of responsibility, but only for a certain mode of it. As we explained above, many people predicate "morally responsible" of a naughty three-year-old child and of a felonious president in different senses, denying that the former made a free choice and claiming that the latter did so. Whether or not such a claim can be correct, the meaning of "morally responsible" which includes "free choice" is given in the very making of the claim.

A soft determinist might grant that the child and the president are called "morally responsible" in different senses, but maintain that both senses are susceptible to an analysis consistent with *Nfc*. But some *PSfc* might claim that in asserting moral responsibility of the president he uses "moral responsibility" in a sense which includes "free choice" in its definition. Surely, such a claim is *intelligible* even if it is in principle false because *Nfc* is true. One who makes this claim wishes to insist that the president could have avoided obstructing justice but freely chose to obstruct it—"freely chose" as defined in chapter one, section B.

A soft determinist might point out that inasmuch as he has been able to provide analyses of many senses of "can" which are compatible with *Nfc*, further analysis might show that even the sense of "can" involved in the definition of "free choice" is compatible with *Nfc*.[6] This suggestion, however, depends on the view—which is a curious view of the relationship between the meaning which speakers intend when they use language and the meaning which analysis can uncover—that analysis can show that words really mean the contradictory of what speakers in using them mean to say.

Of course, analysis can show that a speaker's expressions convey meanings he did not intend. What a person says often has implications to which he fails to attend. If such implications are pointed out, a person often withdraws his original statement and substitutes for it one which avoids the unintended implications. But analysis cannot show that a speaker's expression has a "true meaning" which is logically incompatible with the meaning he consciously intends to express by using the precise language he does.

In the preceding paragraphs, we have been trying to understand why the soft determinist assumes that his articulation of meanings of "free"—and some related expressions—compatible with *Nfc* rules out the senses of these expressions which involve free choice. The preceding clarification reveals the inadequacy of some possible reasons for this assumption. But the inadequacy is so glaring that there must be a different reason why most soft determinists make this assumption.

In fact, there is a different reason: Soft determinists believe *Nfc* true. Some of them, like Hobbes, accept *Nfc* on metaphysical grounds; many others, like Locke and Hume, accept it as a deliverance of science. Considering the historical context in which soft determinism has flourished, one can understand how universal determinism has seemed an obvious truth admitted by all men. Thus, as we have noted at the outset of this section, determinism is generally assumed by soft determinists.

Even more basic than the influence of its historical context, however, is the context of controversy in which the reconciliationist project has its place. Reconciliation is called for only if seemingly incompatible data are given. If *Nfc* were not assumed to be true, there would be no need to reconcile human freedom with something else. Nothing would oppose *Sfc*. Thus, soft determinism is not an initial position in the controversy over free will, but is rather a countermove, an attempt to meet objections to an initial position which includes *Nfc*.[7]

The assumption of *Nfc* by the soft determinist also is revealed by the fact that a soft determinist frequently makes statements which are commonly made by a *PNfc* in arguing for his position. For example, soft determinists say that there can be no doubt that every choice is caused, that a free choice would be a random and unintelligible event, that responsibility requires that one's choices be determined by one's character, and so on.

Clearly, the soft determinist's assumption of the truth of *Nfc* provides no ground for excluding the meaning of "free" required to affirm *Sfc*. If one of the contradictory propositions is true, the other, even if false, is meaningful. The truth of *Nfc* would provide no ground for regarding the use of expressions needed to state its contradictory as suspect or confused.

Nothing in our discussion of soft determinism presupposes the truth of *Sfc*. Our point merely is that "free choice" is meaningful and that *Sfc*/*Nfc* cannot be dissolved by talking about kinds of freedom the admission of which is compatible with *Nfc*.

B. The double-aspect theory

Soft determinism is not the only attempt to show that *Sfc*/*Nfc* is a misformulation of the controversy over free will. There is another form of compatibilism which has been adopted by many philosophers since Kant. We call this form of compatibilism "the double-aspect theory."[8]

On this view, determinism does not involve *Nfc*, because the language appropriate to determinism cannot be used to refer to choice. One can refer to choice only from the standpoint of the agent or in the practical language of action. Determinism is a thesis about events; it can make reference only from the standpoint of an observer or in a theoretical language such as that of science. The two distinct aspects have been called "distinct levels of description and explanation," "diverse language strata," "different bodies of discourse," "separate domains," and so on.

A contemporary example of the double-aspect theory is found in A. I. Melden's *Free Action:*

> Where we are concerned with causal explanations, with events of which the happenings in question are effects in accordance with some law of causality, to that extent we are not concerned with human actions at all but, at best, with bodily movements or happenings; and where we are concerned with explanations of human action, there causal factors and causal laws in the sense in which, for example, these terms are employed in the biological sciences are wholly irrelevant to the understanding we seek. The reason is simple, namely, the radically different logical characteristics of the two bodies of discourse we employ in these distinct cases—the different concepts which are applicable to these different orders of inquiry.[9]

Melden's statement of this theory is typical of expressions of it by many other authors.[10]

It is possible to hold the double-aspect theory for reasons irrelevant to the controversy over free choice. One might hold that there is nothing about either domain incompatible with *Sfc*. One might also hold that both domains exclude *Sfc*. The latter view might take the form of maintaining causal determinism for events and determination by reasons for actions. Such a view clearly would include *Nfc*. Thus, it is not a form of compatibilism. In the remainder of this section, we are concerned only with proponents of a double-aspect theory who think that the distinction of two domains permits them to assert the compatibility of freedom with determinism, and thus to avoid the contradictory 'alternatives expressed in our formulation of the controversy.

Construed in this way, the double-aspect theory still requires clarification. What is the relationship between the two domains? Is the distinction between the two bodies of discourse merely a matter of fact? That is, can the distinction be eliminated by a more adequate understanding of the rules by which each body of discourse might be translated into the other? If so, the double-aspect theory does not dissolve *Sfc/Nfc*. The *PNfc* will be able to look forward to the discovery of the required translation rules so that he will be able to use theoretical language to refer to choices and to affirm *Nfc*.[11] The *PSfc*, for his part, can admit that theoretical language might be used to refer to choice, but he will use such language to deny the truth of *Nfc* and whatever other theoretical propositions he must deny to maintain *Sfc*.

On another interpretation, the double-aspect theory claims that the two bodies of discourse are in principle irreducible to one. On this interpretation, each language is indispensable for certain purposes and neither language can be translated into the other. Such a view can take either of two forms.

In one form, it might involve the claim that reference, truth, and explanation are possible in only one body of discourse—that appropriate to talking about events theoretically and in terms of factors which exclude *Sfc*.[12] On this approach, the body of discourse appropriate to action contains no statements and thus allows neither the *PSfc* nor the *PNfc* to affirm anything other than what can be expressed in theoretical language. It follows that this interpretation of the double-aspect theory does not permit the claim that freedom and determinism are compatible by virtue of the distinction between bodies of discourse.

In another form, the double-aspect theory which holds that there are irreducible bodies of discourse allows truth-claims to be made in both of them. Only on this approach can the double-aspect theory permit both freedom and determinism to be truly affirmed, yet avoid the seeming contradiction between them by positing the irreducibility of the domains proper to each. But even in this form, the double-aspect theory will not put to rest *Sfc/Nfc*.

The *PNfc* can admit the irreducibility of the language of action to that of causally determined events. Still, he might argue, the former language is dispensable and there are good reasons to dispense with it, at least to the extent that it is not translatable into deterministic language.[13] Such reasons might include the explanatory purposes of science, the promotion of reform of criminal law, and the practical confusion arising from the use of the language of action. For his part, the *PSfc* must of course resist any attempt to eliminate the language of choice.

Thus, this form of the double-aspect theory fails to dissolve *Sfc/Nfc*. It fails because the analysis of the use of ordinary language cannot by itself settle a substantive philosophical question. Of course, such analysis is essential for the accurate formulation of the issue. We grant that it is significant that ordinary language about human actions articulates the phenomena of choice in such a way that this language is not altogether reducible to scientific discourse. It does not follow, however, that the *PNfc* is necessarily misguided or wrong-headed. The most which follows is that if *Nfc* is correct, people should more or less radically revise the way they talk about human actions.

Some advocates of the double-aspect theory would point out at this juncture that their view is not merely descriptive of the way language does work. They would claim that the irreducibly distinct bodies of discourse regarding actions and regarding events are indispensable because without them and their distinction one cannot speak coherently about human behavior. Such a claim expresses in terms of language the same thesis which Kant expresses by speaking of the irreducibility of theoretical and practical thinking.[14] The conditions of the possibility of meaningful discourse and of coherent thinking either are the same or—at least in respect to this problem—precisely analogous. It is no accident that many proponents of the double-aspect theory remind one of Kant even if they do not mention him.

Because Kant's treatment of this form of the double-aspect theory is clear and well-developed, we first consider the proposal in his own terms.

In the *Critique of Pure Reason* (A444-445=B472-473), the thesis of the third antinomy is: "Causality in accordance with laws of nature is not the only causality from which the appearances of the world can one and all be derived. To explain these appearances it is necessary to assume that there is also another causality, that of freedom." The antithesis is: "There is no freedom; everything in the world takes place solely in accordance with laws of nature."[15]

The arguments Kant proposes for the thesis and the antithesis are not important for our present purpose. What is important is the solution he offers to the antinomy. Because of its difficulty, this solution has been interpreted in various ways. We offer the following as a plausible interpretation, relevant to the double-aspect theory.

Kant's solution to the antinomy begins (A532=B560) with the assertion that there are two and only two kinds of causality conceivable by the human mind: causality according to nature and causality according to freedom. Causality according to nature presupposes time, and it leads to a causal chain or network covering all the facts of the natural world. Causality according to freedom is the power of initiating something spontaneously.

Having made this distinction, Kant proceeds to argue that if all causality in the sensible world were mere nature, then there would be no room for practical freedom, which presupposes that something can happen which *ought* not to have happened. He attributes to man a power of free choice which can be affected by sensuous impulses but which cannot be coerced by them (A533-534=B561-562).

The key to a solution, according to Kant, is not that there is any gap in the solid network of natural causality. Rather, he thinks, the key is that the whole of nature is a world of appearance, not of absolute reality. If nature is not ultimate reality, something nonnatural can be the term of a relationship of a natural event. Thus, Kant is able to formulate the problem in the following terms: "Is it a truly disjunctive proposition to say that every effect in the world must arise *either* from nature *or* from freedom; or must we not rather say that in one and the same event, in different relations, both can be found?" (A536=B564).

Kant next argues that the causality of a person can be regarded from two points of view. To the extent that the person is an appearance in the sensible world, its causality can be regarded from one point of view. To the extent that the person also has a faculty which is not an object of sensible intuition, but through which it can cause appearances, its causality can be regarded from another point of view. Considered as a causality of a thing in itself, this causality is *intelligible* in its action. But considered as a causality belonging to an appearance in the natural world, this causality is *sensible* in its effects.

Thus, for Kant, the human person has an empirical aspect, and according to this aspect the person's causality and effects in the world of nature are altogether determined by antecedent causes. At the same time, this same person has an intelligible aspect, and according to this aspect nothing happens to the person, no action begins in the person, and there can be no change in the person, "but we may yet quite correctly say that the active being *of itself* begins its effects in the sensible world. In so doing, we should not be asserting that the effects in the sensible world can begin of themselves; they are always predetermined through antecedent empirical conditions . . ." (A541=B569).

Might it not be the case that in certain instances the empirical causality is an effect of an intelligible causality (A544=B572)? Of course, one would have to assume that "the *action* of these causes *in the appearance* is in conformity with all the laws of empirical causality" (A545=B573). Man knows himself in respect of intelligence and reason to be a purely intelligible entity (A547=B575). The fact that reason has causality is evident from imperatives which persons impose on their active powers; nature knows only "is," "was," and "will be," not "ought" (A547=B575).

Having reached this point, Kant's attempted explanation breaks down. "Ought" expresses a conceptual ground of action; a merely natural action always has an empirical causal condition. "The action to which the *'ought'* applies must indeed be possible under natural conditions," Kant affirms. But the conditions do not determine the will. Whatever is willed, whether the pleasant or the good, "reason will not give way to any ground which is empirically given," for it follows its own order of ideas "to which it adapts the empirical conditions." If sensuous impulses impel me to will, they cannot give rise to an "ought"; reason declares actions to be necessary, "although they have never taken place, and perhaps never will take place" (A548=B576).

Here Kant is discussing two different things. On the one hand, reason may issue its own demands, whether these be fulfilled or not. Reason says what ought to be, and this necessity, Kant points out, is irreducible to natural requirements and conditions. On the other hand, actions which are presumably caused by reason occur in the empirical world. This world must be such as to allow for their possibility; the empirical conditions must be adaptable to the intelligible causality. This discussion leaves unclear how empirical conditions which are woven into the unbroken fabric of the totality of nature can be adapted for particular acts.

Reason itself, Kant goes on, must have an empirical aspect. This can be completely investigated from experienced actions, which reveal the subjective principles of an individual's will. But if we compare the acts—which from an empirical point of view are inevitable—to reason as a cause, Kant says that perhaps what inevitably happened ought not to have happened. Then Kant makes the remarkable statement: "Sometimes, however, we find, or at least believe that we find, that the ideas of reason have in actual fact proved their causality in respect of the actions of men, as appearances; and that these actions have taken place, not because they were determined by empirical causes, but because they were determined by grounds of reason" (A550=B578).

The problem with this statement is not whether it is true, but whether it can make sense at all on Kant's own principles. On the one hand, the only actions which can be known are effects in the world of experience; everything in that world is not *more or less* determined, but *completely* determined. Yet Kant is saying that some actions have taken place "not because they were determined by empirical causes." On the other hand, "ought" points to an intelligible causality, and nothing happens to this principle in itself—it is an unchanging principle. But actions which take place in the empirical world—a world uniformly determined as a completely interlocking system—sometimes are determined by grounds of reason and sometimes are not. Kant here breaks down his own distinction between the two domains; he treats the causality of nature and the causality of the noumenal self as if they were each necessary conditions but only together a sufficient condition for those empirical effects which are human actions.

A confirmation of the correctness of our criticism is found in a footnote in which Kant argues that since a person does not know the intelligible character except by its empirical effects, he can never know the real morality of actions, even of his own. "Our imputations can refer only to the empirical character. How much of this character is ascribable to the pure effect of freedom, how much to mere nature, that is, to faults of temperament for which there is no responsibility, or to its happy constitution (*merito fortunae*), can never be determined . . ." (A551=B579). Kant should keep the two modes of causality distinct; in this footnote, he mingles them.

In the text, Kant goes on to argue that the causality of reason is outside time; it therefore can be a spontaneous starting point of a new series of effects. The same cause—man, the moral agent—belongs to nature, and from this point of view "no given action (since it can be perceived only as appearance) can begin absolutely of itself" (A553=B581). To say that the act as part of nature cannot begin absolutely of itself is an understatement on Kant's principles; he should say that the act does not at all begin of itself, but is wholly determined by antecedent conditions.

Kant illustrates his point with the example of a voluntary action, a malicious lie. He says that one can trace the empirical aspect of the action to its sources, but "we none the less blame the agent" disregarding conditions "just as if the agent in and by himself began in this action an entirely new series of consequences." One proceeds on a law of reason according to which the agent can and ought to have determined, irrespective of all the empirical conditions, to act otherwise.

> This causality of reason we do not regard as only a co-operating agency, but as complete in itself, even when the sensuous impulses do not favour but are directly opposed to it; the action is ascribed to the agent's intelligible character; in the moment when he utters the lie, the guilt is entirely his. Reason, irrespective of all

empirical conditions of the act, is completely free, and the lie is entirely due to its default. (A555=B583)

Here, the moral judgment, the possibility of which is denied four pages previously, is firmly made. Moreover, whereas four pages previously Kant says that imputations can be made only to the empirical character, here the action is ascribed to the agent's intelligible character.

It might be thought that Kant's difficulties arise only because of certain distinctions not yet clearly made in the first *Critique,* distinctions which Kant made later on. For our present purpose, it is not essential that the analysis of Kant's works be complete. To answer the objection, it is sufficient to quote the following from Lewis White Beck, a leading scholar sympathetic to Kant:

> If by "freedom" we mean noumenal causation and assert that we know no noumena, then there is no justifiable way, in the study of phenomena, to decide that it is permissible in application to some but not others of them to use the concept of freedom. The uniformity of human actions is, in principle, as great as that of the solar system; there is no reason to regard statements about the freedom of the former as having any empirical consequences. If the possession of noumenal freedom makes a difference to the uniformity of nature, then there is no uniformity; if it does not, to call it "freedom" is a vain pretension.[16]

In his effort to dissolve *Sfc/Nfc*, Kant assigns determinism to the natural sequence of causes and effects, while he postulates free choice in the principle of action of a moral subject. This separation would be sufficient to solve the problem only if the two domains were kept completely distinct. The danger is in attempting to use the two viewpoints simultaneously in order to provide something like a stereoscopic view of the reality of human action.

But Kant precisely makes such an attempt. He wants to be able to look at human actions which occur within experience and to consider them at the same time as effects of a causality outside the unbreakable network of natural causes and effects.

The result is that sometimes Kant thinks of action precisely as an appearance; he then relates it to other appearances, and announces that no one can ever know the moral quality of anyone's action, including his own. Sometimes, however, Kant thinks of action as an expression of moral agency, and then he is willing to say that the malicious liar is guilty regardless of the whole sequence of conditions which made his act—as a piece of empirical behavior—as inevitable as anything in nature can be. Kant also sometimes tries to relate an action simultaneously to empirical causes and to moral agency, regarding the action as somehow composite and as somehow an effect of both sorts of principles—for example, when he speaks of mitigated responsibility.

When Kant is consistently looking at action from a single point of view, it is difficult to see how he could establish any empirical criteria according to which any observable sequence of behavior would count as a "malicious lie," or, in general, what criteria Kant could offer for distinguishing any set of phenomena and regarding it as an act to be imputed to a moral agent. When Kant does not consistently look at action from a single point of view, it is difficult to see how he overlooks the inconsistencies into which he falls.

Kant could avoid these inconsistencies and maintain a place for both *Sfc* and *Nfc* only if he firmly refused to allow anything whatsoever to fall into both domains. Yet he wishes to use his distinction to deal with human action and he does not wish to restrict action to one of the two domains.

One reason why Kant's version of the double-aspect theory is interesting is that in itself it is a theory not of two bodies of discourse, but rather of two standpoints for thinking. In reading Kant, one easily notices the distinction between ordinary language and the conditions for the possibility of meaningful discourse. Kant continually uses ordinary language in a way which violates the requirements of his double-aspect theory. We think that recent proponents of the double-aspect theory make a similar mistake, but their lack of explicitness in stating their position conceals the mistake, for it is hard to tell whether they are maintaining a thesis about ordinary language or about what is necessary for any meaningful discourse about human behavior.

A proponent of the double-aspect theory might answer that the inconsistencies we have pointed out in Kant's text are peculiar to Kant and reveal no underlying problem with the double-aspect theory. We admit that Kant's approach has its idiosyncracies. But we think that Kant's inconsistencies are a symptom of a problem which confronts the double-aspect theory as such.

If the incompatible predicates, "free" and "determined," can be said of the same human behavior or anything necessarily related to the same behavior, then there will be something of which it is possible to say that it is both free and determined. Thus, even if Kant's inconsistencies are avoided, similar inconsistencies will emerge—or, at least, the double-aspect theory will not preclude their emergence. To preclude such contradictions, the bodies of discourse must be separated to such an extent that nothing whatever can be the common referent of the relevant expressions in the distinct languages. Thus, the theory requires what J. R. Lucas calls "a thorough-going schizoglossia which is blatantly at variance with the facts."[17]

But if the two bodies of discourse are separated to this extent, it will not be possible to refer to anything which is a piece of human behavior as the referent or as a component of the referent of "free" and "determined." In this case, the double-aspect theory is pointless. It is pointless because the apparent contradiction which the double-aspect theory was intended to remove could never arise if it were not possible—at least mistakenly—to refer to the same thing as both "free" and "determined."

But the proponent of the double-aspect theory might object that the whole point of his approach is to eliminate confusion by showing that expressions of the two bodies of discourse do not have the common reference often mistakenly assumed for them. This objection involves a very strange view: that without making any false affirmations one can use expressions to make affirmations and be mistaken about their reference by supposing that two expressions have a common reference which they do not have. The double-aspect theorist is trying to tell a *PNfc*, not that he is in error in affirming that actions are determined, but that when he says "actions" he is really referring to something other than actions.

The implausibility of the double-aspect theorist's view can be made clear by an example. Imagine a prosecutor outlining his case at the opening of a murder trial: "Discovering that he would inherit his uncle's estate, the defendant deliberately planned to kill the victim, his uncle. He took a gun, held the gun to his uncle's head, and pulled the trigger. The victim's brains spilled out, and he died instantly." The double-aspect theorist must defend at least the following proposition: It involves a category mistake to say, even falsely, that in the circumstances precisely as they were, the trigger moved *because* the nephew deliberately planned to kill his uncle.

A philosopher might try to maintain this proposition, but to do so would be to deny the very possibility of any necessary relationship between the victim's death (a physical event) and the murderer's deliberate plan—part of a human act. In short, the trouble with the double-aspect theory is that even if human acts are not precisely physical events, there is a necessary relationship in given circumstances between certain physical events and a certain human act. The logic of the double-aspect theory demands that its proponents say that the uncle's death and the nephew's deliberate plan had nothing to do with each other.[18]

Thus, Kant's difficulty was not due to any idiosyncracy. Whether one uses Kant's phenomenon/noumenon distinction, or whether one uses a reasons-language/causes-language distinction, or some other distinction, one nevertheless has the same basic difficulty as Kant, provided that the two domains are defined by their opposition and are distinguished precisely in order to avoid the contradiction which would otherwise arise.

Of course, as we said in the earlier part of this section, someone might use such a pair of expressions to make a distinction not meeting the specified conditions. In particular, he might distinguish reasons-language from causes-language without assigning determinism to the latter and some principle incompatible with determinism to the former. But in this case even the appearance of compatibility between determinism and freedom is lost. Our formulation of *Sfc/Nfc* is not shown to be mistaken.

A double-aspect theorist might object at this point that our entire discussion of the double-aspect theory thus far has been based upon a misunderstanding of it. He might claim that he can slip between the horns of the dilemma we have posed for him. The common reference he needs is achieved while the contradiction we point out is avoided, if the same thing can be considered in two bodies of discourse from different points of view. He believes this possible and holds that in one perspective a piece of human behavior can be seen as a determined event while in another perspective the same thing can be seen as a free act. The behavior seen as the trigger being pulled in the event-perspective is seen in the action-perspective as the pulling of the trigger. The difference in perspective removes the contradiction, without precluding common reference.[19]

But this approach does not remove the contradiction; it only appears to do so. The appearance is created by the metaphor of "different points of view." The notion of points of view is based on an analogy between vision and propositional knowledge.

Different visual points of view on the same object present, so to speak, different pictures of one and the same thing. These pictures can be radically different—for example, the view of a coin on edge and the view of the coin's face. Yet these pictures do not contradict one another; they are simply different. They do not conflict precisely because they are *pictures* of the object; they make no claims about the object itself.

Propositional points of view are like visual points of view in some ways, but are different in a crucial respect: The propositions which collectively constitute a point of view on some subject matter are not pictures of the subject matter. If they are affirmed, they are *claims* about the subject matter itself. It is one thing to say that a coin on edge looks like a two-dimensional rectangle; it is another thing to affirm that the coin on edge *is* a two-dimensional rectangle.

What perhaps lends plausibility to the analogy is the way in which certain propositions are expressed. For example, "He was standing to the right of the desk" and "He was standing to the left of the desk" seem to be contradictory, but both could be true, if stated by persons who viewed the situation from different visual points of view. But this use of the expression "different points of view" is simply another way of expressing the requirement of the principle of noncontradiction usually expressed by "in the same respect."

Thus these two statements, if both true, are *not* expressions of contradictory propositions. Either they are not fully explicit statements of the same proposition or they are not fully explicit statements of different propositions. If they are statements of the same proposition, then the difference in point of view has been discounted and no contradiction is involved; if they are statements of different propositions, then the points of view are included in the propositions as part of the states of affairs being described. In the latter case, since the subjects of predication are different, the propositions cannot be contradictory.

Thus, the difference of points of view construed in this way is of no use to the double-aspect theorist; *Sfc* and *Nfc* are contradictories; they refer to the same thing in the same respect.

The flaw in the points-of-view analogy can now be explicated. Different visual points of view produce different pictures of the same thing. By treating propositional knowledge as if it were vision, one easily takes for granted that contradictory propositions are merely different pictures of the same thing. On this analogy, contradictory propositions would be incompatible only if they were affirmed from the same point of view. If they are affirmed from different points of view, however, such propositions are only different pictures of the same thing.

But here the analogy is carried too far. A proposition affirmed from a given propositional point of view about something other than the point of view itself does not characterize the point of view. Instead, someone uses it it pick out some other state of affairs and affirms that this state of affairs obtains—obtains independently of the conditions of one's knowing it and talking about it. Thus, the contradictory propositions affirmed about the same state of affairs from different propositional points of view are no less contradictory for their being affirmed from these different points of view. These propositions are not about the points of view from which they are affirmed, but about some other state of affairs; what they articulate is that state of affairs, independent of anyone's knowing it and talking about it. If it happens that the point of view of one affirming a proposition is confused by him with what he is talking about, then he makes false statements about the world.[20]

Our point can be restated more briefly. The difference between visual points of view depends on the conditions for seeing, not on what is seen. Propositional knowledge about something, however, claims to articulate states of affairs, not the conditions of one's knowing them to be so. Different propositional points of view are precisely different conditions for one's knowing and talking about things. Hence the difference of points of view in this case makes no difference at all; differences in propositional points of view are precisely excluded by the claim involved in the affirming of any proposition: that the state of affairs which it picks out obtains.

The application of this analysis to the example of the two expressions, "the pulling of the trigger" and "the trigger's being pulled," makes clear that they do not belong to different bodies of discourse whose distinction allows statements which would otherwise be contradictory to be affirmed without contradiction. The two expressions can be used in stating the same proposition; if so, only a single statement is made. This difference of point of view is merely grammatical. The two expressions can be used in stating different propositions; if so, they either refer to the same thing or not.

If to the same thing, the two propositions will contradict each other provided that the properties which are attributed are incompatible. Thus, if "The pulling of the trigger was a free act" and "The trigger's being pulled was a determined event" refer to the same thing, then the conjunctive proposition expressed by these two sentences will be logically impossible, assuming that "free act" and "determined event" signify incompatible properties, as they do if something's being a determined event entails that, whatever else it might be, it is not a free act.

If the expressions are used to refer to different things, then the two propositions could not be contradictory and the distinction between viewpoints is unnecessary. If "the pulling of the trigger" refers to a human act and "the trigger's being pulled" refers to an object's movement, then to say that the one is free and that the other is determined does not even seem to be a contradiction.

In sum. The double-aspect theorist cannot escape the dilemma we have pointed out. Either he fails to avoid the contradiction between *Sfc* and *Nfc*, or he avoids contradiction at the price of making his distinction pointless. The double-aspect theory, however subtly developed, is no more successful than soft determinism in its attempt to show the dissolubility of the controversy over free will. Soft determinism includes *Nfc*, while the double-aspect theory fails to preclude it.

In chapter two, we showed that the existing ways of arguing for *Sfc* are unsuccessful. In chapter three, we showed that the case for *Nfc* is a weak one. But we are not skeptics. We think that *Sfc/Nfc* can be resolved in favor of *Sfc*. In chapter five, we articulate the method to be used in refuting *Nfc*. This refutation will provide the key to establishing *Sfc* in chapter six.

5: Preliminaries to the Argument

In this chapter, we set forth the logical structure of the argument we will use in chapter six in our attempt to show that *Nfc* is self-refuting. Thus, our main topics in this chapter are self-referential statements and the arguments which are based upon the ways in which these statements go wrong.

As necessary background for this discussion of self-reference, we devote the first section of this chapter to the common ways in which statements can go wrong. We also consider at the end of the chapter that aspect of the *PNfc's* position which gives rise to the self-referential difficulties we will show in chapter six.

Thus, this chapter has six sections: A) How statements go wrong; B) Self-referential statements; C) How self-referential statements go wrong; D) The falsification of self-referential statements; E) The affirmation of "No free choice"; and F) Rationality norms as conditions for affirmation.

A. How statements go wrong

Since philosophical theories are statements, one can find out how the former go wrong by considering how the latter go wrong. We define a statement—in the sense of a *stating*—as follows: A statement (*S*) includes someone's act (*A*) of affirming a proposition (*P*) by way of a token (usually a sentence) (*T*). A statement, then, includes an affirmation—in the sense of an act of affirming. By "affirmation" we mean all those acts in which someone claims—with whatever degree of conviction—that a proposition is true. Thus, hypotheses and opinions frequently are affirmed. For example, to claim that one position is more reasonable than another is to affirm that position. Commands, questions, prayers, and fictional pretenses are not affirmations. We call affirming, denying, questioning, and other acts upon propositions "propositional acts."[1]

We also distinguish between the act of making a statement, what is stated, and the sentence used to express what is stated. We use the expression "performance of the statement" to refer to the act of affirming what is stated and to the act of uttering the sentence. We use the word "proposition" to refer to what is stated. A proposition has both sense and reference; it is either true or false. We use the word "sentence" to refer to the linguistic entity the utterance of which—by speech or by writing or otherwise—expresses the proposition which is affirmed.

Statements can go wrong because of failure of the proposition, or of the sentence, or of the performance of the statement.

Propositions can be false. The state of affairs picked out by a proposition might not obtain.

Propositions considered in sets can go wrong in another way. Sets of propositions can be formally inconsistent—that is, they can be reduced to propositions of the form *p and not-p*. Since philosophical theories are made up of a number of propositions—some of them unstated assumptions, some of them remote implications—the ordinary tests of formal logic are very important in philosophical discussion. It is worth noting that the discovery of a formal inconsistency does not require one to abandon any *particular* proposition. Since inconsistency obtains between two propositions, one can remove the inconsistency by surrendering either of them.

Statements also can go wrong by a failure of their sentences. A sentence can fail to express a proposition. Frequently, sentences of this sort are called "meaningless." We use "meaningless" to mean a defect either of sense or of reference.

One common way in which a sentence can fail to be meaningful is by being vague or indefinite. Vagueness and indefiniteness are semantic difficulties, because they prevent determinate reference.

Semantic difficulties such as vagueness and indefiniteness are often pointed out by critics of philosophical theories. Perhaps the most common use of the philosopher's question, "What exactly do you mean?" is to demand that the state of affairs under consideration be delineated precisely and fully. Our first chapter exemplifies such semantic clarification. *Sfc/Nfc* has often been confused because of the different meanings of "free." To avoid this confusion these meanings are distinguished. The controversy also has been impeded by the indefiniteness of the expression "free choice." To remedy this indefiniteness the empirical reference of the notion is clarified.

There are philosophical arguments which claim to show that certain philosophical theses have *inherent* semantic difficulties. If such an argument is successful, it warrants the charge that the thesis in question is meaningless. We used such an argument in chapter four in our criticism of the double-aspect theory.

Both Plato's and Aristotle's arguments against the theory that all is flux, and Aristotle's argument against the theory that all is undifferentiated unity are attempts to show that these theories render reference impossible. In a world of undifferentiated unity or in a world of complete flux, no state of affairs could obtain. It would be impossible to refer to such a world.[2]

The examples drawn from Plato and Aristotle are of arguments which seek to show that the theories criticized entail the impossibility of reference—including the reference of these very theories. Our argument against the double-aspect theory showed that this theory either leads to formal inconsistency or makes it impossible to refer to some of the phenomena for which the theory is intended to account.

Statements also can go wrong by a failure of their performances. A performance of a statement goes wrong when the performance cannot achieve its purpose—that is, when the performance is pointless. A performance can be pointless for a number of different reasons. One of these is if the statement lacks a suitable context. As C. K. Grant indicates, utterances must take place in a context—that is, they imply certain propositions about their speaker, their audience, and so on. If the implied propositions are false, then the utterance is irrational. According to Grant, the performance of making a statement has psychological and propositional "pragmatic implications." For example, one using an indicative sentence ordinarily implies that he believes it, that he has an audience, and that he wishes the audience to believe it. These implications do not follow from the proposition affirmed; yet if they are false, the utterance is *pointless*.[3]

Performative pointlessness not only is common in the ordinary usage of speech acts of various kinds; it also explains a philosophically important informal fallacy—that of begging the question. There is nothing formally wrong with the circularity involved in this fallacy. The fallacy arises because the circularity makes impossible the successful achievement of the purpose of the argument. The purpose of an argument is to make its conclusions rationally acceptable by virtue of its relation to grounds which are independently acceptable. If the truth of the conclusion is assumed as part of the premises, then the argument cannot achieve its desired effect of *making* the conclusion acceptable on the basis of something independently acceptable. We have shown in chapters two and three that many arguments for and against *Sfc* are pointless in just this way.

B. Self-referential statements

Self-referential statements can go wrong in all the ways other statements can go wrong. Their self-referential character, however, makes a difference to the logical properties of their going wrong and this difference is philosophically important. Because the notion of self-reference is tricky, we define it and give examples of its various kinds. We also argue that there is nothing inherently wrong with self-referential statements.

A *statement* is self-referential if and only if the proposition which is affirmed refers to some aspect of the statement—that is, either to the sentence, or to the performance of affirming or uttering, or to the proposition itself.

We first consider self-referential statements in which the reference is to the sentence. Smith's statement (*S*), "All Smith's English statements are cases of correct English," affirms a general proposition. Each instance of this general proposition is a proposition which, 1) refers to the sentence used to make a statement of Smith's in English, and, 2) says of it that it is a case of correct English. Let "*T*" name the sentence which expresses the proposition affirmed in *S*. This proposition has a self-referential instance: "*T* is the sentence used to make a statement of Smith's in English and *T* is a case of correct English." We call the self-reference of this statement "sentential." The proposition in *S* would not be sententially self-referential if Smith used a French sentence to make his statement. Nor would the proposition in *S* be sententially self-referential if someone else said: "All Smith's English statements are cases of correct English."

In a similar way, Smith's statement, "All Smith's statements are cases of correct English," is sententially self-referential. The proposition affirmed in this statement is sententially self-referential whenever it is affirmed by Smith. Likewise, "All my statements are cases of correct English" is a sententially self-referential statement. The propositions affirmed in statements made by using these words will be different for each speaker, since "my" will have a different referent in each. Yet the propositions affirmed by these words will all be sententially self-referential, whenever a speaker uses these words to make a statement.

There are self-referential statements in which the reference is to the performance. We call these "performatively self-referential statements." For example, Smith's spoken statement (*S*), "Smith always speaks softly," is performatively self-referential. Let "*U*" name Smith's speaking the sentence used to express the proposition affirmed in *S*. This proposition has a self-referential instance: "*U* is a spoken utterance of Smith's and *U* is spoken softly." The proposition affirmed in *S* need not be performatively self-referential; Smith might express in writing the proposition expressed in *S*, or someone else might express this proposition.

There also are performatively self-referential statements in which the reference is to the affirming rather than to the uttering. For example, Smith's statement, "All Smith's statements are well-founded," is performatively self-referential. The reference is to Smith's affirming.

There also are self-referential statements in which the reference is to the proposition. We call these "semantically self-referential statements." For example, Smith's statement (S), "All Smith's statements are contingently true," is semantically self-referential. Let "P" name the general proposition affirmed in S. Each instance of this general proposition is a proposition, 1) referring to some proposition affirmed by Smith, and, 2) saying of it that it is contingently true. The proposition affirmed in S has a semantically self-referential instance, "P is a proposition and P is contingently true." This statement is semantically self-referential only when affirmed by Smith.

The previous examples might suggest that all self-referential statements contain general propositions. This need not be so. For example, "This sentence contains five words" can be used to express a sententially self-referential statement. "This sentence is printed on paper" can be used to express a performatively self-referential statement. However, semantically self-referential statements cannot be singular; sentences which seem to express the propositions in singular semantically self-referential statements turn out to be paradoxical. We discuss these below.

Thus far we have been considering *statements* which are self-referential. As the examples make clear, the propositions affirmed in these statements are not inherently self-referential—that is, the propositions might be expressed in ways which would not involve self-reference. For instance, the propositions might be affirmed by different speakers, or by way of different sentences.

However, there are certain propositions which are self-referential in any possible stating of them. Such propositions inevitably refer to themselves or to the performances of their statements or to the sentences by which they are expressed. We call such propositions "self-referential propositions"; they should not be confused with the propositions of self-referential statements.

The following are examples of self-referential propositions. "All statements can be made in English" expresses a sententially self-referential proposition. "All affirmations are well-founded" expresses a performatively self-referential proposition. "All propositions are either true or false" expresses a semantically self-referential proposition.

In each of these examples an instance of the general proposition refers to the sentence or performance or proposition. No matter how these propositions are stated, they make reference to the sentence, performance, or proposition. In other words, the self-reference of these propositions is invariant in relation to any change of sentences used to express them, persons who affirm them, and modalities of uttering and affirming them.

As already noted, semantically self-referential statements cannot be singular. Statements such as "This very statement is vague" and "This very statement is false" are puzzling. One wonders just what proposition it is of which the vagueness or falsity is predicated. In fact, "This very statement is false" is a version of the Liar Paradox. If one takes it to be true, then it turns out false, since it says that it is false. If, on the other hand, one assumes it to be false, then it turns out true. Other self-referential statements also lead to paradox—for example, Grelling's paradox concerning "heterologicality." These have been called "semantic paradoxes." Seemingly similar paradoxes arise in the use of certain formal notions to refer to themselves. These are called "logical paradoxes." Russell's paradox concerning the class of all classes which are not members of themselves is a famous example.

The semantic and logical paradoxes of self-reference have given rise to the claim that all self-reference is illegitimate and leads to paradox. We dispute this claim. Analysis of self-referring statements which do lead to paradox does not support the claim that all self-reference is illegitimate; rather the kinds of self-reference which are illegitimate can be shown to be so for specifiable reasons.

The claim that all self-reference must be avoided was first articulated by Russell and Whitehead in *Principia Mathematica*. They contend that all self-referential statements are nonsensical since they all violate what Russell and Whitehead call "the vicious circle principle."

All self-referential statements, they argue, violate this principle by making reference to "illegitimate totalities," such as the one referred to in the paradox of the class of all classes which are not members of themselves. Thus, "All propositions are either true or false" is rejected as nonsensical, as is the statement of the Liar Paradox.[4] Likewise, they apply their principle to the well-known argument that skepticism is self-refuting.

> Similarly, the imaginary sceptic, who asserts that he knows nothing, and is refuted by being asked if he knows that he knows nothing, has asserted nonsense, and has been fallaciously refuted by an argument which involves a vicious-circle fallacy. In order that the sceptic's assertion may become significant, it is necessary to place some limitation upon the things of which he is asserting his ignorance, because the things of which it is possible to be ignorant form an illegitimate totality. But as soon as a suitable limitation has been placed by him upon the collection of propositions of which he is asserting his ignorance, the proposition that he is ignorant of every member of this collection must not itself be one of the collection. Hence any significant scepticism is not open to the above form of refutation.[5]

Thus, *all* self-reference is rejected as illegitimate.

This view has been further articulated by those who regard language as a hierarchy of levels each of which can have as referents only linguistic and nonlinguistic entities lower in the hierarchy. Moreover, the view that all self-reference is illegitimate has been taken as a basis for regarding all arguments which depend on self-reference—including those against *Nfc*—as fallacious.[6]

This claim that all self-reference is illegitimate and must be avoided involves a number of widely recognized difficulties.[7] Several of these difficulties are crucial.

The prohibition of self-reference may be stated as follows: "There are no self-referential propositions." This formulation is logically equivalent to (S): "All propositions are non-self-referential." If the utterance of S expresses the affirmation of a proposition (P), then this proposition is a general one, whose instances taken collectively make reference to all propositions. One of these instances makes reference to P; this instance is "P is a proposition and P is non-self-referential." In other words, P is semantically self-referential in virtue of the fact that it is about *all* propositions. However what P says about all propositions, including itself, is that they are non-self-referential. It follows that either S does not express a proposition, or P falsifies itself.

On the one hand, if S does not express a proposition, then S can make no truth-claim; it cannot *deny* that there are propositions which contain self-reference. Thus S has no cognitive purpose; it is simply not a truth-claim. On the other hand, if a proposition is affirmed in S, then the proposition is self-referential and falsifies itself. Any attempt to avoid this dilemma by limiting the scope of the prohibition would allow for *some* self-reference.[8]

The second decisive objection to the complete prohibition of self-reference as illegitimate is that the prohibition ignores the differences between kinds of self-reference. Russell and Whitehead regard as identical in kind the self-reference of the application of formal notions to themselves, the self-reference of the semantical paradoxes, and the performative self-reference of skepticism. These are clearly different, as are the paradoxes which arise in each case.

Logical paradoxes, such as Russell's, are not genuine antinomies by which one is driven to hold both elements of a contradiction. The class of all classes which are not members of themselves will be a member of itself if one assumes that it is not; it will not be a member of itself if one assumes that it is. But one can remove the paradox by noticing that it depends upon the assumption that there is a class of all classes which are not members of themselves. If, rather than making this assumption, one asks whether there could be such a class, what was stated as a paradox can be seen to be a reductio ad absurdum argument to support a negative answer to the question. This argument shows that the notion of a class of all classes which are not members of themselves is incoherent. There can be no such class.[9] There appears to be a paradox only because of the way the issue is formulated. That there is such a class is erroneously taken as given, not stated as an assumption to be proved or disproved.

Quine points out that semantic paradoxes, unlike logical paradoxes, do lead to genuine antinomies.[10] These too, however, depend upon an assumption, although one of a different sort than in the logical paradoxes. The assumption on which all the semantic paradoxes rest is that the sentences which generate them express propositions. This assumption is false.

With regard to the putative statement, "This very statement is false," one can ask what proposition it is of which the falsity is predicated. A similar question can be asked with regard to such puzzling sentences as "This very statement is true" and "This very statement is vague." Ordinarily, when someone asks for semantic clarification, a straightforward answer is possible; the speaker can indicate what he is talking about. The speaker can name it or pick it out by a definite description. This is also the case when the object referred to is a proposition. Thus, if someone asks which proposition a speaker is claiming to be true, or vague, or false; the speaker can express the proposition in some other way, name it, or describe it.

These procedures fail for statements which lead to semantic paradoxes. If someone says "This very statement is false" and is asked what proposition he is talking about, his answer, "This very statement," or his repeating the statement, or anything else he might do is no help since such a reply cannot indicate a referent. Unless it can be shown that the subject, "This very statement," does in fact refer to a proposition, then this sentence does not express a proposition—it has no reference.

For example, someone might ask whether "This very statement" in "This very statement is false" has a referent. Any attempt to show that the referring expression, "This very statement," does in fact refer to a proposition expressed in "This very statement is false" gives rise to the same question. Thus, "This very statement" might be said to refer to "This very statement is false" giving rise to "The statement, 'This very statement is false,' is false." But clearly the very same question can be raised about the referent of "This very statement" as it appears in the included sentence. And a similar question could be asked ad infinitum about any possible referent of "This very statement," since its referent would always include a referring expression, and the reference would always be to the referring expression just inasmuch as it is referring.[11]

In short, the semantic paradoxes are due neither to the fact that they arise in self-referential statements nor to the fact that the self-reference is semantic. The precise difficulty is that there are no propositions expressed in these supposed statements; there is nothing definite to which the referring terms might refer. Like a mirage, the supposed referent continually recedes. Thus, until one sees that the semantic paradoxes are only putative statements, the semantic difficulties posed by such paradoxes cannot be removed.

Other self-referential statements, including the statements of semantically self-referential propositions, need not share these difficulties. "All propositions are either true or false" is semantically self-referring. "The proposition, 'All propositions are either true or false,' is either true or false" is an instance of this proposition. This self-referential instance is not paradoxical; there is no difficulty in indicating its referent. Indeed, the proposition is true.

In the case of sententially and performatively self-referential statements, one does not find paradoxes formally like the logical and semantic paradoxes. Both the latter kinds of paradox are similar in form to the Liar Paradox, the statement of which—if it stated a proposition—would state a proposition which would be true if assumed to be false and false if assumed to be true. Performatively self-referential statements need not be paradoxical. For example, "I always write correct English" is not paradoxical.[12] Those performatively self-referential statements which might be called "paradoxical" can go wrong in a quite different way than logical or semantic paradoxes. "I never write correct English" might be called "paradoxical," but it is not true if false and false if true. As soon as one considers whether the self-referential instance of this statement is true, one discovers that it is not. The sentence used to make the statement is evidence that the self-referential instance of the proposition is not true, and noticing this falsity ends one's perplexity. The air of paradox here is due only to the fact that the proposition is falsified by the very sentence used to express it.

Also distinct from the logical and semantic paradoxes are performatively self-referential statements which go wrong performatively. The skeptic, for example, if he is to be consistent, must consider his own affirmation to be as groundless as all others. One cannot achieve anything by affirming a proposition which one admits to be groundless.

Nevertheless, performatively self-referential statements also can go wrong semantically. Such statements have difficulties similar to the difficulties of those semantically self-referential statements which cannot indicate a referent. For example, "This very affirmation is well-grounded," which is performatively self-referential, has the same kind of difficulty as "This very statement is vague." Since an affirmation is the affirming of a proposition, if one is to indicate the referent of the referring expression, "This very affirmation," in the statement, "This very affirmation is well-founded," then one must also be able to indicate the proposition which is affirmed. This, clearly, cannot be done.

However, in many cases it is neither impossible nor even difficult to indicate what is referred to in performatively self-referential statements. In performatively self-referential statements as well as in sententially self-referential statements the subject matter—that is, the act of affirming the proposition or uttering the sentence used in making the self-referential statement—can be identified by naming it or picking it out by a definite description.

In summary. There is nothing inherently illegitimate about statements which refer to themselves. It is now necessary to consider more systematically how those that go wrong do so.

C. How self-referential statements go wrong

Self-referential statements can go wrong in the same ways as other statements. The propositions expressed in such statements can be false or inconsistent with other propositions; the performances of such statements can be pointless. Sentences which seem to express self-referential statements can turn out to be meaningless.

The breakdown of self-referential statements insofar as they are self-referential is peculiar because some aspect of the statement itself, as referent of the proposition affirmed in the statement, gives rise to the falsity, meaninglessness, or pointlessness.

We have shown how some semantically self-referential statements can be such that it is impossible to indicate the propositions to which they allegedly refer. Since the very propositions which are supposed to be expressed in such statements are what they purport to refer to, these semantic difficulties justify the claim that such a putative statement expresses no proposition.

Semantically self-referential statements can also lead to performative difficulties. For example, "All propositions are false" is a pointless, semantically self-referential statement. It must be noted that "This proposition is false" is not an instance of the preceding general proposition. Its self-referential instance is " 'All propositions are false' is false." Thus, if someone affirms "All propositions are false," his purpose is necessarily thwarted. He affirms a proposition which he must regard as false if he is to be consistent.

Finally, semantically self-referential statements can be falsified by their own propositions. We have shown that any statement of a general prohibition of self-reference is semantically self-referential. An instance of the proposition expressed in this prohibition refers to the proposition itself and says of it that it is non-self-referential. But this instance does refer to the proposition. Thus, the proposition is self-referential, and this fact falsifies the proposition. Likewise, assuming that propositions themselves are metaphysical entities, "No proposition can refer to a metaphysical entity" is falsified by its own proposition. Since this proposition refers to all propositions, it has an instance which refers to itself. Thus, the self-referential instance of the general proposition is falsified by the proposition itself.

Performatively and sententially self-referential statements also can go wrong in all of these ways. We have already shown that performatively self-referential statements can fail semantically by lacking reference. For example, "This very affirmation is well-founded" seems to be a performatively self-referential statement, but it can have no definite reference.

Performatively self-referential statements also can be performatively pointless; pointless statements of this sort are aptly called "self-defeating." We have already seen that skepticism is self-defeating in this way.[13]

The self-referential arguments for *Sfc* which we considered in chapter two, section E, are for the most part attempts to show that any statement of *Nfc* is self-defeating. If these arguments were successful, the affirmation of *Nfc* would be seen to be pointless when its self-referential instance is considered. James Jordan is very clear about this; he points out several times that his argument does *not* show that *Nfc* is false. He thinks it shows only that if *Nfc* is true, then there is no good reason to believe any thesis, including *Nfc*. Thus Jordan regards his argument as a practical, not a theoretical, argument for *Sfc*.[14] The truth of *Nfc* remains possible.

Jordan is correct in thus limiting the claim he makes for his argument. In our own use of an argument of this form in chapter six, section G, we will take care to respect this limitation. If this kind of argument is successful, performative pointlessness is a characteristic of the affirming of *Nfc*, not of *Nfc* itself. Even if it is self-defeating for a *PNfc* to affirm *Nfc*, this does not show *Nfc* false. Likewise in the case of the skeptic: Even if his affirmation is groundless, it might still be true that all affirmations are groundless.

Because the effect of arguments similar to these two is to show the pointlessness of the opponent's act of affirming his thesis rather than to show the thesis false, arguments of this sort have been called "ad hominem." David Wiggins has thus characterized a standard self-referential argument against marxism.

> The reply [that marxist beliefs also are conditioned] is no better than *ad hominem* because it leaves perfectly open the possibility that beliefs, capitalist, marxist, and all others, are *uniformly* tainted by the causality which determines them. It cannot tell against this that if it were so then nobody would have the knowledge of this fact but at best an accidental true belief. Perhaps that is how things are.[15]

Wiggins's criticism is correct to the extent that such arguments do not show any proposition to be false, but only show its affirmation to be self-defeating. Wiggins's criticism is not correct, however, to the extent that by calling such arguments "ad hominem" he suggests that they are necessarily fallacious. Such arguments are not ad hominem in the usual sense; they do not attack in some irrelevant respect the one affirming a position, but they attack the one affirming a position precisely insofar as he is affirming it. If one who uses this type of argument thinks he falsifies the position against which he is arguing, he is mistaken. For example, if those whom Wiggins criticizes suppose that their argument against marxism proves that theory false, they are mistaken. However, it is quite possible to employ this type of argument and fully recognize its limitations. Jordan does not think that his argument that the affirming of *Nfc* is self-defeating demonstrates the falsity of *Nfc*.

Performatively self-referential statements can also be *falsified* by the aspect of their performance to which they refer. We shall try to show in chapter six that if *Nfc* can be rationally affirmed—that is, if the attempt to rationally affirm it is not self-defeating—then it is falsified by any rational affirmation of it, no matter how it is stated. For this reason, we next consider the falsification of performatively self-referential statements.

D. The falsification of self-referential statements

We define the falsification of a performatively self-referential statement as follows: A self-referential statement (S) in which there is an affirming (A) of a proposition (P)—where P is not a logical truth—by an uttering (U) of a token (T) will be performatively falsified if and only if there is a property (Q) such that either A or U has Q and "A has Q" or "U has Q" is inconsistent with P. For example, the stating of "This statement is not printed on paper" is falsified by its being printed here. The method of expressing the statement has a property—being printed on paper—such that the statement that this expression has this property is inconsistent with the proposition stated. Of course, this proposition would not be falsified by the way of expressing it if it were spoken.

In addition to performatively self-referential statements there are performatively self-referential *propositions*; such propositions are performatively self-referential no matter how they are performed. Some of these propositions are such that they are falsified by their performance and would be falsified by *any* performance of them. A performatively self-referential proposition (P) is performatively falsified if and only if there is a property (Q) such that *any* affirmation (A) of P or any utterance (U) of any token (T) used to express P has Q and "A has Q" or "U has Q" is inconsistent with P. For example, an instance of the general proposition expressed by the statement (S), "No utterance can be used to express a proposition," is performatively self-referential. It refers to the utterance used to make S. This instance is falsified by this utterance. This utterance has a property—of expressing a proposition—such that its having this property is inconsistent with the performatively self-referential instance of the general proposition affirmed in S. Moreover, it is clear that this proposition will have a self-referential instance in any statement of it and that this instance will be falsified by the utterance in any statement in which the proposition is stated.

The falsity of performatively self-referential propositions which are performatively falsified can be philosophically important. If a philosophical theory goes wrong in this way, the theory should be rejected *as false*. The proposition affirmed in any statement of the theory is falsified by any performance in which it is stated. Thus, if a philosophical theory has a performatively self-referential instance, and if that instance is falsified by the performance of the statement, or, to be more precise, is such that it would be falsified by any performance of stating the theory, then the theory is inevitably falsified.

We call philosophical arguments which show a theory to have self-referential difficulties "self-referential arguments." In some cases, the self-referential instance is shown by the argument to be inevitably falsified. In others, the self-referential instance is shown by the argument to render self-defeating any statement of the theory.

Descartes's *cogito* can be construed as a self-referential argument.[16] "I do not exist" is falsified by its own affirmation, since affirmations and all other propositional acts have the property of being made by someone who does exist.

The well-known argument that the statement of the verifiability criterion is self-refuting can also be understood as a self-referential argument. The verifiability criterion can be construed as the claim that there are more utterances than there are utterances expressing propositions. It is a proposal of a criterion to distinguish these. Thus, its self-reference will be performative; it refers to utterances as purported statements.

Assuming, for the sake of this example, that the statement of the verifiability criterion affirms a proposition, we state the self-referential argument against the verifiability criterion as follows:

1) The verifiability criterion is the proposition (V) which states: Any sentence (S) which expresses a proposition necessarily has the property (Q)—that is, the property of expressing an analytical truth or an empirical hypothesis.

2) Any statement of V is a case of S, and a statement of V will express a proposition if and only if it has Q.

3) Any statement of V lacks Q. (The statement of V must lack Q in order to perform its function of excluding as meaningless all sentences which lack Q. In other words, the statement of V must lack Q if the statement is to achieve its purpose. If it has Q then it will be pointless. If the statement of V is an empirical generalization about utterances which have been discovered to be meaningless, it cannot exclude the possibility that meaningful utterances not having Q will be discovered. If the statement of V is a stipulation or definition, it cannot exclude the possibility that there are sentences which are meaningful by some other definition of meaning.)

4) It is not the case that any sentence used to express V expresses a proposition.

5) But V is a proposition.

6) Any sentence used to express V expresses a proposition.

(1) is a statement of the verifiability criterion. (2) is a statement of its self-referential instance. (3) is a description of the statement of V which is required for this statement to be a purposeful statement. (4) is entailed by (2) and (3); it is what the verificationist must say about his own sentence if he is to remain consistent and to achieve the purpose of his statement. (5) is true by assumption. (6) states what is true of the sentence used to express V on this assumption. (6) and (4) are contradictories. (6) states a fact about the sentence used to express V; (4) states what follows from V together with the conditions for the

purposeful affirming of *V*. (6) falsifies (4). Any statement of *V* is thus falsified by its own performance.

In establishing inevitable falsity, self-referential arguments of the kind exhibited in the two previous examples are different from self-referential arguments by which someone seeks to show that a philosophical statement is self-defeating. The latter kind of argument does not demonstrate the falsity of the proposition in question, even though it can show that any act of affirming the proposition is inevitably self-defeating. Arguments by which someone seeks to show the falsity of a performatively self-referential proposition bear, not merely upon the affirming of it, but upon its truth.

There are several objections to self-referential argumentation. First of all, someone might object that self-referential arguments leave open the possibility that the opposed thesis could be true. This objection might be based upon a confusion between self-referential arguments which reveal falsity and self-referential arguments which show a statement to be self-defeating.

This objection might also be based on a confusion between logical impossibility and the inevitable falsity which certain self-referential arguments reveal. The proposition refuted by a self-referential argument which reveals the self-referential falsity of it is logically coherent; it picks out a possible state of affairs. The objection we are considering might be based on the assumption that since the proposition picks out a possible state of affairs, it remains possible that the proposition be true. One knows, however, that this state of affairs does not obtain, because the proposition is falsified by its own performance. In fact, where a performatively self-referential *proposition*—in contrast with statement—is falsified, one knows that the falsity is inevitable. There is no way in which the proposition can be stated which does not also provide the falsification of the proposition. Still it is not logically impossible that the state of affairs obtain.

In other words, performatively self-referential propositions which are falsified are not logically impossible nor are their contradictories logically necessary truths. Their falsity is in some respects like that of a falsified scientific theory; one does not regard such falsity as indicating a mere contingency, but rather as revealing a kind of necessity about the world. One expects that the theory will be falsified in all instances which are essentially like those that first falsified it. A scientific theory does not merely *happen* to be false.

Likewise, performatively self-referential propositions which are falsified by their own performance do not merely *happen* to be false. The falsity reveals a kind of necessity. However, unlike scientific theories, performatively self-referential propositions which are false carry with them, in their very statement, the fact which falsifies them. The falsification is inevitable.

Another possible objection to self-referential arguments is that there is a simple and effective way to blunt their force. A philosopher whose thesis is criticized by a self-referential argument can avoid the force of the criticism by limiting the scope of his thesis so that the self-referential instance does not arise.[17] Thus, the self-referential argument does not terminate the philosophical controversy.

But to limit the scope of a thesis which has been refuted by a self-referential argument is implicitly to admit that the original thesis was indefensible. The claim is no longer the same. Perhaps other instances of the thesis are true. But by this limitation the self-referential instance is admitted to be indefensible. The fact that the philosophical discussion continues in no way shows that the self-referential argument has not been decisive. The discussion can go on but with a difference; the thesis originally affirmed has been admitted to be indefensible. Both parties to the discussion can continue the controversy. The critic can ask by what principle the self-referential instance is abandoned although others are still claimed to be true. To abandon the self-referential instance because it has been shown indefensible while still claiming that the thesis holds in other instances is to make an arbitrary move, unless one provides a basis for distinguishing the falsified instance from the others. If one provides such a basis, his new position is clearly different from the original thesis he affirmed.

Of course, neither of the preceding objections against self-referential arguments disputes the claim that the performatively self-referential proposition at issue is indefensible. But one can dispute this claim. Self-referential arguments can beg the question. They can do this by ascribing to the performance a property which one who affirms the proposition need not ascribe to it.

The examination and criticism in chapter two, section E, of previous attempts at a self-referential argument against Nfc revealed that these attempts are question-begging. The $PNfc$ can legitimately answer these arguments by pointing out that they assume what he need not admit—namely, the incompatibility between something's being a reason for belief and its being wholly determined by causal conditions.

However, the fact that some self-referential arguments are question-begging does not mean that all are. In fact, there are some cases in which ascribing a property to the performance which renders the statement indefensible cannot be question-begging. This will be the case whenever the one making the performatively self-referential statement must either regard his performance as having the property in question or become inconsistent.

A proponent of the verifiability criterion might object that it is question-begging to assume—as we do in our criticism of it—that the verifiability criterion is a proposition. He might say that the verifiability criterion is a rule of meaning, not a proposition. In saying this, he could be correct; it is possible that his utterance does not express a proposition; it might be significant in some noncognitive way. It might, for example, express the feelings of verificationists about metaphysics or it might be an exhortation. However, the verificationist could wish to make some claim for the truth or adequacy of his position. As we have shown, if he does affirm his position, then no matter how he affirms it, he makes some sort of truth-claim for it, and in making this claim he states a proposition. Of course, his statement will not meet his own criterion for stating a proposition, but he nevertheless will make a claim for something. In this sense he states a proposition. If he does not admit this, his utterance has no cognitive force, and thus he cannot thereby deny the cognitive meaningfulness of utterances which do not meet his criterion. In short, the verificationist must admit that his thesis is a proposition if he is to achieve his purpose. Nor can the verificationist, without defeating his purpose, admit that his statement is either an empirical hypothesis or a definition.

Our argument against verificationism stands in contrast to the attempted self-referential arguments which we criticized in chapter two, section E, against the affirmation of *Nfc*. In that case, the *P Nfc* was able to deny without rendering his argument pointless that the performance of his statement has the falsifying property. He was able to explain that although his affirming of *Nfc* is itself causally determined it can nevertheless be rationally performed. Thus, the only effect of those self-referential arguments was to elicit a clarification of the theory criticized.

Since many attempts to demonstrate *Sfc* have been question-begging, we shall be especially careful to avoid this fallacy. In formulating our argument against *Nfc*, we shall try to show—in terms of forms of argumentation clarified in the present chapter—that if *Nfc* can be rationally affirmed, then it is performatively falsified, and that if it cannot be rationally affirmed, then any attempt to affirm it will be inevitably self-defeating.

Another possible objection to the force of self-referential arguments is that even if the propositions which they show to be false are inevitably falsified by their own performance, they *might,* nevertheless, be important truths which, unfortunately, cannot be stated.

There is something very strange about the notion of "important truths which, *unfortunately,* cannot be stated." The difficulty which arises in stating propositions which are inevitably self-defeating or falsified is not a mere misfortune —that is, an avoidable accident. The falsity or self-defeating character of such propositions is established by *any* stating of them. They can be stated; they are stated; they are falsified or they defeat their own purpose in being stated. To say that they cannot be stated is merely to say that whenever they are stated, they are falsified or shown to be pointless.

We do not deny that there might be a true proposition which cannot be stated. But if there is any such proposition, clearly it cannot be one such that if it could be stated, it would be inevitably falsified by its own affirmation. Any such proposition is false. It *might* be true only in the sense that it is not logically false.

When the objector says in respect to propositions which are self-referentially falsified, "They *might,* nevertheless, be important truths," this claim can be taken in either of two senses.

In one sense, it means that the propositions shown to be inevitably false by their own performance are logically possible. To say that a proposition is logically possible is to say that it could be either true or false. To be able to be either true or false is just to have propositional sense and reference. Therefore, a proposition which could not be true in this sense is logically impossible. It follows that if the objector means his objection in this sense, then when he says "They *might,* nevertheless, be important truths" what he says is equivalent to "They might, nevertheless, be important falsehoods."

In another sense, "They might, nevertheless, be important truths" could mean something other than that self-referentially falsified propositions are logically possible, that is, neither necessary nor impossible. In this other sense, a preference for the truth of falsified propositions is expressed. Such a preference can hardly be rational.

Someone might accept the preceding response with respect to propositions which are self-referentially falsified, but object that if the proposition is only shown by a self-referential argument to be performatively self-defeating, it might—in a more significant sense—still be true and important. We admit that such propositions might be true in a more significant sense than that in which a falsified proposition might be true. A falsified proposition is merely logically possible; a proposition shown to be self-defeating is not falsified, and there remains an ontological possibility that it be true.

Nevertheless, a proposition shown by a self-referential argument to be performatively self-defeating cannot be used as a premise or defended as a conclusion in a rational discussion. Rational discussion involves both propositional acts such as affirming and speech acts such as uttering. In our argument in chapter six, nothing turns upon reference to utterances. Thus we reply here to the objection only insofar as it applies to self-defeat arising from reference to the act of affirming.

To claim a proposition true is to affirm it; to rely in reasoning upon the fact that a proposition has not been falsified is to weakly affirm it. There can be no point in affirming, even weakly, a proposition whose affirmation is inevitably self-defeating. It must be noted, moreover, that rational discussion can occur in an individual's own thinking. Thus, if it is pointless for a person to affirm a proposition in an argument with another, it is pointless for him to think the proposition true in his heart, while avoiding embarrassment by not uttering it aloud.

E. The affirmation of "No free choice"

If *Nfc* is true, then no one's affirmations and utterances can be freely chosen acts. Affirming and uttering certainly are among a person's acts, but if *Nfc* is true, no one can freely choose to do these acts any more than he can freely choose to do any other acts. If no one's affirmations and utterances can be freely chosen acts, then no *PNfc's* affirming or uttering can be a freely chosen act. The *PNfc* is a man among men; if no one can make a free choice, neither can he. If no *PNfc's* affirming or uttering can be a freely chosen act, then no *PNfc's* stating of *Nfc* can involve a freely chosen act. Whenever a *PNfc* states his thesis, he performs an instance of the kinds of acts which are affirmations and utterances. Thus, if *Nfc* is true, any statement of it, in excluding the possibility of free choice generally, excludes free choice from the very act which affirms it.

A proposition's truth or falsity depends upon whether the state of affairs it picks out obtains. Whether or not the state of affairs a proposition picks out obtains, the reference of the proposition remains the same. Thus, the reference of *Nfc* remains the same whether it is true or false. *Nfc* has an instance referring to any possible human act; thus, it has an instance referring to any possible act of affirming or uttering, and so to any possible act of affirming *Nfc* and uttering sentences which express *Nfc*. Hence, it is clear that *Nfc* is a performatively self-referential proposition.

We argue in chapter six that *Nfc* is self-refuting—that any affirmation of *Nfc* relevant to *Sfc/Nfc* either falsifies *Nfc* or renders the affirming of it self-defeating. To prepare for this argument, we now clarify what is involved in the affirming of *Nfc*. To do so, we must clarify what is involved in making any grounded affirmation.

At the beginning of this chapter, we defined an "act of affirming" as any propositional act by which someone holds a proposition to be true or reasonable to accept. Assenting to a proposition by faith, accepting it as a hypothesis which has some likelihood, and asserting it are among the ways of affirming it. Thus, one affirms a proposition whenever he holds it to be true or more likely to be so than not.

"To affirm" sometimes is taken to mean to publicly assert a proposition as absolutely certain. In this sense of "to affirm," its contrary is "to disavow"; one only denies a proposition in this sense if one publicly rejects the proposition as certainly false. Between affirming and denying in these strong senses, there obviously are many propositional acts which involve holding a proposition true or likely. By contrast, according to the definition of "affirming" which we have adopted, any propositional act by which one holds a proposition to be true or reasonable to accept is an affirmation of the proposition.

One can consider any proposition either by itself or in relation to other propositions to which it is related truth-functionally. One also can perform propositional acts which have nothing to do with the truth or falsity of a proposition—for example, one can include a proposition in a fictional narrative. We are not interested at the moment in propositional acts which bear upon propositions in truth-functional relations, and we are interested only in propositional acts which bear upon a proposition's truth or falsity. Considering a proposition by itself and with respect to its truth or falsity, one is capable of only three kinds of propositional acts. First, one can merely entertain the proposition as one whose truth or falsity—or even likely truth or falsity—is yet to be discerned; second, one can hold the proposition true or regard it as more likely true than not; third, one can hold the proposition false or regard it as more likely false than not. The second kind of propositional act is what we call "affirming"; the third, what we call "denying." Obviously, on these definitions, one never affirms or denies without doing both, for whatever proposition one affirms, one denies its contradictory.

Thus, even if one only thinks privately that a proposition might be true, he affirms it. If one says to himself, "I am inclined to think that p," he affrms p; perhaps p is a most tentative belief which he would not wish to mention to anyone else, yet he affirms p. Expressions such as "Don't you think that p might be true?" and "I take it that p cannot easily be denied" and "It is my personal feeling that p" and "Isn't it perhaps more realistic to think p" and "No one today can take *not-p* very seriously" and "I think it clear that the time has come to rethink the traditional view that *not-p*" can be and often are used to affirm p.

It follows that one affirms if and only if he also denies. Thus, if one expresses a possible belief but admits that the contradictory is equally likely to be true, he is not affirming the belief. Sometimes a hypothesis is put forward without being affirmed; hypotheses can be proposed as questions or included in the design of a research project without any judgment being made with respect to their truth. On some theories of practical and theoretical procedure, it is even possible to make use of hypotheses while admitting that their contradictories are equally likely to be true. In such uses of hypotheses to control the environment or to organize a region of experience, the hypothesis is not proposed for acceptance as true or more likely, and its contradictory is not regarded as any less reasonable to suppose true.[18] Thus, expressions of possible beliefs and proposals of hypotheses can occur without any propositional act of affirming. In such cases, the proposition is proposed with no more claim about what is the case than would be made if one articulated the propositions in a purely fictional account.

For the sake of clarity, we now make several points which we do not expect any *PNfc* to dispute.

In *Sfc/Nfc*, it is clear that the *PNfc* must affirm *Nfc*. If one merely proposes the proposition as an interesting possibility, neither affirming it nor denying it, he is not a *PNfc*, for his propositional act in respect to the proposition is no more that of a *PNfc* than that of a *PSfc*. In a dispute about which ot two contradictor; propositions is true, one cannot be located on either side unless one expresses at least very tentatively a propositional act leaning toward one side.

To put the same point in other words. *Nfc* describes a world from which the ability to make free choices is absent. If any such world exists, then in that world no one can make a free choice. But the mere proposition, *Nfc,* does not claim that the actual world excludes *Sfc*. This claim is made only when someone holds *Nfc* true or likely true of the actual world—in other words, only when someone affirms *Nfc*. The mere proposition, *Nfc*, can be doubted or denied as well as affirmed. One who doubts it or denies it does not exclude free choice from the actual world, but leaves room for it.

Affirmations can be made in different ways; they can be groundless or they can be grounded.

A groundless affirmation is a gratuitous preference for one of a pair of contradictories. One of the pair is held without any epistemic warrant to be true or more likely. For example, a person knowing nothing about space exploration might affirm that travel to distant stars will be achieved within the next century, and another equally ignorant person might dispute this by saying that such travel is impossible. Of such groundless affirmations and denials, barroom arguments are made. One also can make an affirmation despite the availability to him of grounds for making the contradictory affirmation. For example, a person who is told that he is dying of incurable cancer might affirm for many months that he is not seriously ill and that he surely does not have cancer.

In such cases, the groundless affirmation and the irrational affirmation remain affirmations. One proposition is held to be true or likely; its contradictory is held to be false or unlikely. A person who publicly affirms a proposition without grounds asks others to accept it and to reject its contradictory, but if anyone asks why the proposition should be accepted, no reason can be given for accepting it. The reasonableness of accepting it, or even of considering it, is not shown.

If the *PNfc* affirmed his position in this way, he would exclude *Sfc* only by an ipse dixit. However, *Sfc/Nfc* is a controversy to which the parties are scientists, philosophers, theologians, and others who are, or who at least claim to be, engaged in the serious pursuit of truth. In such company, anyone who makes arbitrary affirmations is ignored as soon as the arbitrariness of his affirmations becomes clear. Thus, the *PNfc* not only affirms *Nfc* but also proposes it as a grounded affirmation.

Affirmations can be grounded in different ways: by direct evidence, by logical insight or analysis, and by other procedures—for example, inductive argument.

If one has direct evidence for a proposition, one's affirming of it will be epistemically legitimate. For example, if one sees rain falling, one's affirmation that rain is falling has epistemic legitimacy. In such a case, the grounds for the affirmation are immediately given. If one has evidence of this sort, it is reasonable to affirm the proposition for which one has it, but it is not merely more reasonable to affirm the proposition than its contradictory. It is unreasonable and perhaps impossible to deny a proposition for which one has such evidence.

If one understands the formula of a logically true proposition, one's affirmation of it also will be epistemically legitimate. For example, if one understands $6 + 7 = 17 - 4$, then one's affirming of the equation has epistemic legitimacy. The same can be said for one's affirming of the conclusion of a more complex logical or mathematical proof. Here again the claim is not that it is more likely that the proposition is true or more reasonable to accept, but rather that it is perhaps impossible not to assent to it.

Statements of fact based on immediate evidence and statements of logically true propositions are not the only sorts of grounded affirmations. There are many statements—for example, interpretations of data, generalizations, and hypotheses—which one reasonably affirms, although they are based only somewhat indirectly on evidence. There are also propositions which are shown to be true by the analysis of language or by conceptual clarification which are reasonably affirmed, although they are neither self-evident nor logically necessary. There also are propositions supported by authority which one reasonably affirms. A great many—if not most—of the truths people think they know are propositions which they affirm on the authority of parents, teachers, friends, neighbors, journalists, technical experts, scientists, religious leaders, and so forth.

We define as "rational affirmations" all affirmations which are grounded otherwise than by direct evidence or by insight into logical truth. One affirms rationally if and only if the proposition he affirms is one more reasonable for him to hold true or likely than its contradictory. The contradictory of a rational affirmation remains consistent both with the direct evidence one has and with the logically necessary propositions one knows.

In the present work, we are concerned with a controversy regarding a set of facts—the phenomena of choice. In chapters two and three we pointed out that some on each side of the controversy have suggested that the affirmation of their position is based upon direct evidence. But neither of these claims succeeds; both depend upon a failure to recognize the limits of what can be derived from the data alone. Nor does an appeal to logically necessary truths settle the controversy. A clear example of this is the failure of the fatalist attempt to derive *Nfc* from logical truths alone. It remains that the affirmation either of *Sfc* or of *Nfc* can be at best a rational affirmation.

Thus, as we have seen, *Nfc* is affirmed as a hypothesis by physical and psychological determinists. Some psychological determinists and some who attack the intelligibility of free choice seem to regard clarification of the phenomena of choice or conceptual analysis as an important ground for their affirmation of *Nfc*. Operationalists consider their affirmation of *Nfc* to be justified rationally by its fruitfulness. Religious believers who affirm *Nfc* think their assent to it is justified by the authority of their faith.

In chapter six, we argue that any attempted rational affirmation of *Nfc* either falsifies *Nfc* or renders the attempt to affirm it self-defeating. Our argument will rest on the claim that there are necessary conditions for rationally affirming *Nfc*—that is, conditions which must be fulfilled if the attempt to rationally affirm it is to succeed. To clarify the notion of *conditions for rational affirmation,* we note that many human acts have conditions which must be met if these acts are to be what they are intended to be.

As we mentioned previously, C. K. Grant points out that making a statement has what he calls "pragmatic implications," and that if these implications are false, the making of the statement is irrational. Somewhat similarly, John R. Searle explains that an illocutionary act such as promising has a set of conditions which must be satisfied for a successful and nondefective act.[19]

In law, conditions are laid down for the success of acts such as making a contract or a will, indicting a person, passing sentence on a convict, and so on. If the conditions are not met, the attempted legal act can be held null and void. In religion, likewise, there are conditions for the validity as well as, for the licitness of ritual acts, such as sacraments; the ritual is believed to be pointless if conditions for its validity, at least, are not satisfied.

It seems reasonable to suppose that there are analogous conditions for the propositional acts of affirming and denying. If there are such conditions and they are not fulfilled, then acts of affirming and denying will be defective in some way. Such conditions for rationally affirming a proposition would be neither a function of the meaning or truth of the proposition nor of the meaningfulness of the language used in stating it.

Assuming there are conditions for making rationally grounded affirmations, then if these conditions are not fulfilled an attempt to make such an affirmation fails to be what it was meant to be—a rational affirmation. Of course, one's affirming can succeed in this respect—when these conditions obtain—and one's statement can still go wrong in some other way. For example, one can succeed in affirming a false proposition or a proposition inconsistent with other propositions of which one is more certain. One might have rational grounds for affirming a proposition—for example, one might have evidence which confirms a plausible hypothesis—yet the evidence itself might consist in faulty observations. For these reasons, an attempt to make a rational affirmation can succeed, although the proposition one affirms is false, inconsistent with other propositions which one should prefer to it, or actually without the ground one supposes one has.

Thus, it seems that certain conditions must obtain if one is to be successful in rationally affirming a proposition such as *Nfc*. Inasmuch as we regard *Sfc* as true, we obviously consider *Nfc* false and think there are many propositions inconsistent with *Nfc* which one should prefer to it. Moreover, in chapter three, we have disputed the soundness of all the grounds we know of on which *Nfc* has been affirmed. However, we have not disputed—in fact, we have made clear—that *Nfc* is rationally affirmed. Thus, we assume that the conditions for rationally affirming *Nfc* can obtain. We next consider certain of these conditions.

F. Rationality norms as conditions of affirmation

In each of the sections of chapter three, we examined one of the main lines of argumentation for *Nfc*. We ended each section with a summary of the *PNfc's* argument. These summaries included explicit articulations of certain principles which the various arguments presuppose.

The following principles are excerpted from the summaries. A full description of the data is to be preferred to a partial description. A generalization based on meticulous observation is to be accepted. Logical principles are to be adhered to in all one's thinking, even when doing so requires one to give up beliefs based upon experience. Any view which meets the criteria of simplicity, predictive success, and explanatory power . . . is to be accepted. Relevant facts are not to be ignored in a theoretical dispute. A method of interpretation which is successful is to be relied upon in further, similar cases. An account of phenomena is not to be accepted if it requires something inconsistent with the data for which it is supposed to account. Nothing inexplicable is to be admitted as possible. If one accepts a goal, a view of things helpful for achieving that goal is to be preferred—other things being equal—to a view of things which blocks effective pursuit of it. If one is reasonable in accepting traditional faith, then all its doctrines, without qualification, are to be accepted as meaningful and true.

We maintain that these principles—or some such principles—are necessary conditions for rationally affirming *Nfc*. We call principles of this sort "rationality norms." While the rationality norms used in arguments for *Nfc* might be refined, we do not maintain that the *PNfc* is unreasonable in appealing to these or similar principles. We do maintain that the rationality norm or norms which a *PNfc* presupposes in any argument for his position must be in force, not null, if the act of rationally affirming *Nfc* is to succeed—that is, if it is to be a valid and not a mere putative rational affirmation.

Rationality norms guide one in affirming propositions. They bear directly on the affirming, not on the proposition affirmed. They do not describe facts which might confirm the proposition, nor are they generalizations from which the proposition might be deduced. Rationality norms are *norms*; they say what *is to be,* not what *is.* They direct one's steps in moving toward making an affirmation and in making it, so that one's affirming will be grounded, even though the proposition one affirms is neither logically true nor a matter of evident fact. In rationally affirming a proposition, one assumes rationality norms, not as premises from which one might deduce conclusions about the world, but as licenses or warrants legitimating the moves one makes in taking one proposition rather than its contradictory as more likely to be true of the world.

In one respect, rationality norms are like the rules of formal logic. Both bear upon the legitimacy of the relationship between grounds and a conclusion; rationality norms are concerned with the relationship of evidence or reasons to a proposition which they rationally support somewhat as rules of formal logic are concerned with the relationship of premises to a conclusion which they entail. Neither a rationality norm nor a logical rule such as *modus ponens* is any part of what is affirmed in the proposition on whose affirmation it bears.

However, the rules of formal logic differ from rationality norms. The rules of formal logic show how propositions and formally distinct parts of propositions are formally related, while rationality norms indicate only that certain sorts of reasons and evidence provide adequate grounds for affirming a conclusion.

Of course, *Nfc* can be deduced from some more general propositions. For example, universal determinism entails *Nfc.* But universal determinism itself gains its plausibility from a scientific theory of physical determinism; as we shall explain more fully shortly, the affirmation of such a theory presupposes a rationality norm—for instance, a simplicity-rule. Even if *Nfc* could be deduced from the laws of logic, as the fatalist attempts to do, the affirmation of *Nfc* on such a basis would require justification, because such an affirmation would involve a preference for logical truths over other grounds for belief.

Another consideration further clarifies the distinction between the rules of formal logic and rationality norms, and the bearing of the latter upon the *act* of affirming. One who violates a law of logic eventually finds himself in formal incoherence; he loses his ability to *mean* anything and to *say* anything. One who violates a rationality norm does not thereby become formally incoherent. If the violation is clear, he will be unreasonable, but he can still talk in a way which makes *sense.* His propositions are coherent, but his affirming of them is somehow out of order. He can be called "foolish," "rash," "careless," "dim-witted," "silly," or something of the sort.

Thus rationality norms bear upon the act of affirming; one who follows them makes affirmations rationally, while one who ignores or violates rationality norms proceeds unreasonably in making affirmations.

Thus, we claim that there are nonformal norms of affirmation, presupposed by the *PNfc's* affirming of *Nfc*. This claim is not ad hoc, and the *PNfc* is by no means alone in presupposing such nonformal norms.

Similar norms also function in the arguments for *Sfc* which we criticized in chapter two. The argument for *Sfc* based upon experience proceeds on the principle that if something seems to be so, then it is to be taken to be as it seems. The argument from moral responsibility proceeds on the principle that the presuppositions of commonly held beliefs and important institutions are to be assumed to obtain. The argument proposed by Thomas Aquinas assumes that a position which is consonant with one's entire worldview is to be accepted. William James's argument supposes that if belief in a position contributes to the moral quality of life, then that position is to be preferred to one which detracts from such quality. The argument that *Nfc* is self-defeating assumes that any self-defeating position is to be given up.

Moreover, our own argument in chapter six, section I, insofar as we attempt to establish *Sfc*, appeals to certain rationality norms.

Many philosophers in recent times have articulated principles for inquiry and rational affirmation, and pointed out that these principles—to which they have given various names—are neither descriptive statements nor formal logical rules.

Wilfrid Sellars, for example, emphasizes that anyone who engages in conceptual activity must recognize norms and standards:

> . . . if one gives to "practical" the specific meaning *ethical* then a fairly sharp separation of these activities can be maintained. But if one means by "practical" *pertaining to norms,* then so-called theoretical reason is as larded with the practical as is practical reasoning itself.[20]

Sellars makes clear that the epistemic *values* of theoretical reasoning bring it into close relationship with practical reason. A full theory of practical reason "would also recognize the inseparability, yet distinguishability, of theoretical and practical reason in all dimensions of human life."[21]

Roderick Chisholm also emphasizes the normative dimension of epistemology. Throughout his writings in this field—a field which many regard as wholly theoretical—he presses the analogy between epistemic and ethical judgments. Some of the epistemic principles he formulates are very similar to some of the rationality norms we have listed. He also speaks of "epistemic obligations" and talks of a proposition's being "worthy of belief." Chisholm clearly thinks that the moves governed by such norms are neither standard deductions nor inductions, and that the norms themselves are neither descriptive statements nor mere conventions.[22]

Other philosophers who do not speak as explicitly as Sellars and Chisholm do about the normative principles of theoretical inquiry and affirmation nevertheless sometimes mention such norms. Quine, for example, formulates an empiricist rule about the leaps which are to be taken from what is given: "Don't venture farther from the sensory evidence than you need to."[23] Arthur Murphy points out that a theorist should avoid infatuation with his theory if his theorizing is to be "a serious activity, responsibly carried on, and subject to practically normative standards for its right performance."[24] Max Black, in explaining why one should accept the conclusions of inductive arguments, points out that human beings belong to the "inductive institution" and are thus subject to "norms of belief and conduct imposed by the institution."[25]

We hold that *Nfc* could not be rationally affirmed without implicitly assuming if not explicitly invoking some rationality norm or other. If we are right, it follows that any *P Nfc's* affirmation of his position is conditioned by at least one rationality norm. Several considerations indicate the correctness of this contention.

First, the ways in which *Nfc* is affirmed in *Sfc/Nfc* make clear the essential role of rationality norms in the affirming of it.

Often *Nfc* is affirmed as part of a larger theory or worldview. Such a theory or worldview gains whatever credibility it has insofar as it is a hypothesis which plausibly accounts for a certain range of data, or insofar as it is an interpretation of experience as a whole. However, there are many competing theories and worldviews, and a person prefers one to another only insofar as one is simpler, more far-reaching, more pleasing, more useful, or something of the sort. But preference by such criteria assumes that a hypothesis or interpretation of experience which meets them *is to be preferred* to one which fails to meet them or meets them less well.

As we explained in chapter three, sections A and C, it is not surprising that *Nfc* comes to be affirmed in the context of a general theory or worldview. It is a universal, negative proposition about a certain conceivable human capacity; it says that no one has that capacity. Such a proposition is not simply descriptive; it is not merely a generalization; and, since it is a claim about the world, it is not merely a logical truth. A claim such as this needs some sort of indirect justification, and one way to give it such justification is by fitting the proposition to be affirmed into a special or general theory which seems reasonable insofar as it meets the criteria established by some rationality norm.

This point can be made more specific by considering the affirmation of *Nfc* as part of the hypothesis of physical determinism, and by seeing the role of a rule of simplicity in the affirmation of such a hypothesis.

If a proposition is affirmed as a hypothesis, alternatives to it remain possible; its contradictory is logically possible and its contradictory can admit the very same data, for any hypothesis goes beyond immediate evidence. Thus, logic and immediate evidence alone do not compel one's assent to a hypothesis.

The purpose of a hypothesis is to account for the data. The only justification for admitting factors into a hypothesis is that they serve this purpose. Moreover, if a theorist admits any unnecessary factors into his hypothesis, he assumes an unnecessary liability. From these considerations it follows that —other things being equal—a more economical account of the data is to be preferred. Of course, there can be arguments about which of two or more hypotheses is more economical. Moreover, economy is not the only desideratum in inquiry; someone can argue for a less economical account if it better satisfies some other criterion. Still, at least some degree of conformity to a rule of simplicity is necessary for a proposition if it is to be rationally affirmed as a hypothesis.

Clearly, when a physical determinist affirms *Nfc* as part of his general hypothesis, he implicitly appeals to a simplicity rule.[26] The phenomena of choice do provide some ground for judging that one has made a free choice. However, the physical determinist supposes that admitting such an ability would complicate unnecessarily his coherent view of nature. The citadel of will would be holding out after everything else had surrendered to deterministic theory. In this case, a deterministic account is preferred because it excludes a property—the ability to make free choices—which would be diverse in kind from any other natural property. This peculiar property is not directly given in experience. It seems reasonable to hope that man's physical and biological functions can account for all human behavior, rendering unnecessary the supposition of so odd a property. The appeal to a rule of simplicity is seldom made explicit in so many words. But the appeal clearly is implicit in the arguments of the physical determinist.

Thus, it is clear that even if a *PNfc's* version of physical determinism were to vary more or less from the typical examples of it we considered in chapter three, section C, any version of this position would have to appeal to some sort of simplicity rule. In some cases, the simplicity rule might be assumed into a demand for predictive success or fruitfulness in practical application.

We also considered in chapter three, sections D and E, arguments for *Nfc* based upon a clarification of the role of purposes in choice and upon the inexplicability or mysteriousness of choices if they are free. Such arguments need not appeal to a simplicity rule, for they do not account for the data in the same way a hypothesis does. But arguments for *Nfc* on these other bases also attempt to rule out *Sfc* as oversimplified, incomplete, or unintelligible. As we saw, all such criticisms involve the application of criteria of preference for *Nfc* and an implicit appeal to the norms which demand that these criteria be met.

Many of the arguments for *Nfc* depend upon an implicit appeal to the principle of sufficient reason. Historically, this principle often has been thought of as an a priori truth, a basic law of being and of knowledge. However, Kant was on the right track, we think, in regarding it as a regulative principle. It does not function in arguments otherwise than as a rationality norm. Richard Taylor, who accepts the principle, treats it as a "datum—not something which is provably true, but as something which all men, whether they ever reflect upon it or not, seem more or less to presuppose."[27] It seems clear that the principle of sufficient reason makes a normative demand: An adequate reason why anything is so rather than otherwise *is to be expected.* If this demand is qualified by an additional phase—*unless one has a reason not to expect such a reason*—the principle of sufficient reason loses its metaphysical ring but becomes a plausible norm for rational inquiry and affirmation.

The preceding clarification of the conditions for affirming *Nfc*, whether as a hypothesis or not, indicates that some rationality norm or other must be presupposed in any rational affirmation of this position. We doubt that any *PNfc* would deny this, for such norms have a pervasive role in inquiry. They are required for what Wilfrid Sellars calls the "material moves" which are necessary in any scientific language:

> Everyone would admit that the notion of a language which enables one to state matters of fact but does not permit argument, explanation, in short *reason-giving,* in accordance with the principles of *formal logic,* is a chimera. It is essential to the understanding of scientific reasoning to realize that the notion of a language which enables one to state empirical matters of fact but contains no material moves is equally chimerical. The classical "fiction" of an inductive leap which takes its point of departure from an observation base undefiled by any notion as to how things hang together is not a fiction but an absurdity. The problem is not "Is it reasonable to include material moves in our language?" but rather "*Which* material moves is it reasonable to include?"
>
> Thus, there is no such thing as a problem of induction if one means by this a problem of how to justify the leap from the safe ground of the mere description of particular situations, to the problematical heights of asserting lawlike sentences and offering explanations. The sceptics' notion that any move beyond a language which provides only for the tautologous transformation of observation statements is a "venture of faith" is sheer nonsense. An understanding of the role of material moves in the working of a language is the key to the rationale of scientific method.[28]

What Sellars says of science holds a fortiori of any attempt to rationally affirm a philosophical position which claims to be serious about the way the world is.

If the *PNfc's* need for some rationality norm or other were not important to our argument, what we have said thus far would suffice. However, the argument in chapter six turns on just this point. Therefore, we attempt a general proof that any rational affirmation of *Nfc* will be conditioned upon some rationality norm.

We have said that rationality norms are necessary conditions for rational affirmations. Rational affirmations are a sub-class of grounded affirmations —they are the grounded affirmations which are not grounded in immediate evidence and/or in truths of logic. Since a proposition which is rationally affirmed is not *directly* derived from what grounds it, a justification—something like a warrant or a license—is needed for affirming the proposition on its more or less remote ground.

If one could bring the grounds for a rational affirmation into immediate relation to it by deduction from evident premises or by reduction to immediate data, then the affirmation would not be a "rational" one in our sense. Instead, it would be one of the stronger sorts of affirmation which philosophers do not argue about. Therefore, without a justification—something like a warrant or a license—no proposition of the sort which philosophers argue about can be affirmed. If the ground could not be linked with the affirmation, the ground would be irrelevant and the affirmation would be groundless.

Of course, it is easy enough to express the link between the ground and the affirmation in logical form. The simplest formal way of doing this would be to make the proposition or propositions which pick out the ground of the affirmation the antecedent of a conditional proposition, and the proposition which is to be affirmed the consequent of the same conditional proposition. Then, since the truth of the ground is given—or assumed—the affirming of the consequent is warranted deductively. However, this formulation of the relationship—or any more complex formulation of it—does not dissolve the difficulty, which merely becomes a question about the truth of the conditional proposition. In many cases, reasons for the truth of the conditional can be given, and the reasoning process can be expressed in further conditionals. But unless the content with which one is dealing is reduced to evidential immediacy or logical equivalence, the question will always remain: Is it reasonable to affirm the proposition in which one was originally interested on its more or less remote ground?

Rationality norms help one to bridge this gap. Whether one prefers with Sellars to call this bridging a "material move" or with Quine a minimal "leap," or whatever, affirmation under such conditions is an act which can be done reasonably or unreasonably. Rationality norms direct one to a better act of affirming. Rationality norms attempt to say what sorts of characteristics are —to adopt some apt language from Chisholm—" 'evidence-making characteristics,' or 'reasonability-making characteristics,' or even 'epistemically-better-making characteristics.' "[29]

Thus, since *Nfc* is affirmed in the context of *Sfc/Nfc* as a rational affirmation, and since all such affirmations are conditioned by rationality norms, any *P Nfc's* affirmation of his position will be conditioned by such a norm.

One more point about rationality norms is important for our argument. They can be in force or not.

We have made clear that rationality norms are conditions for acts of affirming. In general, conditions for anything can obtain or not, and what they condition obtains only if its necessary conditions obtain. Norms are peculiar conditions; they cannot fail to obtain in the way that empirical conditions can fail to be given. Yet norms can fail to obtain if they are null. Norms can be null, without force, if their being in force entails a state of affairs which itself does not obtain.

Rationality norms, like other norms and rules, regulate. Norms regulate by making a special kind of demand. In the case of many norms, including rationality norms, this demand is not a physical or a psychological exigency. The demand of such norms is that a certain standard be met, although this demand may not be fulfilled. Thus, such norms both set a standard and require that it be met. They not only describe a standard, they prescribe it. But norms cannot actually prescribe anything if the conditions for their fulfillment do not obtain.

Some examples will clarify the notion of actually prescribing—that is, of a norm being in force in contrast with its being null.

One promises his friend, who is in the hospital, to visit on Tuesday. On Monday, the friend dies. One ought to keep one's promises, but in this case the norm is null; that is, it does not actually prescribe. Again, a child is told that he ought to eat his entire doughnut but carefully preserve the hole, since it can be turned in for a free doughnut. Here again, the norm does not actually prescribe; it is null. The child discovers by empirical inquiry that the seeming prescription is incoherent. Again, a professor ought to meet his seminar, but on the way to it his car breaks down. The norm is null; it does not actually prescribe.

In some cases, an apparently valid norm actually is null. An act conditioned upon the norm is performed, and seems to be performed successfully. Yet the act, although done in good faith, is not successful; it is merely putative, and must be set aside. For example, a person is indicted, tried, and convicted of a crime. The charge is based on a section of the criminal code which everyone concerned takes to be in force at the time of the trial. However, the Supreme Court subsequently strikes down this section of the criminal code, by a five to four decision, finding it void because of vagueness. Any person convicted of a crime on a charge laid under this section can obtain a writ setting aside his conviction and ordering his immediate release from prison. His indictment, trial, and conviction were invalid legal acts. They were attempted acts which did not succeed in doing what they were meant to do. They were a merely putative exercise of the processes of justice inasmuch as they were based upon a section of the criminal code which was null and void, a section not in force

—that is, one which did not provide the necessary condition which it seemed at the time to provide for the attempted acts which relied upon it.

In chapter six, we will show what condition must obtain if the rationality norm required for any rational affirmation of *Nfc* is to be in force. In the present discussion, we think we have clarified two points: 1) that in *Sfc/Nfc*, *Nfc* must be rationally affirmed; 2) that the act of rationally affirming *Nfc* is conditioned upon rationality norms, which must be in force if the attempted act of affirming it is to be successful, not merely putative.

6: Free Choice Established

A. Introduction

In this chapter, we attempt to establish *Sfc* as defined in chapter one. In chapter one, we clarified the controversy over free choice and defined *Sfc* and *Nfc* as contradictories; in chapter four, we defended this formulation. In chapter five, section E, we showed that the *P Nfc* must seek to rationally affirm *Nfc*. In the present chapter, we argue that if *Nfc* can be rationally affirmed, then *Nfc* will be falsified by any rational affirmation of it. We also argue that if *Nfc* cannot be rationally affirmed, then any attempt to rationally affirm *Nfc* will be self-defeating. We call "self-refuting" any statement which is necessarily either self-referentially falsified or self-defeating.

We argue in this chapter that the self-refutation of *Nfc* together with other considerations establishes *Sfc*. In attempting to rationally affirm *Nfc*, the *P Nfc* necessarily accepts conditions which entail free choice. If these conditions obtain, as we assume in sections B through F, then *Nfc* is falsified. In section G we assume, for the sake of argument, that these conditions do not obtain—an assumption shown in section F to be equivalent to *Nfc*. On this assumption, the *P Nfc's* attempt to rationally affirm *Nfc* cannot succeed; his act of affirming will be merely putative. A thesis which cannot be rationally affirmed is self-defeating. In sections H and I, we supply further considerations which warrant the inference from the self-refuting character of *Nfc* to the truth of *Sfc*.

Because of the complexity of this chapter, we provide the following detailed outline.

In sections B through F, we assume that the conditions for rationally affirming *Nfc* do obtain—that is, that *Nfc* can be rationally affirmed. Our purpose in B through F is to show that on this assumption every statement of *Nfc* is inevitably falsified by its own affirmation.

In B we give the first formulation of the argument. In C we establish two key premises of the argument in B, numbers (7) and (11). In D we lay the ground for the second formulation of the argument which we give in E. In F we argue that free choice is entailed by the normativity to which the *PNfc* appeals in rationally excluding *Sfc*. Thus, in F we defend a key premise of the argument formulated in E—that is, premise (7*). Section F completes the phase of our argument against *Nfc* which assumes that *Nfc* can be rationally affirmed.

In G we grant—for the sake of argument—the opposite assumption: that the conditions required to rationally affirm *Nfc* do not obtain. We show that if these conditions do not obtain, then any attempt to rationally affirm *Nfc* is self-defeating.

In H we consider the objection which naturally arises against any attempt to refute *Nfc*—that any attempt to refute it is question-begging. In this case the objection is formulated as the claim that the *PNfc* need not attempt to rationally affirm *Nfc*. We show that the *PNfc* cannot remain in *Sfc/Nfc* if he does not rationally affirm *Nfc*. In I we show how the self-refuting character of *Nfc* together with other considerations grounds the rational affirmation of *Sfc*.

In chapter two, we considered many previous attempts to refute *Nfc* and to establish *Sfc*. We showed these attempts to be question-begging. In J we return to a consideration of these previous attempts and we show that while these attempts fail, each of them includes an important insight which is part of the total solution of *Sfc/Nfc* on the side of *Sfc*. We also show that the limitations of each of the previous attempts to refute *Nfc* are overcome by our refutation. In K we make some concluding remarks.

B. First formulation of the argument

In this section we assume that the conditions necessary for the rational affirmation of *Nfc* do obtain. We also argue from an analysis of various modes of normativity which we will provide in section C. This formulation of the argument also has an empirical premise that there are only certain modes of normativity consistent with *Nfc*. This premise will be eliminated in the second formulation of the argument.

The proposition we attempt to prove in this section is: If *Nfc* can be rationally affirmed, then *Nfc* is falsified by any rational affirmation of it.

1) The *PNfc* rationally affirms *Nfc*. (By assumption.)

2) If *Nfc* is rationally affirmed, then the conditions obtain whereby *Sfc* can be rationally excluded. (By the clarifications in chapter five, section E.)

3) The conditions obtain whereby *Sfc* can be rationally excluded. (From [1] and [2].)

4) If the conditions obtain whereby *Sfc* can be rationally excluded, then some rationality norm must be in force. (By the clarifications in chapter five, section F.)

5) A rationality norm adequate to warrant an affirmation which excludes *Sfc* is in force. (From [3] and [4].)

6) If any norm is in force, its normativity does not require the truth of *Sfc* for the norm to be in force. (Entailed by *Nfc*.)

7) Paradigmatic, creative, logical, and technical normativity meet the condition specified in (6). (To be established in section C.)

8) Only the kinds of normativity mentioned in (7) meet the condition specified in (6). (Empirical premise discussed below.)

9) The normativity of any rationality norm appealed to by one who rationally affirms *Nfc* is such that *Sfc* is not a necessary condition for that norm's being in force. (From *Nfc* as its performatively self-referential instance.)

10) The normativity of any rationality norm appealed to by one who rationally affirms *Nfc* must be either paradigmatic or creative or logical or technical normativity, or some combination of these. (From [8] and [9].)

11) The normativity of the types specified in (10) cannot rationally exclude *Sfc*. (To be established in section C.)

12) No rationality norm adequate to warrant an affirmation which excludes *Sfc* is in force. (From [10] and [11].)

13) (5) and (12) are contradictories.

14) (5) falsifies *Nfc*. ([5] states a property of any rational affirmation of *Nfc*. [12] states a proposition entailed by the conjunction of *Nfc* with other propositions a *PNfc* must grant.)

The following observations are intended to clarify the argument.

The fact which falsifies *Nfc* is that its affirmation rationally excludes *Sfc*. This fact falsifies *Nfc* because any kind of normativity consistent with *Nfc* cannot rationally exclude *Sfc*.

As we explained in chapter five, section D, a proposition is falsified by its own performance if and only if the performance has a property such that the statement that the performance has this property and the statement of the proposition itself are inconsistent with each other.

Steps (1) through (5) of the argument show that the rational affirmation of *Nfc* has a property—the property of being conditioned by a rationality norm which is in force and which is adequate to rationally exclude *Sfc*. The statement made in (5)—that the rational affirmation of *Nfc* has this property—is inconsistent with *Nfc*.

Steps (6) through (11) show that any *PNfc* must affirm (12), which is inconsistent with (5). If the normativity which conditions the act of affirming *Nfc* is limited to the kinds specified in (8), then the statement in (10) is a necessary consequence of *Nfc*.

In other words, the fact that the rational affirmation of *Nfc* rationally excludes *Sfc* is inconsistent with *Nfc*. But by assumption the rational affirmation of *Nfc* does rationally exclude *Sfc*. Therefore, there is a property of the very act of rationally affirming *Nfc*—its property of rationally excluding *Sfc*—which falsifies *Nfc* whenever it is rationally affirmed. Since the kinds of normativity specified in (8) cannot exclude *Sfc*, another kind of normativity must be involved in any rational affirmation of *Nfc*.

Steps (7) and (11) are defended in section C. There we show the consistency of certain types of normativity with *Nfc* and their inadequacy to condition a rational exclusion of *Sfc*.

Steps (8) and (10) are based upon an empirical assumption. The types of normativity listed in (7) are the only types we know of consistent with *Nfc*. The only other type of normativity we know of entails *Sfc*, as we shall show in section F. This empirical assumption seriously weakens the argument in its present formulation. However, we dispense with the empirical assumption in the second formulation of the argument in section E. We will be able to dispense with it because the analysis we will carry out in section D will show what kind of normativity the *P Nfc* requires if he is to rationally exclude *Sfc*.

C. Normativity consistent with "No free choice"

In this section we do two things. First, we distinguish several types of normativity consistent with *Nfc* and show their consistency with it. Second, we show the inadequacy of these types of normativity to fill the role of the normativity required to rationally affirm *Nfc*. The first part of this section establishes step (7) of the argument in B. The second part of this section establishes step (11) of the argument in B.

We distinguished various meanings of the word "ought" in chapter two, section B. These are the only types of normativity we know of. All but one of them is consistent with *Nfc*. Here we deal only with the types of normativity consistent with *Nfc*.

A kind of normativity is consistent with *Nfc* if and only if it does not entail *Sfc*. A kind of normativity would entail *Sfc* only if *Sfc* were a necessary condition for the norm to be in force. *Sfc* would be a necessary condition for a norm to be in force only if the norm could not be fulfilled unless *Sfc* were true.

The normativity of what we call a "paradigmatic norm" is the normativity of certain characteristics of a class vis-à-vis members of the class. These characteristics are taken to be normal or expected and they are a standard for evaluating the members as proper or normal members of the class.

This kind of normativity does not entail *Sfc*. The alternatives which it distinguishes are not, of themselves, alternatives for choice or action. The alternative to meeting a paradigmatic norm is to be abnormal. "The roses ought to bloom in the spring" exemplifies this kind of normativity. It is characteristic of roses to bloom in the spring; if they fail to bloom as expected, they are regarded as abnormal specimens. However, this kind of normativity does not entail that a specimen which fails to conform to it could conform by choice or action. Thus, paradigmatic normativity is consistent with *Nfc*.

The normativity of what we call a "creative norm" is the normativity of the product of creative activity vis-à-vis its own components.

This product, to the extent that it is creative, establishes norms for evaluating its own components as they are unified in the work. For example, "The red at the top of the painting ought to be more intense" evaluates a painting by a standard which in this case was not realized. The peculiarity of this norm is the fact that it is given—often imperfectly—only as a consequence of the activity whose outcome it evaluates. This kind of normativity does not entail *Sfc*. The alternatives, one of which it prescribes, are not alternatives for choice, because these alternatives are known as alternatives from the norm consequent upon the activity. Before the standard is in some way understood—that is, before the creative act—this normativity is not operative. Therefore, the normativity of creative norms is consistent with *Nfc*.

The normativity of what we call "logical norms" is the normativity of the demand that one be consistent and avoid incoherence. Logical norms prescribe how one is to think and talk if one is to do so in a coherent manner.

The normativity of logical norms does not entail *Sfc*. This normativity does not prescribe one of a set of alternatives which are open to choice. The normativity of a logical rule excludes one alternative as incoherent; what is incoherent cannot be an alternative for choice. The alternative excluded by a logical norm remains possible only so long as one is unaware of the incoherence involved in violating the norm. This is not to say that one cannot choose to overlook a contradiction. Overlooking is a possibility; even assuming *Nfc*, it is within one's power. But it is not within one's power to choose what one knows to be impossible. Therefore, the normativity of logic is consistent with *Nfc*.

The normativity of what we call "technical norms" is the normativity of consistently pursuing one's desires. These norms prescribe necessary conditions for achieving one's purpose. They are sometimes called "hypothetical imperatives." Their normativity can be seen by contrasting them with factual conditional statements. "If you wish to get to Chicago quickly, then you should fly" contains a prescriptive element which is lacking in "If you wish to get to Chicago quickly, then you will fly." The latter states only a matter of fact; the former, while no doubt based in part upon the latter, states a rule of action.

The normativity of technical norms does not entail *Sfc*. There are alternatives here, but they need not be possibilities for choice. The possibilities are alternative means for achieving a purpose. The purpose, which is assumed, can determine which alternative will be pursued.

Someone might object that if the possibilities are not really open, then there is no difference between a factual conditional statement and a technical norm. The "ought" in a technical norm suggests a possibility of nonfulfillment. There are two grounds for this possibility. First, the complexity of the world and the limitations of human knowledge render it possible that a definite goal not specify a necessary means with its definiteness. Second, the multiplicity of definite goals pursued by an individual renders it possible that a conflict occur such that the necessary means to one goal is not employed because of priority given to another goal.

Neither of these two possibilities, however, necessarily implies Sfc. The first indeterminacy can be settled by weighing probabilities—a purely cognitive procedure. The second possibility can be eliminated by the predominance of an individual's motivation toward one goal rather than another. Therefore, the normativity of technical rules is consistent with Nfc.

In summary, there are four kinds of normativity we know of consistent with Nfc. Next we show why none of these four kinds will be adequate to fulfill the role of the normativity required as a condition for affirming Nfc if it is to rationally exclude Sfc.

The normativity of paradigmatic norms cannot exclude Sfc. Using this notion of normativity, someone might affirm Nfc because it is the expected or the normal position to accept. This kind of normativity cannot, of itself, exclude a position as less reasonable. To do this, one must have a further norm which states that what is normal or expected is more reasonable. Without such a norm, this normativity states only a fact about what does and what does not measure up to the standards set by the defining characteristics of a certain kind of object. Clearly, then, this kind of normativity cannot of itself exclude any proposition as less reasonable. This kind of normativity might exclude the $PSfc$ as abnormal, but does not exclude Sfc as less reasonable. Therefore, if the normativity involved in the affirmation of Nfc is understood as the normativity of a paradigmatic norm, then the affirmation of Nfc does not rationally exclude Sfc. Paradigmatic normativity would exclude an affirmation as less reasonable only if one assumed that every rational preference is the normal preference and showed one act of affirming to be more nearly normal than the other.

The normativity of creative norms cannot exclude Sfc. The possibilities for the evaluation of which a norm is required define Sfc/Nfc; they are shared by all who argue either side. Hence any difference in creativity between the $PSfc$ and the $PNfc$ cannot affect the quality of their positions, although such a difference might well affect the quality of their efforts to articulate and defend their positions. Thus, a *P Nfc* could only implausibly appeal to a creative norm. He might argue, for example, that his work—or some *P Nfc's* work—presents a creative achievement of the intellect by which other attempts to argue either side in *Sfc/Nfc* are to be judged. Such a norm could justify a claim that efforts to argue for *Sfc* have been uninspired, but not that *Sfc* is less reasonable. This is made clear by the fact that an even more creative effort might some day be made by a *PSfc*. Therefore, if the normativity involved in the affirmation of *Nfc* is understood as the normativity of a creative norm, then the act of affirming *Nfc* does not rationally exclude *Sfc*.

The normativity of logic cannot exclude *Sfc*. As already noted, the norms of logic can exclude only inconsistency and the nonsense which arises from it. The norms which condition the affirmation of *Nfc* are not in this sense logical norms. They are norms for preferring one account, description, or interpretation over coherent alternatives. Suppose, however, that these norms could be understood as logical norms. In this case *Sfc* would have to be excluded as self-contradictory—as, for example, the fatalist attempts to do. If *Nfc* were a logical truth, then *Sfc* could no longer be a coherent hypothesis, description, or interpretation of the world. But as has been shown in chapter three, section B, the contradictory of *Nfc* is not self-contradictory, nor is *Nfc* a logical truth. Therefore, if the normativity involved in the act of affirming *Nfc* is understood as logical normativity, then the affirmation of *Nfc* does not exclude *Sfc* as less reasonable.

The normativity of technical norms might seem the most likely candidate for the role of the normativity by which the affirmation of *Nfc* excludes *Sfc*. Clearly, any of the rationality norms which might be assumed in affirming *Nfc* are prescriptions for carrying on inquiry and making affirmations. Thus, a rationality norm might appear to be a technical rule which states what must be done to achieve one's theoretical goal. But the normative force of technical norms is also insufficient to exclude *Sfc*. A necessary condition for the force of a technical norm is that one share the purpose of the activity which it directs, since the norm states what is necessary to achieve this purpose. The force of such a norm is always conditional. But such a conditional norm could rationally exclude *Sfc* only conditionally. If a *PSfc* shares the very same purposes as the *P Nfc*, then this condition will be fulfilled and he will feel the force of this kind of normativity. It could be reasonable for such a *PSfc* to give up his position. But it is indeed unlikely—as we showed in chapter three, section F—that every *PSfc* will share the precise purposes of the *P Nfc*.

If the *P Nfc* presents the *PSfc* with a technical norm, and if this norm is in force for the *PSfc*, then the *PSfc* in fact shares the goal upon which the norm is grounded. In this case, the actual prescriptivity of the norm arises from the irrationality—which amounts to inconsistency—of wanting a certain end more than any other yet still rejecting a necessary means to it. In other words, the prescriptivity of a technical norm in this case is reducible to matters of fact and rules of logic.

Someone might object that certain technical norms might have a normativity other than that which we have attributed to them. Such norms would prescribe one of two coherent alternatives, such that the openness of these alternatives would not arise merely from the complexity of the world nor from the multiplicity of purposes—all equally reasonable to pursue—which various individuals do pursue. The openness of the alternatives would arise on some ground which nevertheless established one of the possible purposes as unconditionally more reasonable to pursue. We will show in section D that precisely this sort of normativity is required to rationally exclude *Sfc* in the rational affirmation of *Nfc* by a *PNfc*. We show in section F that this sort of normativity entails *Sfc* and thus is unavailable to the *PNfc* even if the rule which he uses to express it takes the form of a hypothetical imperative.

In sum. Technical normativity actually prescribes only if the one to whom a technical norm is proposed shares the goal on which its prescriptivity is conditioned and has no conflicting goal to which he gives priority. This fact limits the usefulness of technical norms in rationally excluding one of a pair of contradictory propositions. Whenever it is rational for a particular person not to share in desiring a certain purpose, then no technical norm derived from that purpose is in force for him. Thus, he is not unreasonable if he ignores the norm and any affirmation which is conditioned by it. Therefore, if the normativity involved in the affirmation of *Nfc* is that of a technical rule, then the act of affirming *Nfc* does not rationally exclude *Sfc*, except in cases in which the normativity which happens to be formulated in a technical norm is of the peculiar sort discussed in the preceding paragraph.

The preceding discussion of the inadequacy of technical rules to rationally exclude *Sfc* can be illustrated as follows.

There might be a social scientist who became convinced by the evidence available to him that belief in *Nfc* has socially bad consequences—for example, that it lessens individual initiative and the sense of social responsibility. From this he might conclude that *Sfc* is the more reasonable position, although a deterministic hypothesis is more attractive in other respects. As a social scientist, such an individual would have basically the same goals of describing, explaining, and controlling behavior as any *PNfc*. He is not rationally required, however, to respond to a *PNfc's* appeal to rationality norms which they both agree upon, because this hypothetical social scientist considers one of these norms for inquiry—namely, that explanations should be morally and socially useful—to be overriding in this situation. Like the determinist, his purpose is partly theoretical. Yet his concrete idea of what theoretical inquiry is to achieve is different, and this gives rise to his use of different rationality norms.

The *PNfc* cannot exclude such a position as unreasonable, if his normativity is only that of technical norms which state necessary conditions for achieving goals of inquiry which he happens to want most strongly to achieve, but which not everyone need share.

D. Normativity required to affirm "No free choice"

Step (8) of the argument in section B is an empirical assumption. In the present section we replace this empirical assumption by means of an analysis of the normativity required to rationally affirm *Nfc*. This analysis will yield a positive characterization of the requisite normativity. This positive characterization of the properties of the normativity required to rationally affirm *Nfc* will enable us to dispense with the empirical assumption in B and thus to formulate a definitive proof in E. The proof in E will not depend upon the characterization in C of types of normativity compatible with *Nfc*; hence, it makes no difference if there are types of normativity compatible with *Nfc* not considered in C.

Someone might observe that in C we did consider a type of normativity which might fill the role of the normativity required by the *PNfc* to rationally affirm *Nfc* and exclude *Sfc*. The normativity in question would be of a sort which meets three conditions. First, it could be expressed by a technical rule; second, it is grounded in a purpose which allows that there be alternative ways of acting in respect to it; and third, it prescribes one of these ways as unconditionally more reasonable to follow. We agree with this observation. In the remainder of this section we show that the normativity necessary for rationally affirming *Nfc* prescribes unconditionally and prescribes one of two open but incompatible possibilities. We show in section F that this sort of normativity entails *Sfc*; if this sort of normativity is in force, then *Sfc* obtains.

The arguments in C that the kinds of normativity compatible with *Nfc* are inadequate to rationally exclude *Sfc* already provide some indication—a negative one—of the properties of the normativity necessary to rationally affirm *Nfc*.

Unlike the normativity of a paradigmatic norm, the normativity required to rationally affirm *Nfc* must prescribe an alternative as more reasonable and not simply as a proper member of a certain class. Unlike the normativity of a creative norm, this normativity must prescribe an alternative which is unconditioned by a given product. Unlike the normativity of a logical norm, this normativity must prescribe one of two alternatives, both of which are logical possibilities. Unlike the normativity of a technical norm, this normativity must prescribe unconditionally; a person must not be able to escape the force of the norm merely because he happens to have different—but equally reasonable—goals and priorities. There emerge here certain features of the normativity required to rationally affirm *Nfc* insofar as this rational affirmation excludes

Sfc. These features suggest a description in positive terms of the required normativity.

The normativity involved in the affirmation of *Nfc* has properties partly common to the normativity of logical norms and technical norms.

Like a logical norm, the norm required to rationally affirm *Nfc* has an unconditional force. Logical norms are conditioned neither upon one's purposes nor upon contingent states of affairs. Whatever one might wish to do or to think, one must be consistent. The exclusion of *Sfc* in the rational affirmation of *Nfc* is also unconditional.

However, the normativity needed to exclude *Sfc* is like that of a technical norm in that it prescribes one from among a set of coherent alternatives. *Sfc* is coherent, yet it is rationally excluded by the rational affirmation of *Nfc*.

Thus, the normativity required to rationally exclude *Sfc* unconditionally prescribes one of two coherent and incompatible alternatives. However, the unconditionality of this prescribing is distinct from that of logical norms. Also, the openness of the alternatives presupposed by this prescribing is distinct from the openness of the alternatives presupposed by technical norms.

The unconditionality of a logical norm consists in the fact that its violation is irrational in the sense of being incoherent. The unconditionality of the normativity required to rationally exclude *Sfc* consists in the fact that the *PSfc's* violation of it—as the *PNfc* sees it—is irrational in the sense that it violates a rationality norm which both the *PSfc* and the *PNfc* must respect.

The alternatives, one of which is prescribed in rationally affirming *Nfc*, are not only logically coherent, but also physically and psychologically possible, and they are not such that either of them is indispensable for achieving a purpose necessarily shared by everyone. There are open alternatives; both *Sfc* and *Nfc* can be affirmed. However, if the affirmation of one alternative is rational, the other alternative is not open to a person who is committed to the rational pursuit of truth.

A *PNfc* might object to the foregoing analysis by saying that the normativity of the rationality norm which he assumes in affirming *Nfc* either precludes open alternatives to his affirmation or prescribes only conditionally. However, as we showed in chapter five, section E, in the context of *Sfc/Nfc*, *Nfc* must be *rationally* affirmed. Unlike other grounded affirmations—those based on immediate evidence and/or derived from logical truths—a rational affirmation does leave an alternative open as a possibility, but as one less reasonable to accept. Moreover, the *PNfc* who attempts to ground his affirmation by an appeal to a technical rule for achieving a particular purpose rather than to a rationality norm finds that he cannot exclude rational opponents. We made the latter point clear in our analysis and critique of operational grounds for affirming *Nfc* in chapter three, section F.

In this section we have shown that in rationally excluding *Sfc* the *PNfc* requires a normativity which prescribes unconditionally and between open alternatives. This clarification of the kind of normativity required to rationally exclude *Sfc* permits us to dispense with the empirical assumption we made in our first formulation of our argument in section B. The second formulation of our argument will show that if the conditions obtain which are necessary to rationally affirm *Nfc*, then *Nfc* is inevitably falsified by any rational affirmation of it. After stating this argument in E, we will show in F that the prescriptivity of the *PNfc's* rational exclusion of *Sfc* cannot be in force unless *Sfc* is true.

E. Second formulation of the argument

1) The *PNfc* rationally affirms *Nfc*. (By assumption.)

2) If *Nfc* is rationally affirmed, then the conditions obtain whereby *Sfc* is rationally excluded. (By the clarifications in chapter five, section E.)

3) The conditions obtain whereby *Sfc* can be rationally excluded. (From [1] and [2].)

4) If the conditions obtain whereby *Sfc* is rationally excluded, then some rationality norm must be in force. (By the clarifications in chapter five, section F.)

5) A rationality norm adequate to warrant an affirmation which excludes *Sfc* is in force. (From [3] and [4].)

(The preceding steps are identical with the corresponding steps in the first formulation in B; the following steps are different.)

6*) Any norm by which a *PNfc* can rationally exclude *Sfc* has a normativity which prescribes unconditionally and prescribes one of two open alternatives. (Established in D.)

7*) Any norm which prescribes unconditionally and prescribes one of two open alternatives is in force only if the person to whom it is addressed can make a free choice. (To be established in F.)

8*) Any norm by which the *PNfc* can rationally exclude *Sfc* is in force only if the person to whom it is addressed can make a free choice. (From [6*] and [7*] together with the clarifications in chapter five, section F.)

9*) Someone can make a free choice. (From [5] and [8*].)

10*) *Nfc* is inconsistent with (9*).

11*) *Nfc* is falsified by (9*). ([9*] states what the *PNfc* does in rationally affirming *Nfc*, assuming that the conditions obtain whereby one can rationally affirm *Nfc*.)

The present formulation differs from the formulation in B; the present argument is based upon a statement of the property of any rational affirmation of *Nfc* in virtue of which the *PNfc's* act of rationally affirming *Nfc* performatively falsifies *Nfc*. This property entails *Sfc* as we shall show in F; yet no rational affirmation of *Nfc* can lack this property. Thus, if the conditions obtain whereby the *PNfc* can rationally affirm *Nfc*, *Nfc* is inevitably falsified. We consider in G what follows if these conditions do not obtain.

The argument depends upon an explication of the property of any rational affirmation of *Nfc*. We have provided a clarification in D which reveals this property; we do not refute *Nfc* by imposing conventions upon the *PNfc*. We assume nothing which any *PNfc* can deny.

The argument in B rested upon an empirical premise—namely, that the only kinds of normativity consistent with *Nfc* are the kinds dealt with in C. We admitted that this empirical premise leaves open the possibility of another kind of normativity compatible with *Nfc* and adequate to rationally exclude *Sfc*. However, the clarification in D permits us to dispense with that empirical premise. Thus, the present argument makes clear, as the argument in B does not, why any rational affirmation of *Nfc* is falsified by a necessary property of the *PNfc's* own act of affirming his position.

Our present argument includes (7*) as a key premise. The proposition in (7*) is one of the most important theses in this work. If it is true, then no *PNfc* can avoid appealing in his very attempt to deny *Sfc* to a norm which entails *Sfc*. We next prove (7*).

F. Normativity and free choice

In this section we show that a norm which prescribes unconditionally between open alternatives has, as a necessary condition for its being in force, the ability to make a free choice on the part of the person directed by such a norm. We do not argue in the present section that *Sfc* is true. We are concerned here only with a conceptual relationship—that between a certain kind of norm and free choice. We express the necessity in this relationship by saying that this kind of normativity "entails" free choice.

There clearly is some sort of close connection between the relevant normativity—the normativity required by the *PNfc* in his rational exclusion of *Sfc*—and free choice. A choice is free if and only if there is a choice between open alternatives such that there is no factor but the choosing itself which settles which alternative is chosen. The normativity in question directs a person with respect to an act which he might choose as one of two open alternatives, and this norm directs him by prescribing unconditionally.

Nevertheless, the relationship between such normativity and free choice is not one of mutual entailment. If choices which are experienced and naturally judged to be free actually are free, then among such choices are many to which no normative demand seems relevant. For example, one might have the experience of choosing between staying in town over a weekend to entertain a visiting friend and going on a weekend vacation with another friend. One experiences such a choice as his own and experiences nothing requiring either alternative, not only in the sense that he is aware of no condition determining him but also in the sense that he experiences no normative demand to choose one alternative rather than the other. In fact, his experience is simply that both possibilities are attractive, but the two are incompatible, and there is no way to settle which to do except by choosing.

Although the relationship between free choice and a norm which prescribes unconditionally between two open alternatives is not one of mutual entailment, still it is clear that if one is free, he could be bound by the kind of demand which the *PNfc* makes in rationally affirming *Nfc*. If one is free, then the two alternatives must be regarded as open; one can choose either of them. Yet one of them is prescribed—that is, one is rationally preferable.

For our argument, the important aspect of the relationship between free choice and a norm which prescribes unconditionally between two open alternatives is that free choice is a necessary condition for the fulfillment of such a norm. We argue for this thesis as follows. If one is determined by any factor whatsoever either to fulfill the norm or not to fulfill the norm, then there are not two open alternatives. The alternative to which one is determined will be the only one which can be realized, whether or not he is aware of this fact. But the sort of normativity relevant here is just the sort which implies that there are open alternatives; this was shown in D. Thus, nothing *determines* the fulfillment or the nonfulfillment of the norm. Although nothing can determine the fulfillment of the norm, still the norm does prescribe; it prescribes unconditionally. Thus, the norm must be able to be fulfilled, but it cannot be fulfilled by a necessitated or determined response. In other words, if the norm actually prescribes, then the person to whom it is addressed both must be able to bring it about that the norm be fulfilled and must be able to bring it about that the norm not be fulfilled—that is, he must be able to choose freely.

The preceding argument can be stated in another way. If a norm which prescribes unconditionally and between open alternatives is such that the one to whom it is addressed can fulfill it, but is not determined to fulfill it, then he can choose to fulfill it. Clearly, if one *can* but *need not* choose one of the alternatives, then he is free in that choice. The norm in question *is* such that a person directed by it can fulfill it but need not fulfill it; if he were determined, then the alternatives would not be open. We showed in D that the alternatives of affirming either *Nfc* or *Sfc* are open. If one were determined either to fulfill or not to fulfill the norm, then the norm would not prescribe unconditionally. We showed in D that the norm does prescribe unconditionally.

It has often been argued that when someone says: "This is what you ought to do," the person addressed intuitively takes the speaker to mean: "You have two alternatives; you can do either; you ought to do this one." Kant argues in this way in the *Critique of Practical Reason*.[1] But our argument in the present

section is different from Kant's argument, which depends upon the unconditional—that is categorical—character of moral norms. If a norm prescribes
conditionally, then its fulfillment depends upon natural conditions. According to Kant, a norm can be unconditional only if it is based upon a reason.
Kant's argument clearly begs the question vis-à-vis the *PNfc*; Kant assumes a
reasons/causes distinction which no *PNfc* need admit. Moreover, there is at
least one type of normativity—logical normativity—which prescribes unconditionally and which can actually prescribe even if the person who is directed by
it could not make a free choice. A logical norm prescribes the only coherent
alternative; thus there are no open alternatives and no need for choice.

Our use of the fact that the norm is unconditional is different from Kant's. In
our analysis, it is the fact that the norm prescribes among *open* alternatives
which precludes either of the alternatives being determined. The *unconditional*
character of the norm according to our analysis requires that—if the norm is to
be in force—it *can* be fulfilled even though, because the alternatives are open, it
cannot be determined to be fulfilled.

Thus, Kant was correct in observing that "ought" implies "can." His
oversight was in not noticing that there are several meanings of "ought" which
correspond to distinct meanings of "can." In this section, we have shown that
the "ought" which expresses the normativity required for any rational affirmation of *Nfc* implies the "can" which is included in the expression of *Sfc*.

G. "No free choice"—either false or self-defeating

In the argument in sections B through F, we have assumed that the conditions
for rationally affirming *Nfc* obtain. We have shown that on this assumption,
although the *PNfc* can rationally affirm *Nfc*, it is inevitably falsified. Thus on
this assumption, *Sfc* is established.

The self-referential argument in sections B through F catches the *PNfc* in
action. But it is often conceded that even those who hold *Nfc* true cannot avoid
thinking and talking as if they were free when they actually engage in some
activity requiring deliberation and choice. Thus, it seems possible that the
argument merely shows an instance in which the *PNfc* cannot help thinking and
talking as if *Sfc* were true.

In other words, we assume in B through F that the conditions obtain whereby
Nfc can be rationally affirmed. But there is another possibility. Perhaps the
conditions required to rationally affirm *Nfc* do not obtain; if so, *Nfc* cannot be
rationally affirmed. If any one of the conditions necessary to rationally affirm a
proposition does not obtain, then the proposition in question cannot be rationally affirmed. If any of the necessary conditions for each and every rational
affirmation never obtains, then in no case can *Nfc* be rationally affirmed.

The possibility we consider in the present section is that *Nfc* is true. But if a free choice can never be made, then *Nfc* cannot be rationally affirmed. If *Nfc* cannot be rationally affirmed, then the argument against *Nfc* in B through F is inadequate, since that argument proceeds on the assumption that the *PNfc* can rationally affirm *Nfc*.

Thus, the *PNfc* might admit that at times he inconsistently thinks and acts as if *Sfc* were true. But the *PNfc* will insist that even if he, like all men, must at times think and act *as if Sfc* were true, still this inevitable state of affairs does not count against the truth of *Nfc*. Among the states of affairs in the world, all of which the *PNfc* regards as determined, the *PNfc* recognizes mistakes and illusions, even inevitable illusions.

We respond to this line of reasoning by showing why on this alternative assumption, the *PNfc's* attempt to rationally affirm *Nfc* is inevitably self-defeating.

A performatively self-referential proposition is self-defeating if the self-referential instance renders the affirmation of the proposition pointless. For example, unrestricted skepticism is self-defeating in this way. The performatively self-referential instance of "All affirmations are groundless" is "The affirmation that all affirmations are groundless also is groundless." Thus, skepticism renders any act of affirming it pointless; any ground one might have for affirming skepticism is removed by the assumption, implicit in that affirmation, that skepticism is true.

Any rational affirmation of *Nfc*—assuming *Nfc* true—is self-defeating in this way. *Nfc* implies that at least one condition required to rationally affirm *Nfc* never obtains. The reason why one condition for rationally affirming *Nfc* never obtains if *Nfc* is true is that the truth of *Nfc* entails the falsity of *Sfc*. The falsity of *Sfc* in turn entails the impossibility that the norm to which any *PNfc* must appeal in attempting to rationally affirm *Nfc* can be in force. The impossibility of this norm being in force entails that the rationality norm required for a rational affirmation of *Nfc* cannot be in force; thus the truth of *Nfc* entails the impossibility of rationally affirming *Nfc*.

As we have just shown, the performatively self-referential instance of *Nfc* requires that any rational affirmation of *Nfc* be impossible. If *Nfc* is assumed to be true, then it cannot be rationally affirmed. One might seem to rationally affirm it, but one's act would be putative, not genuine, for it would be conditioned upon a norm which was itself void inasmuch as what it required for its validity could not be given. The performatively self-referential instance of *Nfc* renders ineffectual any attempt to rationally affirm it. This instance requires that any affirmation of *Nfc* not be a rational affirmation, since any rational affirmation is conditioned upon a norm which cannot be in force unless *Sfc* is true. Thus, if *Nfc* is true any attempt to rationally affirm it is self-defeating.

Someone might object that if we are to be consistent with our stated assumption in the present section, then we must grant for the sake of argument that *Nfc* is true. If *Nfc* is true, then surely it must be rational to affirm *Nfc*. For what could be more rational than to affirm a proposition which is, in fact, true?

But we have not conceded that *Nfc* is in fact true. The assumption—for the sake of argument—that *Nfc* is true is not equivalent to knowledge that *Nfc* is true. If one grants a proposition for the sake of argument, then one must grant whatever follows from the *proposition*; in other words, granting an assumption is granting whatever would obtain if the proposition were true. However, the claim to know that *Nfc* is true presupposes that the conditions obtain whereby the proposition *can be known* to be true. Thus, the claim to know that *Nfc* is true—that is, the claim that *Nfc* can be rationally affirmed—implies more than that the state of affairs obtains which would obtain if *Nfc* were true.

Our point here can be illustrated by a certain sort of agnosticism with respect to the existence of God. Some Christians hold that precisely because God exists and utterly transcends human reason, no one can know whether God exists or not. This position obviously is coherent. It would not be so if the truth-conditions of a proposition were identical with the conditions for affirming that proposition.

Inasmuch as any attempt to rationally affirm *Nfc* is self-defeating, the *PNfc's* inconsistency in thinking and acting as if *Sfc* were true when he tries to rationally affirm *Nfc* is not an avoidable inconsistency. The activity of rationally affirming is unlike other activities in which a *PNfc* might engage while inconsistently acting and thinking as if he were free. If *Nfc* is true, then the implicit appeal by the *PNfc* to a normativity which entails *Sfc* is futile. The norm cannot actually prescribe; the attempt to affirm *Nfc* necessarily fails. What is more, only if the attempt to affirm *Nfc* necessarily fails can the *PNfc* avoid the inevitable falsification which—the argument in B through F has shown—occurs on the assumption that *Nfc* can be rationally affirmed.

H. The inescapability of the dilemma

In G we compared skepticism with *Nfc*. Any attempt to affirm skepticism is self-defeating. Unless *Nfc* is false, any attempt to rationally affirm it is self-defeating. The question is: Need the *PNfc* attempt to *rationally* affirm *Nfc*? Perhaps he can affirm *Nfc*, without rationally affirming *Nfc*. If so, the *PNfc* can escape. *Nfc* is not falsified merely because the *PNfc* affirms it, but only if he *rationally* affirms it. Likewise, *Nfc* is not self-defeating merely because the *PNfc* attempts to affirm it, but only if he attempts to rationally affirm it. It is only in attempting to *rationally* affirm *Nfc* that the *PNfc* must appeal to the normativity which entails *Sfc*.

The *PNfc* is faced with a dilemma. If his attempt to rationally affirm *Nfc* can succeed, then *Nfc* is inevitably falsified, as we have shown in B through F. If

Nfc cannot be falsified—because it is true—then any attempt to rationally affirm *Nfc* inevitably fails, as we have shown in G. Faced with this dilemma, the *P Nfc* has only one escape. He can claim that he can affirm *Nfc* to be true, but that he need not attempt to rationally affirm *Nfc* in the sense of "rationally affirm" which we clarified in chapter five, section E.

However, the clarifications in chapter five, section E, show that our use of the expression "rationally affirm" is not a convention established arbitrarily to refute *Nfc*. Rational affirmations are a sub-set of affirmations having epistemic legitimacy—that is, of grounded affirmations. Other sub-sets of this set are affirmations of formal truths and affirmations of propositions which articulate immediately experienced states of affairs. Affirmations lacking epistemic legitimacy are those wholly without warrant.

Thus, if the *P Nfc's* claim has epistemic legitimacy without being a rational affirmation in the sense defined, then *Nfc* must be either a formal truth or an immediately evident fact. As we showed in chapter three, sections A and B, it is neither of these. Moreover, *Nfc*, insofar as it is a general proposition about the world—*No* one *can* make a free choice—not only depends upon evidence, but also upon grounding the affirmation in the evidence. Rationality norms do this as we explained in chapter five, section F. Affirmations conditioned by such norms, as we showed in chapter five, section E, are rational affirmations.

There remains only one possibility. Perhaps *Nfc* can be affirmed, although the affirmation of it is not warranted. An affirmation which is not warranted might nevertheless be true. We agree that someone might affirm *Nfc* without claiming epistemic legitimacy for his affirmation. Necessarily lacking any rational ground, a *P Nfc* might claim that *Nfc* is true. This position, if our argument in sections B through F is correct, is the only position the *P Nfc* can take. To affirm one's position in this way, however, is to withdraw from the philosophical controversy.

Once more, we might be accused of question-begging. The preceding argument presupposes that the *P Nfc* must *somehow* affirm *Nfc*. Perhaps he need not affirm it at all.

We admit that *Nfc* need not be affirmed. It can be posed as a question or included in fictional dialogue. Whether *Nfc* is true or not, its utterance can be considered to be part of a technique useful for solving social problems. *Nfc* can be used as a heuristic device, even by someone who considers *Nfc* false.

Someone might utter *Nfc* as part of a program of conditioning people to forget *Sfc*. Of course, this would not be an affirmation—that is, a claim that *Nfc* is or even might be true. If the utterance included any expression of a leaning toward *Nfc* rather than *Sfc*, then, as we showed in chapter five, section E, it would be an affirmation. But it need not be.

However, such an utterance of *Nfc* is not inconsistent with the affirmation of *Sfc*. Only an affirmation of *Nfc* can exclude the affirmation of the contradictory proposition (*Sfc*) as false, less reasonable to believe, or in any way less likely to be true than *Nfc* itself.

Therefore, if any *P Nfc* wishes to propose *Nfc* as true—or as at all more likely to be true than *Sfc*—then the *P Nfc* must affirm *Nfc*. As we explained in chapter five, section E, "affirm" need not imply a claim of certitude. Thus, anyone who wishes to consider the possibility that *Nfc might* be true as anything more than a mere possibility is in a strange position. He either must avoid affirming *Nfc*, however weakly, even when talking to himself, or he must affirm *Nfc* without any warrant whatsoever.

We say, "He must avoid affirming *Nfc*, even when talking to himself." For rhetorical reasons, we speak of the *PSfc* and the *P Nfc* as if they were distinct persons. However, this distinction is irrelevant to the logic of our argument. As Plato says, reasoning can be a dialogue of the soul with herself. To affirm is not primarily to perform an act of communication, but to perform a propositional act, an act by which one seeking truth prefers one proposition to its contradictory. Whether one wishes to gain agreement with his affirmation or not, whether he even expresses it in speech, the conditions necessary for making it must obtain. Insofar as a rational affirmation depends upon a rationality norm, the act of rationally affirming a proposition can succeed only if the norm is in force. If *Sfc* is false, the rationality norm on which any successful rational affirmation of *Nfc* would depend never could be in force. Thus, no one could affirm *Nfc* rationally, but only groundlessly, even when talking to himself.

This is not to say that someone might not entertain *Nfc* without affirming it. In fact, he might express his thought to others. But there could be no argument between someone who affirmed *Sfc* and someone who nonaffirmatively expressed *Nfc*. The latter is not making a claim. This option, then, is not open to one who wishes to suggest that *Nfc* is true. Moreover, it follows that someone in this position cannot accuse his opponent of begging any questions. His "position" is not a position defended in argument; he takes no stand on a question which might be begged. In other words, this "*PNfc*" is not a *PNfc* at all. He utters *Nfc* but does not affirm it and thus does not deny *Sfc*. Only one who denies *Sfc* joins issue in *Sfc/Nfc*.

At this point there is another move which someone might wish to make. He might claim that he is not making an affirmation of *Nfc* because on his own theory affirmations cannot be made. His utterance *could* be nothing more than, for example, a conditioning device.

This position is not necessarily incoherent, but it is questionable whether anyone consistently maintains it. Either of two possible attitudes might be involved. One would be consistent, avoiding any attempt to rationally affirm any proposition, and withdrawing altogether from any attempt to participate in philosophic or other intellectual discussion. The other would be an inconsistent attitude, denying the possibility of rationally affirming propositions to the extent necessary to render his own position impregnable to self-refutation, but at the same time assuming—perhaps, even, pretending, the better to condition us—that some possibility of rational controversy remains, and that a position such as this one could be considered, taken seriously, and perhaps even affirmed within such a controversy.

I. Free choice affirmed

We have shown in sections B through F that any rational affirmation of *Nfc* is inevitably falsified, unless the act of affirming it fails because the normativity it requires is not in force. We have shown in G that the attempt to rationally affirm *Nfc* inevitably fails; every such attempt is self-defeating. We have shown in H that the *PNfc* must attempt to rationally affirm *Nfc*. Thus, we can say without qualification that *Nfc* is self-refuting—that is, necessarily either self-falsifying or self-defeating. Yet we have not shown that *Nfc* is certainly false.

Since *Sfc* and *Nfc* are contradictory propositions, if the argument in B through H had shown *Nfc* false, it also would have shown *Sfc* true. However, the weaker conclusion we have thus far established—that *Nfc* is either self-falsifying or self-defeating—does not by itself entitle one to affirm *Sfc* as a proposition which is firmly established. We now show how the self-refuting character of *Nfc* together with certain other considerations does warrant a rational affirmation of *Sfc*. Our claim is that one can be said to "know" that *Sfc* is true in a very strong sense—in the same sense in which one can be said to "know" that there is an external world.

We showed in F that there is a kind of normativity which is in force only if *Sfc* is true. We showed in D and in G that in trying to rationally affirm *Nfc*, the *PNfc* cannot help assuming some norm or other having this kind of normativity. We did not invent this normativity nor did we characterize it by stipulation. Rather, we found it by explicating what is necessarily involved in the *PNfc's* own attempt to rationally exclude *Sfc*.

Inasmuch as the normativity which entails *Sfc* is something one *finds,* it is a datum. Of course, it is not a sense datum, but it is given in the experience of engaging in rational controversy—in particular, in the experience of attempting to rationally affirm *Nfc*. The *PNfc's* appeal to some rationality norm or other is a fact; moreover, it is an inescapable fact for him unless he ceases to be a *PNfc*. The normativity of the norm to which the *PNfc* must appeal is an aspect of this inescapable fact. In this sense, the normativity which entails freedom is a datum. One experiences this normativity somewhat as one experiences the normativity of rules of formal logic. Anyone who understands, follows, and appeals to any rationality norm—that is, anyone who makes or even considers making any rational affirmation whatsoever—has the phenomenon of this normativity present to his awareness.

The phenomenon of the normativity which entails *Sfc* is both like and unlike the phenomena of choice, of which the *PSfc* and the *PNfc* offer contradictory interpretations. These phenomena are alike in that the normativity of rationality norms prescribes the making of a choice and thus entails that *Sfc* is true, and the phenomena of choice provide a person with grounds for judging that he is making a free choice. They also are alike in that both the givenness of the normativity which entails *Sfc* and the givenness of the experience of choosing are logically compatible with *Nfc*. In other words, one can admit both data, yet affirm *Nfc* without contradicting himself.

But while the data of the experience of choice and the datum of the normativity which entails *Sfc* are similar in some ways, they differ in an important respect. Consideration of their difference yields results even more interesting than those yielded by consideration of their likeness.

The data of the experience of choice ground the judgment that one is making a free choice partly by something negative—that in making a choice a person *does not* experience anything making him make the choice he makes. Thus, these data are of evidential value only insofar as one considers them in a framework of expectation according to which what is not given is taken as significant by its absence. The normativity of rationality norms, insofar as this normativity is a phenomenon, has no similar negative aspects. One's experience of this normativity is not an awareness of something involving the absence of an awareness of something else. Thus, the phenomenon of the normativity which entails *Sfc* points to its truth without presupposing a framework of expectation according to which what is not given is taken as significant by its absence. In other words, the normativity assumed by one who attempts to rationally affirm *Nfc* entails *Sfc* no matter what other state of affairs obtains or does not obtain.

Thus, the data of the experience of choice and the datum of the normativity of a rationality norm present different obstacles to the *PNfc*. The *PNfc* must *explain* the data of the experience of choice; he succeeds in explaining them if he establishes *Nfc* and gives a plausible account of why people are unaware of the determining factors which make them choose precisely as they do. Thus, the evidential value for a *PSfc* of the data of the experience of choice can be undercut by the *PNfc*, without the latter having to dismiss the data as illusory. However, even if the *PNfc* could fully account for the datum of the normativity which entails *Sfc*, his explanation would in no way undercut the evidential value of this datum for a *PSfc*. No matter how the datum of the normativity of rationality norms originates, the *PSfc* can show, as we have shown in F, that this normativity entails *Sfc*. An account by a *PNfc* of the genesis of this normativity would be irrelevant. We ourselves think this normativity is prior to any free choice. But its being so is of no help to the *PNfc*. The normativity which entails *Sfc* is relevant precisely insofar as it functions as evidence. The

P Nfc certainly is in no position to suggest that the fact that evidence and reasons derive entirely from factors other than a free choice provides any ground for thinking such evidence and reasons impotent to establish the conclusion of the argument.

Nevertheless, the datum of the normativity which entails *Sfc* does not by itself entail the *truth* of *Sfc*. The phenomenal normativity establishes *Sfc* only if the norm is in force—that is, if it actually prescribes, if it is not null, if it can be fulfilled. We have shown in F that if *Nfc* is true, the normativity cannot be fulfilled. If *Nfc* is true, then the phenomenon of a normativity which demands that *Sfc* be true must be an illusory phenomenon. Only if the phenomenon of this normativity is illusory is the normativity in principle null.

The normativity which entails *Sfc* might be rendered null in a particular case by a merely contingent fact. For example, a norm which demands temperance might be rendered null by the psychological incapacity of an addict to restrain himself. But the evidential value for the *PSfc* of the phenomenon of the normativity of rationality norms is in no way lessened by the possibility that the norms be nullified by contingent facts. Only if *Nfc* were shown to be true would the evidential value of the phenomenon of this normativity be undercut.

Arguments which proceed from experience take for granted that appearances are to be accepted at face value except to the extent that there is some reason for not so taking them. This assumption is a rationality norm: Phenomena are to be regarded as real unless there is some reason to distinguish between appearance and reality. On this rationality norm, the normativity which entails *Sfc* is to be regarded as real unless there is some ground to distinguish between appearance and reality. Moreover, since the phenomenon in this case is of evidential value without considering it in a framework of expectation according to which what is not given is taken as significant by its absence, a distinction between appearance and reality in this case can be made only if the phenomenon is an illusion. Thus, the rationality norm requires us to suppose that *Sfc* is true unless there is a reason to reject the phenomenon of the normativity of rationality norms as illusory.

Might the phenomenon be an illusion? Yes. The phenomenal normativity fails to demonstrate that *Sfc* is true because one can accept the normativity as phenomenon and yet affirm *Nfc* without contradicting himself. This phenomenon and the existential fact that someone has the ability to fulfill the norm's demand are distinct in such a way that they might exist apart without any logical absurdity. Facts are not logically necessary, and the givenness of one fact does not render absurd the supposition that a distinct fact not be given. Thus, the phenomenon of the normativity which entails *Sfc* might be an illusion —"might" here signifying mere possibility.

However, the conclusion that *Nfc* is self-refuting does establish something about *Sfc*. The *P Nfc* attempts to rule out *Sfc* by showing that there is something about choice or about man or about the world or about the nature of things which excludes this peculiar capacity. But we now know that the *P Nfc's* project is impossible in principle. Thus, *Sfc* is a proposition having a peculiar status. One might call it "epistemically necessary," meaning by this that it *cannot* be rationally denied. An epistemically necessary proposition might still be false, but its possible falsity is irrelevant in a rationally conducted controversy.

We have already shown that a very stringent rationality norm requires that *Sfc* be accepted as true unless there is a reason to reject the phenomenon of the normativity of rationality norms as illusory. It is possible that this normativity be an illusion, precisely insofar as it is possible that *Nfc* be true. But propositions which articulate mere possibilities give one no reason whatsoever for questioning data, much less for regarding them as illusory. Thus *Sfc* must be accepted as true. To refuse to affirm it is to groundlessly reject as necessarily illusory a phenomenon—the phenomenon of the normativity of rationality norms.

Someone who cares nothing for rational discourse might take his stand on the mere possibility that *Nfc* is true and that the phenomenon of the normativity of rationality norms is illusory. He might arbitrarily and groundlessly refuse to accept the truth of *Sfc* and even irrationally and dogmatically insist that *Nfc* is true. Such a person might at the same time pretend to participate in rational discourse; he might play the role of sophist. If the normativity of rationality norms were illusory, not only would one be unable to rationally affirm *Sfc*, one would be unable to rationally affirm any proposition whatsoever. The rational grounds for all discourse in science, philosophy, history, criticism, theology, and the practice of every liberal art and profession would be merely apparent. A sophist might rejoice in such a prospect; no sincere participant in the intellectual life can entertain it.

The conclusion that *Sfc* must be accepted as true is a conclusion about the world. The *P Nfc* attempts to exclude a conceivable human capacity from the world. *Sfc*, then, not only means that there is a possibility that someone might make a free choice, it means that there is a person who has the capacity to make free choices.

Who is this person? At least anyone who understands rationality norms, who is aware of their normativity, and who is guided by them in a conscious pursuit of truth is such a person. At least anyone who deliberately engages in the intellectual life can make free choices. It is not a special capacity, like creative genius, reserved to a few. It is a common human capacity, possibly absent only from those who cannot make any rationally grounded affirmations in the context of a purposeful effort to reach truth.

There is a further question: Do people make free choices? Is the capacity to make free choices exercised?

To answer this question we must return to a consideration of the phenomena of choice. People do experience making choices. This experience also is not something special, reserved to a few. It is a common human experience which most people have on many occasions during their lives.

In the experience of making a choice, as we explained in chapter three, section D, a person confronts purposes which are not commensurable. Prior to choice, one lacks an order of priorities sufficient to establish one alternative as preferable to another. In making a choice, a person does not simply experience himself ending deliberation and initiating action. He does experience this, of course, but in choosing the person who makes a choice also experiences himself setting a criterion, making commensurable what was not commensurable. A person experiences his endorsement of other necessary conditions for his choice; he experiences setting a priority which will stand unless he alters it by a subsequent choice.

In choosing a person has a sense of freedom because of all that is positive in his experience; he judges that he is making a free choice because he does not experience anything making him make the choice he makes, and he assumes that what he does not experience is not operative. The *PNfc* has an initially plausible case insofar as he points out that this framework of expectation could be undercut. One's judgment that one is making a free choice could be mistaken without the experience being illusory if one's choice actually were determined by some factor of which one remained unaware.

However, the person who makes a choice is by no means unreasonable in supposing that he is making a free choice; his judgment is rationally warranted until it is challenged. The rational warrant for the initial judgment that one is making a free choice when one has the experience of choice is simply that the apparent should be taken at face value unless there is some reason for supposing otherwise. In other words, the same rationality norm we stated previously in showing the evidential value of the normativity of rationality norms also applies to the experience of choice itself.

However, there is a difference. The experience of choice could be an inadequate warrant for the judgment that one is making a free choice without this experience being illusory. This is so precisely inasmuch as a person's judgment also depends upon his taking as significant his lack of awareness of any determining factor. However, since *Nfc* is self-refuting, there cannot be any way to displace in principle the framework of expectation. In other words, one could only show that a person never makes free choices when he judges that he does make them if one could show *Nfc* true, and this cannot be shown since *Nfc* is self-refuting, and its character as self-refuting together with the normativity which demands free choice establishes *Sfc* as true.

Thus, in general, if a person supposes that he is making a free choice, there is no reason to think that he is not making one.

Still, one can ask whether the judgment that one is making a free choice might not be mistaken in particular instances. In one sense, the judgment might be mistaken, for a person could fail to attend to his own experience, not have all that is involved in the experience of choice—for example, settle an issue by previously established priorities—yet afterwards think he has made a free choice. Similarly, a person can choose freely but not have as many available alternatives as he might suppose. These possibilities have been discussed in chapter three, section D. But what if a person does have the experience of choice, including the experience of determining himself to one alternative by establishing a priority which makes previously incommensurable purposes commensurable? Can a person with this experience be mistaken in judging that he is making a free choice?

We think a mistake in such a case is a logical possibility, but no more than that. The judgment cannot be undercut by any line of argument which would rule out its correctness on some general principle, for any such line of argument would include *Nfc*, and *Nfc* is self-refuting. To undercut the judgment that someone has made a particular free choice, one would have to point to some particular factor correlated with his choice and claim that this factor determined the choice. But how could such a claim be made good? A person who understands what free choice is will point out that there are many necessary conditions of his freely choosing as he does, and these conditions will correlate with his choice, but these conditions also are conditions for not making the same choice. To establish the relationship of the supposed determining factor to the choice actually made, one would have to show that without this factor, the choice would not have been made. In other words, one would have to show the truth of a subjunctive proposition about a particular state of affairs, a state of affairs which has a uniqueness—as choices do—such that it cannot be regarded as a mere specimen of a type.

The conclusion of this last line of argument seems to us to show that if a person has all the appropriate data of choice in a particular case, then his judgment that he has made a free choice is no more defeasible than is the general proposition, *Sfc*. The status of such a particular judgment, we admit, is a complex question, and so we are not as confident in this conclusion as we are in the conclusion that *Sfc* must be accepted as true.

In reaching the latter conclusion, we pointed out that to refuse to accept *Sfc* is to groundlessly reject as necessarily illusory a phenomenon which is given. Such groundless rejection is possible only because it remains to deny a truth based upon data when there is in principle no way to show these data as other than what they seem.

Michael Slote, arguing against skepticism with respect to the reality of the external world, points out that the skeptic does not contradict himself. Like us, Slote relies on rationality norms in his argument, although he calls such norms "principles." One of these he calls the "Principle of Illusion and Evidence," which he states as follows:

> . . . one who is (even in the slightest degree) rationally justified in believing any (fairly specific) causal claim must have evidence which he is rationally justified in trusting or using in order to support that claim, and must, therefore, not be rationally justified in believing that all his sense and memory experiences are illusory (non-veridical).[2]

This principle—or one very like it—can be put more briefly: If one cannot possibly have any good reason for rejecting experience as illusory, one ought to accept it as genuine.

It is possible that there be no external world. It is possible that *Nfc* be true. But in either case, one must reject data as illusory and in neither case can one possibly have any reason for doing so. Once this state of affairs becomes clear, it is speculation against the value of rational discourse to ask for proof that there is an external world or that *Sfc* is true. The demand for proof at this point is a demand which in principle cannot be met. It is a demand that one show a position—there is a world; there can be free choices—to be necessary when its contradictory is not logically, but only rationally, absurd. To refuse to affirm as rationally established positions such as these because one's demand for demonstration of absolute necessity is not met is to arbitrarily reject rationally necessary positions by setting an impossible condition for affirming them.

A position which is rationally grounded, which in principle cannot be displaced, and whose contradictory is a mere possibility can be said to be "known." Thus, *Sfc* is established. It is among the truths we know.

J. Previous arguments for free choice

In chapter two, we considered previous arguments for *Sfc*. These were the argument of those who invoked immediate experience, the argument of those who proceed from the awareness of moral obligation, William James's argument, Thomas Aquinas's argument, and the arguments of those before us who tried to develop a self-referential argument against *Nfc*. Of all the self-referential arguments, we gave special consideration to James Jordan's, because of its merits. We concluded in chapter two that all previous arguments failed to establish *Sfc*. Previous arguments either assumed that the evidence of choice by itself established *Sfc* or they required premises which a *P Nfc* need not accept. Thus we concluded that previous arguments failed to accomplish what they attempted.

Despite this failure, previous arguments against *Nfc* are philosophically valuable. Each of these types of argument has a sound insight at its basis, and each of these insights contributes to a full understanding of free choice. It is appropriate at this point to consider these insights and to place them within a comprehensive understanding of free choice, an understanding developed out of our argument against *Nfc* and our characterization of *Sfc*. As we integrate these insights into our own framework it will become clear how the defects in each of the previous attempts are overcome in our work.

Although prior arguments for *Sfc* taken together have almost everything necessary to establish *Sfc*, the errors and limitations of each approach renders impossible any mere synthesis of them. Thus, although we profit from what has been accomplished by others, we think our work makes its own contribution toward securing *Sfc*. This contribution depends to a great extent upon our concern to avoid question-begging against the *PNfc*. Thus, in what follows we take special care to point out how the argument we propose avoids question-begging in the ways in which previous attempts did not.

The argument from immediate experience was sound, at least to the extent that there is an experience of choice; any attempt by a *PNfc* to deny the elements of this experience is mistaken. Moreover, the experience of choice does lead to judgments—"I have made a free choice"—which on the whole surely are sound. These judgments, as we have explained in I, are not undercut and cannot be undercut by theories which attack as in principle mistaken the framework of expectation within which one considers his own experience. We have concluded that the individual who thinks he *knows* he has made a free choice does know it.

The defect in the argument from immediate experience is that it fails to provide any serious response to the challenge of arguments for *Nfc*. Many who defend *Sfc* on the basis of experience proceed as if *Nfc* simply does not exist in the field of philosophical controversy. However, if anyone—*PNfc* or *PSfc*—proceeds as if he simply has no opposition, he is dogmatic. Moreover, those who argue from immediate experience contribute little to the clarification of the nature of free choice or to the issues at stake in *Sfc/Nfc*. Only through developing arguments, we believe, can these issues and concepts be clarified. For our part, we think that in developing the argument for *Sfc* in B through I we have also clarified the concept of free choice.

Thus, if we are correct, our development of the argument for *Sfc* has remedied the defects of the argument from immediate experience.

The argument based upon moral responsibility certainly is correct in claiming that there is a normativity which entails *Sfc*. The normativity to which the *PNfc* appeals when he attempts to rationally affirm *Nfc* is a normativity to which the *PNfc* must appeal if he is to remain in *Sfc/Nfc*. In fact, the same normativity belongs to all rationality norms. All affirming in rational discourse appeals to the same normativity. Thus, it is clear that there are undeniable examples of the sort of normativity which those who pressed the argument from moral responsibility use as their point of departure.

The *PNfc*, often in the role of compatibilist, tries to explain away the normativity to which the *PSfc* points in the argument from moral responsibility. However, the normativity to which the *PNfc* appeals in seeking to rationally affirm *Nfc* cannot be explained by reduction to any other sort of normativity. Thus, the concern of the *PSfc*, who argues for *Sfc* on the basis of moral responsibility, that *Nfc* would undercut morality is not an irrational fear.

The normativity which is discernible in any rational attempt to affirm anything whatsoever embodies a morality immanent in the intellectual life itself. As such, this morality is an epitome of man's moral responsibility in every field of action. This normativity is irreducible to any mere set of natural conditions; one cannot reduce this "ought" to any "is" which does not already embody it. However, the exclusion of naturalistic descriptivism does not require that one abandon the intellectual life—or human life in general—to arbitrary options. The demand of this normativity is both rational and unconditional, although one can choose to disregard it.[3]

The difficulty with the argument from moral responsibility is not that those who develop it appeal to anything unreal as their point of departure. The difficulty is that they simply assume the reality of a sort of normativity which they merely affirm to be incompatible with *Nfc*; they do not exhibit this sort of normativity and show its incompatibility with *Nfc*.

Precisely by showing in D that this sort of normativity is necessary for the *PNfc's* rational affirmation of *Nfc*, and that no other sort of normativity will do, we show the irreducibility of the moral normativity which those who argue from moral responsibility wish to defend.

Moreover, those who argue from moral responsibility generally assume a point which seems intuitively obvious—namely, that "ought" implies "can." We have clarified the soundness of this intuition in F, and we think the point to be in need of the sort of defense we provided for it there.

In clarifying this peculiar sort of normativity, we also have shown in what way it is unconditional. Kant and many others distinguish categorical from hypothetical imperatives. But they fail to distinguish the unconditional demands of logical norms from the unconditional normativity which prescribes one of two open alternatives.

Thomas Aquinas's argument for free choice is based upon a distinction between man's ultimate good and the goodness inherent in any alternatives between which a person can choose. Any particular purpose embodies only a limited goodness, which can never appeal to every aspect of the human personality. Thus, for Aquinas, the goods between which human persons choose are incommensurable in themselves. By establishing a personal order of priorities, choice makes limited goods commensurable with each other. In developing his argument, Aquinas provides one of the most accurate descriptions of the experience of choice. He also has a clear understanding of the normativity which corresponds to free choice and distinguishes this normativity from that of logical and of technical norms.

Aquinas's accurate understanding of free choice was most useful to us in clarifying the controversy. By stressing the special character of moral normativity and the incommensurability of goods, Aquinas provides insights which find their place in our argument's use of the special character of the normativity of rationality norms and in our account of the very possibility of action which is rationally directed but which, nevertheless, is not determined by the reasons which guide it. Aquinas's argument falls short insofar as he lacks the method of self-referential argumentation. Lacking this method, he is unable to show that Nfc is self-refuting. His exposition of free choice fails—if it is taken as a demonstration—to avoid question-begging.

The proponents of previous self-referential arguments saw the potentiality of settling Sfc/Nfc by this method. They contributed to the development of the method itself, and they made an important contribution to the controversy by compelling their opponents to begin to face up to the implications of what a $PNfc$ is doing when he tries to rationally affirm Nfc.

However, previous self-referential arguments against Nfc lacked a fully explicit methodology. Moreover, proponents of previous self-referential arguments generally assumed the distinction between reasons and causes; in doing so their arguments became question-begging. By showing that the normativity involved in any rational affirmation is a type of normativity irreducible to other kinds, we articulated a basis for making a distinction between reasons and causes.

Again, previous proponents of self-referential arguments failed to make clear—as we pointed out in chapter two, section E—the distinction between the prescriptivity of logical norms and the prescriptivity of an unconditional norm which entails Sfc. What many philosophers, such as J. R. Lucas, fail to show is that if man is something more than a merely physical entity, then Sfc is true. This point cannot be taken for granted. Our argument has clarified this matter by distinguishing between logical normativity and that normativity which is required for rational affirmation. Without this distinction, there is a serious danger that, as with Kant, the unconditional normativity of moral requirements will be mistaken as a demand for logical consistency. Such a view makes it impossible to explain how people freely and knowingly choose to do what is morally evil.

Previous self-referential arguments against Nfc also failed to make clear the precise property of the $PNfc's$ affirmation which leads to the falsification or self-defeat of his affirmation or attempted affirmation. We have made clear (in

D) the property of the *PNfc's* act of affirming which leads to the downfall of *Nfc*.

Again, previous self-referential arguments—including our own first attempt—did not take fully into account the way in which the experience of choice enters into the solution of the problem. When one first discovers the technique of self-referential argument, there is a temptation—which ought to be resisted—to suppose that it can yield results of value even if one ignores data other than those included in the position being refuted. We have shown in I how important the experience of choice is, and we have made clear that the refutation of *Nfc* does not of itself establish *Sfc*. The rational affirmation of *Sfc* has a very solid warrant, but this warrant is not independent of the experience of choice nor is it independent of the experience—a datum of another sort—of the normativity of rationality norms.

William James's argument took account of experience. He makes the point that any argument for *Sfc* in a certain way depends upon a free choice. As he says: "Freedom's first deed should be to affirm itself." In other words, James realized that one could, after all, choose to be a *PNfc*. James closely relates these observations to the difference between the world-views of those who affirm *Sfc* and those who deny it. For him, this difference has an important moral dimension; it distinguishes two basic stances toward reality.

James, however, fails to make clear the rational grounds for affirming *Sfc*. He seems to consider *Sfc* and *Nfc* to be on a par. We have shown how far this view is from the truth. While one can opt for either position, the option in favor of *Sfc* is as rational as any option can be, while the option for *Nfc* lacks any rational basis whatsoever.

James also tends to ignore an aspect of the problem most clearly understood by Aquinas—namely, that man must choose among incommensurable purposes, and that not all norms prescribe in the same way. Yet James certainly had a valuable insight. In section H we showed that although the *PNfc* cannot rationally affirm *Nfc*, yet must attempt to do so if he is to remain in *Sfc/Nfc*, still, on the bare logical possibility that *Nfc* could be true even though it is altogether indefensible, someone could continue to think *Nfc* true. James's analysis of opting throws some light on this possibility, especially to the extent that he takes into consideration the fact that *Sfc/Nfc* is not a merely theoretical issue, but also a practical issue, and in some sense a moral issue.

K. Concluding remarks

Philosophy is unsatisfying in many ways, both to its practitioners and to its audience. Philosophical arguments often fail by begging the question; they are based upon assumptions which need not be granted. It is not surprising that philosophical arguments often fail in this way. Other disciplines proceed from stable assumptions agreed upon by competent practitioners of each discipline and seldom questioned by them. Philosophy, by contrast, examines assumptions; ideally, it leaves nothing unquestioned.

Thus, practitioners of philosophy are engaged in continuous reexamination of the presuppositions of their inquiry. This fact gives philosophy its unsettled appearance. Philosophical questions appear never to be satisfactorily answered; the history of philosophy appears to show little progress toward the resolution of any important issue. *Sfc/Nfc* is a case in point.

But the appearance of interminable and futile argument is to some extent deceptive. One can reach definitive conclusions in philosophy; one can make progress in philosophy. We think the argument we articulate in this chapter is an example of what any philosopher can do. Of course, many a philosopher who has labored to produce a serious work has shared the same belief in the possibility of progress and has had the same fond opinion of the fruits of his labor. While we are confident that the argument we present is sound, we entertain the possibility that we are mistaken, for we are aware that our initial attempt to articulate a self-referential argument against *Nfc* was defective in many respects, although it seemed sound to us when we published it. Therefore, we welcome careful, critical examination of the present attempt. We are reasonably confident that the main lines of the argument can withstand criticism.

The method of self-referential argumentation described in chapter five and used in this chapter is not new. Plato used it. But so far as we know, no one has previously formulated it reflectively and applied it systematically. The present work was undertaken partly as an attempt to explore the potentiality of this method. We wished to see whether we could construct a cogent self-referential argument against *Nfc*, an argument which would avoid begging the question. Moreover, we regard *Sfc/Nfc* as one of the most important controversies in the whole of philosophy. The implications for human life—both for the life of the individual and for the life of society—of accepting either side are enormous. Thus, we undertook this work partly for methodological and partly for substantive reasons.

We think it better to *use* a philosophical method which seems to have promise than to limit oneself to describing its logical features and speculating about its promise. One success is more of a basis than many philosophers who have recommended a philosophical method have had for their confident expectation that it would bring about significant progress in the field. To the extent that the present experiment is a success, we think the method of self-referential argumentation gives good promise of further important success. For example, self-referential argumentation might be used to show the irreducibility of propositional knowledge to physical or behavioral events and processes; it might also be used to show the irreducibility of the physical world to phenomena and/or ideas. We have not attempted to articulate a self-referential argument for either of these theses and we know of only sketchy attempts to do so. But in carrying through the present experiment, we have clarified—in ways we ourselves did not expect at the outset—the precise nature and limitations of self-referential argumentation.

Besides resolving *Sfc/Nfc* and clarifying the nature and limits of self-referential argumentation, we think the present work shows another point of considerable importance—namely, the role of rationality norms in inquiry. Other philosophers have noticed that there are such norms, but few have articulated what they are and few have made use of them in full awareness of what they were doing.

Our argument in sections H and I suggests that rationality norms are the ethics of inquiry and rational discourse generally—or, at least, an important part of this ethics. Moreover, we have shown that the ethics of inquiry and rational discourse is more intimately related to the content of reasonable affirmations than many philosophers have supposed. We have shown that rationality norms play a central role in one philosophical controversy —*Sfc/Nfc*.

The *PNfc* refutes himself in attempting to rationally affirm *Nfc*, for he appeals to a norm which is in force only if *Sfc* obtains. Thus, either the rational affirmation of *Nfc* falsifies it or the attempt to rationally affirm *Nfc* is self-defeating. Therefore, it is only by clarifying the implications of the rationality norms required to rationally affirm *Nfc* that our argument makes clear that *Nfc* is self-refuting.

Moreover, the truth of *Sfc* is not established solely by the self-refutation of *Nfc*. The self-refutation of *Nfc* shows that in principle *Sfc* cannot be rationally denied. One must appeal to a rationality norm to draw the further conclusion that *Sfc* must be affirmed. But this rationality norm is stringent. Thus, given that *Sfc* cannot be rationally denied, it is altogether unreasonable to refuse to affirm it, just as it is wholly unreasonable to refuse to affirm that there is an external world.

Of course, someone can choose to violate rationality norms. When one engages in inquiry and discourse, values other than truth are at stake; one can make an immorally excessive commitment to these other values and thus degrade the intellectual life. But anyone who sincerely engages in philosophical controversy is committed to conforming to rationality norms. Thus, the *PNfc* is caught between the implications of his own position, insofar as it is self-referential, and the implications of his participation in the intellectual community, insofar as he is thereby committed to use rational discourse in pursuit of truth.

We are inclined to think that clear understanding of the role of rationality norms in inquiry will help to solve other philosophical problems. Rationalists have regularly treated rationality norms—for example, the principle of sufficient reason—as if they were metaphysical truths. In reaction, empiricists have tended toward skepticism with respect to conclusions rationally grounded by rationality norms. Such conclusions are neither evident matters of fact nor logically necessary truths, and so empiricists have felt free to deny them. At the same time, as our examination of arguments for *Nfc* in chapter three makes clear, empiricists have used—at least implicitly—rationality norms required for their own argumentation as readily and as uncritically as rationalists have used them. Clarification of the ethics of inquiry will make for more consistent reasonableness or, at least, will call attention to practices involving unreasonable inconsistency.

In claiming that we have established a philosophical thesis on a substantive and perennial question, we realize we make a claim which is unfashionable in many quarters. Of course, any *PNfc* will look for a fatal flaw in our argument. But if none is found, not only should the *PNfc* change his position, but also the proponent of the view that philosophy can establish no substantive theses should amend his view.

In claiming that we have established *Sfc*, we are not merely making a claim about how language is used or about how phenomena appear in consciousness. We make an ontological claim: Someone can choose freely. The proposition concerns human beings and their capacity for choice. The making of such an ontological claim is what is unfashionable. Moreover, our claim is especially likely to be unwelcome because it is for *Sfc*. A claim which would seem modest enough if it were made on behalf of a generally accepted position must seem arrogant if it is made on behalf of a position generally assumed to be as unacceptable as the entire worldview of which historically it was a part.

Even in recent years, while most philosophers have officially eschewed theory in philosophy, arguments for *Nfc*—or, what is more common, arguments which take for granted the theoretical truth of *Nfc*—have continued to be offered and to be well received. Yet *Nfc* is a paradigmatic instance of speculative metaphysics. Not only do most arguments for it assume the principle of sufficient reason, but also the thesis itself makes a very ambitious claim —namely, to comprehend the structure of reality sufficiently to exclude from it altogether any capacity of human persons to make free choices.

If *Nfc* is a metaphysical thesis, so is its contradictory. But *Sfc* is a far more limited position; it depends upon no extravagant claim about the whole of reality or the whole of the world. That someone can make a free choice can be rationally affirmed on the basis of limited knowledge such as we human beings are capable of. It is no ambitious piece of metaphysical speculation.

Moreover, we do not suppose that what we have done in the present work is the first stage in some grand, metaphysical synthesis. Metaphysical systems are fascinating, but history does not suggest that they are likely to settle important controversies. Rather, speculative metaphysics creates the controversies which a more socratic approach—an approach at once critical and open—must resolve or dissolve.

Even if, as we believe, the approach we have used in the present work can be used successfully in dealing with other philosophical problems, the result will never accumulate to form a description of the essential features of reality or even a complete inventory of what there is. Self-referential argumentation gets results by making clear the limits of reductionism; a self-referential argument works against a position which maintains "Reality is nothing but . . ." or "There is no room in reality for . . ." or "It is in principle impossible that. . . ."

Of course, not every claim that something is in principle impossible is self-refuting. Some such claims are made on the basis of limited principles which do obtain in the limited regions to which our limited knowledge gives us access. Thus, we claim that it is in principle impossible that *Nfc* be rationally affirmed, but this claim is as far from the claim of a speculative metaphysics as the claims of contemporary physics are from the claims of Laplace, which we discussed in chapter three, sections C and E.

In sum. Philosophy does make progress. Methods of argumentation which can yield substantive results are articulated. The implications of participation in the intellectual community are clarified. Substantive issues are settled, not merely dissolved. Yet we do not think there can be any science of reality as such. As human persons must choose among limited and incommensurable goods, they must be satisfied with limited and incompletely synthesized truths. Only so does one maintain openness to the Good and the Truth Itself.

Notes

1. CLARIFICATION OF THE CONTROVERSY

1. Our analysis of freedom owes much to Mortimer J. Adler, *The Idea of Freedom* (2 vols.; Garden City, N.Y.: 1958, 1961), but in many respects we do not follow him.

2. Karl Popper, "Indeterminism Is Not Enough," *Encounter*, 40 (April, 1973), pp. 20-26, discusses a notion of freedom close to this one.

3. Peter van Inwagen, "A Formal Approach to the Problem of Free Will and Determinism," *Theoria*, 40 (1974), pp. 17-20, provides a definition of "free choice" which if specified suitably would be identical with ours.

4. Richard Taylor, *Action and Purpose* (Englewood Cliffs, N.J.: 1966), pp. 53-55, argues that freedom of choice is not mere causal contingency between possible happenings, but conceptually involves reference to a person acting.

5. C. D. Broad, "Determinism, Indeterminism, and Libertarianism," in *Ethics and the History of Philosophy* (London: 1952), pp. 195-217; Taylor, *op. cit.*, pp. 111-112; Roderick Chisholm, "Freedom and Action," in *Freedom and Determinism*, ed. Keith Lehrer (New York: 1966), pp. 17-24; Frederick Ferré, "Self-Determinism," *American Philosophical Quarterly*, 10 (1973), p. 169.

6. J. L. Austin, "Ifs and Cans," in *Philosophical Papers*, ed. J. O. Urmson and G. J. Warnock (Oxford: 1961), pp. 205-232, calls attention to the distinction between hypothetical and nonhypothetical uses of "can"; Bruce Aune, "Can," *Encyclopedia of Philosophy*, vol. 2, p. 19, gives a clear account of the sense of "can" involved in "free choice."

7. Chisholm, *op. cit.*, pp. 24-25.

8. Russell's remark is cited by John Hospers, "What Means This Freedom?" in *Determinism and Freedom in the Age of Modern Science*, ed. Sidney Hook (New York: 1961), p. 140.

9. Our description of the experience of choice owes much to Yves R. Simon, *Freedom of Choice*, ed. Peter Wolff (New York: 1969), pp. 75-127; Richard Taylor, *op. cit.*, pp. 153-257; Paul Ricoeur, *Freedom and Nature: The Voluntary and the Involuntary*, trans. Erazim V. Kohak (Evanston, Ill.: 1966). For other recent accounts

of this experience see Frederick Ferré, *op, cit.*, pp. 169-171; R. C. Skinner, "Freedom of Choice," *Mind,* 72 (1963), pp. 463-480.

10. J. R. Lucas, *The Freedom of the Will* (Oxford: 1970), p. 82, discusses a closely related point and cites relevant literature.

11. Cf. *ibid.,* pp. 19-20 and 30-32. In discussing deliberation, we are describing *phenomena* which are admitted even by those who assert that all acts are in principle predictable; see, e.g., Alvin I. Goldman, *A Theory of Human Action* (Englewood Cliffs, N.J.: 1970), pp. 194-196.

12. We disagree here with the philosophical tradition exemplified by R. L. Franklin, *Freewill and Determinism: A Study of Rival Conceptions of Man* (London, New York: 1968), pp. 71-79.

13. Douglas Browning, "The Feeling of Freedom," *Review of Metaphysics,* 18 (1964), pp. 123-146, excludes many candidates for the title of "feeling of freedom"; he identifies the feeling with the experience of choice itself (pp. 143-146) and correctly notes that the act of choice is not experienced as a datum (p. 146).

14. Robert Young, "A Sound Self-Referential Argument?" *Review of Metaphysics,* 27 (1973), p. 113, notes that in our earlier treatment of these matters ("Determinism, Freedom, and Self-Referential Arguments," *Review of Metaphysics,* 26 [1972], pp. 3-37), we included an "indeterministic account of the experience of choice" in our definition of determinism. The preceding paragraphs make clear that there is no ground for such an objection against the present work. Young perhaps assumed that to describe the experience of choice is to beg the question in favor of the reality of free choices. Not so. To describe the experience of choice is merely to indicate what the controversy is about.

15. See Carl Ginet, "Can the Will Be Caused?" *Philosophical Review,* 71 (1962), pp. 49-55.

2. ARGUMENTS FOR FREE CHOICE

1. Francisco Suarez, *Disputationes metaphysicae,* XIX, ii, 8-15.

2. David Hume, *Enquiries concerning the Human Understanding and concerning the Principles of Morals,* ed. L. A. Selby-Bigge (2nd ed.; Oxford: 1951), p. 94.

3. *The Philosophical Works of Descartes,* trans. Elizabeth Haldane and G. R. T. Ross (Cambridge: 1967), vol. 1, pp. 174-177.

4. *Ibid.,* vol. 2, pp. 74-75.

5. *Ibid.,* vol. 1, pp. 234-235. For a similar argument proposed by a contemporary philosopher, see R. C. Skinner, "Freedom of Choice," *Mind,* 72 (1963), pp. 463-480.

6. *The Chief Works of Benedict de Spinoza,* trans. R. H. M. Elwes (New York: 1951), vol. 2, p. 75.

7. Joseph Priestley, *The Doctrine of Philosophical Necessity Illustrated, The Theological and Miscellaneous Works* (London: 1818), vol. 3, p. 482.

8. John Stuart Mill, *An Examination of Sir William Hamilton's Philosophy* (Boston: 1865), vol. 2, p. 264.

9. J. M. E. McTaggart, *Some Dogmas of Religion* (London: 1906), p. 148.

10. Moritz Schlick, *Problems of Ethics,* trans. David Rynin (New York: 1939), pp. 154-155 (emphasis his).

11. Keith Lehrer, "Can We Know that We Have Free Will by Introspection?" *Journal of Philosophy,* 57 (1960), pp. 145-146.

12. Mortimer J. Adler, *The Idea of Freedom* (2 vols.; Garden City, N.Y.: 1958, 1961), vol. 2, pp. 318-319, cites Henry Mansel, F. C. S. Schiller, and Hubert Gruender.

13. Brand Blanshard, "The Case for Determinism," in *Determinism and Freedom in the Age of Modern Science,* ed. Sidney Hook (New York: 1961), pp. 20-21.

14. R. D. Bradley, "Free Will: Problem or Pseudo-Problem?" *Australasian Journal of Philosophy,* 36 (1958), pp. 40-41.

15. Lehrer, *op. cit.,* p. 157.

16. Nicolai Hartmann, *Ethics,* trans. Stanton Coit (London, New York: 1932), vol. 3, pp. 146-149.

17. C. A. Campbell, *On Selfhood and Godhood* (London, New York: 1957), p. 216.

18. Hans Kelsen, *What Is Justice?* (Berkeley, Los Angeles: 1957), pp. 335-340.

19. Bertrand Russell, *Human Society in Ethics and Politics* (New York: 1955), p. 80.

20. Ted Honderich, "One Determinism," in *Essays on Freedom of Action,* ed. Ted Honderich (London, Boston: 1973), pp. 205-214, articulates such a frank proposal.

21. Hume, *op. cit.,* p. 95 (emphasis his).

22. A. J. Ayer, *Philosophical Essays* (London, New York: 1954), pp. 274-277. This assumption is false. The position of those arguing for free choice is that the person choosing is a cause whose choice forms his own character; see C. A. Campbell, *In Defence of Free Will* (London: 1967), pp. 48-53. See also Philippa Foot, "Free Will as Involving Determinism," in *Free Will and Determinism,* ed. Bernard Berofsky (New York, London: 1966), pp. 95-108. We treat this matter at length in chapter three, sections D and E.

23. Ayer, *op. cit.,* p. 282. See also Winston Nesbitt and Stewart Candlish, "On Not Being Able to Do Otherwise," *Mind,* 82 (1973), pp. 321-330.

24. Schlick, *op. cit.,* pp. 146-150, quotation from p. 150 (emphasis his).

25. See: *Nicomachean Ethics* iii, 1111a22-b9 and 1114a32-b25.

26. Schlick, *op. cit.,* p. 152.

27. Russell, *op. cit.,* pp. 79-80; other examples are given by Adler, *op. cit.,* vol. 2, pp. 307-309 and 430-437; see also Philippa Foot, *loc. cit.* Russell is mistaken in thinking that motivation is irrational if man is free; most who hold for free choice think it limited by many conditions which restrict the live options among which one can choose.

28. Campbell, *In Defence of Free Will,* pp. 23-25.

29. See Honderich, *loc. cit.*

30. W. D. Ross, *Foundations of Ethics* (Oxford: 1939), pp. 250-251.

31. C. D. Broad, "Determinism, Indeterminism, and Libertarianism," in *Ethics and the History of Philosophy* (London: 1952), pp. 205-206.

32. William James, *Principles of Psychology* (New York: 1890), vol. 2, p. 573.

33. William James, *Pragmatism and Four Essays from the Meaning of Truth* (Cleveland, New York: 1955), pp. 82-85. *Pragmatism* was originally published in 1907.

34. William James, *The Will to Believe and Other Essays in Popular Philosophy* (London, New York, Toronto: 1937), p. 146. "The Dilemma of Determinism" was originally an address, and it was first published in 1884.

35. *Ibid.,* pp. 160-170.

36. *Ibid.,* p. 171.

37. William James, *Essays in Radical Empiricism* (New York: 1912), p. 185.

38. St. Augustine, *De libero arbitrio* ii, 20.

39. St. Thomas Aquinas, II *Sententiarum*, d. 25, a. 2; *Summa contra gentiles,* II, 47; *Summa theologiae,* 1, q. 82, a. 2; 1-2, q. 10, a. 2; *De malo,* q. 3, a. 3; q. 6; *In I Perihermenias*, 14, nn. 23-24; *De veritate,* q. 22, a. 6.

40. Elsewhere (*De malo,* q. 6), Aquinas more carefully points out that the will, being not only animate but also immaterial, cannot be moved by any material efficient cause.

41. An attempt at this type of argument or a favorable discussion of it will be found in the following works: Wilbur Marshall Urban, *The Foundations of Ethics* (New York: 1930), pp. 418-419; H. W. B. Joseph, *Some Problems in Ethics* (Oxford: 1931), pp. 14-15; James McTaggart, *Philosophical Studies* (London: 1934), p. 193; A. E. Taylor, "Freedom and Personality," *Philosophy,* 14 (1939), pp. 259-280; A. E. Taylor, "Freedom and Personality Again," *Philosophy,* 17 (1942), pp. 26-37; Paul Weiss, *Nature and Man* (Carbondale, Ill.: 1947), pp. 23-26; C. S. Lewis, *Miracles* (New York: 1947), pp. 23-31; Paul Tillich, *Systematic Theology* (Chicago: 1951), vol. 1, pp. 200-201; E. L. Mascall, *Christian Theology and Natural Science* (London: 1956), pp. 212-219; A. C. MacIntyre, "Determinism," *Mind,* 66 (1957), pp. 28-41; Morris Ginsberg, *On the Diversity of Morals* (London: 1962), p. 82; Lionel Kenner, "Causality, Determinism and Freedom of the Will," *Philosophy,* 39 (1964), pp. 233-248; Warner Wick, "Truth's Debt to Freedom," *Mind,* 73 (1964), pp. 527-537; J. D. Mabbott, *Introduction to Ethics* (London: 1966), pp. 115-116; Sir Malcolm Knox, *Action* (London, New York: 1968), pp. 68-80; Norman Malcolm, "The Conceivability of Mechanism," *Philosophical Review,* 77 (1968), pp. 45-72; James N. Jordan, "Determinism's Dilemma," *Review of Metaphysics,* 23 (1969), pp. 48-66; J. R. Lucas, *The Freedom of the Will* (Oxford: 1970), pp. 114-172; William H. Davis, *The Freewill Question* (The Hague: 1971), pp. 74-79; Noam Chomsky, "The Case against B. F. Skinner," *New York Review of Books*, December 30, 1971, pp. 20-26; A. Aaron Snyder, "The Paradox of Determinism," *American Philosophical Quarterly*, 9 (1972), pp. 353-356; William Hasker, "The Transcendental Refutation of Determinism," *Southern Journal of Philosophy,* 11 (1973), pp. 175-183.

42. See John Laird, *On Human Freedom* (London: 1947), p. 127; G. E. M. Anscombe, "A Reply to Mr. C. S. Lewis' Argument that 'Naturalism' is Self-Refuting," *Socratic Digest,* 4 (1948), pp. 7-16; Margaret Knight, "Consciousness and the Brain," in *Science News,* vol. 25, ed. A. W. Haslett (Harmondsworth: 1952), pp. 98-103; Adolf Grünbaum, "Causality and the Science of Human Behavior," in *Readings in the Philosophy of Science,* ed. Herbert Feigl and May Brodbeck (New York: 1953), pp. 775-776; A. J. Ayer, *The Concept of a Person* (London: 1963), pp. 266-267; Antony Flew, "A Rational Animal," in *Brain and Mind,* ed. J. R. Smythies (London: 1965), pp. 111-128 and 135; Lucas, *op. cit.,* p. 116; David Wiggins, "Freedom, Knowledge, Belief and Causality," in *Royal Institute of Philosophy Lectures,* vol. 3, *Knowledge and Necessity* (London: 1970), pp. 132-154; Adolf Grünbaum, "Free Will and the Laws of Human Behavior," *American Philosophical Quarterly,* 8 (1971), pp. 309-310; Ted Honderich and J. A. Faris, "A Conspectus of Determinism," *Proceedings of the Aristotelian Society,* supp. vol. 44 (1970), pp. 210-214 and 230-234.

43. Jordan, *op. cit.,* pp. 53-54.

44. A. E. Taylor, "Freedom and Personality Again," p. 28.

45. Weiss, *op. cit.,* p. 25.

46. Kenner, *op. cit.,* p. 247.

47. Knox, *op. cit.,* p. 73.

48. Lucas, *op. cit.,* p. 115; it should be noted that Lucas mentions but does not himself accept this view.

49. Snyder, *op. cit.*, p. 354.

50. Grünbaum, "Free Will and the Laws of Human Behavior," pp. 309-310 (emphasis his); see also Wiggins, *op. cit.*, p. 143.

51. Ayer, *The Concept of a Person*, pp. 266-267; see also Laird, *op. cit.*, p. 127.

52. Jordan, *op. cit.*, pp. 60-61.

53. Taylor, "Freedom and Personality Again," p. 29.

54. *Ibid.*, p. 28.

55. Jordan, *op. cit.*, p. 62; cf. Wick, *op. cit.*, pp. 534 and 537; Kenner, *op. cit.*, pp. 246-248.

56. Kenner, *op. cit.*, p. 247.

57. Lewis, *op. cit.*, pp. 29-30.

58. Lucas, *op. cit.*, pp. 144 and 166.

59. *Ibid.*, pp. 165-166.

60. *Ibid.*, pp. 130-133 and 144-145.

3. ARGUMENTS AGAINST FREE CHOICE

1. John Stuart Mill, *An Examination of Sir William Hamilton's Philosophy*, selection reprinted in *Free Will*, ed. Sidney Morgenbesser and James Walsh (Englewood Cliffs, N.J.: 1962), p. 60.

2. Brand Blanshard, "The Case for Determinism," in *Determinism and Freedom in the Age of Modern Science*, ed. Sidney Hook (New York: 1961), p. 21.

3. Steven M. Cahn, *Fate, Logic, and Time* (New Haven, London: 1967), defines (pp. 1-14) fatalism; he also provides an introduction to relevant literature. See especially Richard Taylor, "Fatalism," *Philosophical Review*, 71 (1962), pp. 56-66; *Metaphysics* (2nd ed.; Englewood Cliffs, N.J.: 1974), pp. 58-71. Our analysis of fatalism owes much to Vaughn R. McKim, "Fatalism and the Future: Aristotle's Way Out," *Review of Metaphysics*, 25 (1971), pp. 80-111.

4. Taylor, *Metaphysics*, p. 70. It is worth noting that while Taylor here distinguishes his position from that which depends upon the modal argument, he states (p. 68) his position in terms of the law of excluded middle, and argues in his article, "Fatalism," pp. 63-65, that one must give up the law of excluded middle to avoid fatalism. We recognize, of course, the distinction between the "can" of ability and other sorts of "can," but Taylor's emphasis on the ability-sense of "can" is not formally relevant to the force of the argument, for talk of human ability merely specifies the state of affairs (*R*) in our formulation of the argument. Raziel Abelson, "Taylor's Fatal Fallacy," *Philosophical Review*, 72 (1963), pp. 93-96, makes this point, but Taylor in his response—"A Note on Fatalism," *Philosophical Review*, 72 (1963), pp. 497-499— seems not to see its force.

5. Cahn, *op. cit.*, pp. 102-117, discusses the point and cites relevant literature; his interpretation of Aristotle seems to us poor compared with that proposed by McKim, *loc. cit.*

6. J. R. Lucas, *The Freedom of the Will* (Oxford: 1970), pp. 69-70, makes this point about two meanings of "true"; see also the works he cites.

7. Pierre Laplace, *Essai philosophique sur les probabilités* (Paris: 1814), p. 2 (trans. by Bernard Carroll, S.J.). For recent definitions of "determinism" in the relevant sense, see Richard Rudner, *Philosophy of Social Science* (Englewood Cliffs, N.J.: 1966), p.

91; Peter van Inwagen, "A Formal Approach to the Problem of Free Will and Determinism," *Theoria,* 40 (1974), p. 11.

8. Lucas, *op. cit.,* p. 84.

9. Henry Sidgwick, *The Methods of Ethics* (7th ed.; New York: 1966), pp. 62-63. See also Lucas, *op. cit.,* pp. 84-106, for an exposition and critique of physical determinism; Richard Taylor, "Determinism," *Encyclopedia of Philosophy,* vol. 2, pp. 363-365, for a brief exposition. Hobbes, *On Human Nature,* vol. 4, *The English Works of Thomas Hobbes,* ed. Sir William Molesworth (London: 1840), gives a classic exposition of this view; see especially chapter 12, pp. 67-70. J. J. C. Smart, *Philosophy and Scientific Realism* (New York, London: 1963), provides a typical, recent example; see esp. pp. 8, 15, 47, and 68.

10. Paul Rée, "Determinism and the Illusion of Moral Responsibility," in *A Modern Introduction to Philosophy,* ed. P. Edwards and A. Pap (3rd ed.; New York: 1973), pp. 14-15.

11. Jonathan Glover, *Responsibility* (New York: 1970), pp. 21-23, defines determinism as an empirical hypothesis about human behavior.

12. R. B. Brandt and J. Kim, "Wants as Explanations of Actions," *Journal of Philosophy,* 60 (1963), p. 435.

13. See Max Black, "Making Something Happen," in Hook, ed., *op. cit.,* pp. 44-45; "I have been arguing that 'cause' is an essentially schematic word, tied to certain more or less stable criteria of application, but permitting wide variation of specific determination according to context and the purposes of investigation. Now, if this is so, any attempt to state a 'universal law of causation' must prove futile. To anybody who insists that 'nothing happens without a sufficient cause' we are entitled to retort with the question, 'What do you *mean* by "cause"?' It is safe to predict that the only answer forthcoming will contain such schematic words as 'event,' 'law,' and 'prediction.' These, too, are words capable of indefinite further determination according to circumstances—and they are none the worse for that. But universal statements containing schematic words have no place in rational argument. The fatal defect of determinism is its protean capacity to elude refutation—by the same token, its informative content is negligible. Whatever virtues it may have in encouraging scientists to search for comprehensive laws and theories, there can be no rational dispute about its truth value. Many of the traditional problems of causation disappear when we become sufficiently clear about what we mean by 'cause' and remind ourselves once more of what a peculiar, unsystematic, and erratic notion it is."

14. Bernard Berofsky, *Determinism* (Princeton: 1971), has dealt with many objections which attempt to show determinism meaningless; see esp. part 3, pp. 273-324. See also Glover, *op. cit.,* pp. 21-28.

15. See A. C. MacIntyre, "Determinism," *Mind,* 66 (1957), pp. 39-40: ". . . if determinism rests its hopes on this complex pattern of explanation I find it difficult to see how determinism could ever be verified or falsified. For suppose that the determinist is able to supply a complete explanation of my behaviour in causal terms. Suppose also that my behaviour is rational, that whatever strong reasons are adduced for acting in a certain way I act in that way, that I am infinitely flexible and resourceful in meeting new contingencies. Then no test will be available to decide whether I act as I do because it is the rational way to act or because it is the way in which my deeds are causally determined. For on either supposition I will do the same things. To try and include my reasonableness in a story about causal factors is to try and produce a story about my behaviour sufficiently comprehensive to include everything."

16. Glover, *op. cit.*, p. 23.

17. See, e.g., Arthur Holly Compton, *The Freedom of Man* (New Haven: 1935), pp. 38 ff.; Clark Glymour, "Determinism, Ignorance, and Quantum Mechanics," *Journal of Philosophy*, 68 (1971), pp. 744-751; J. M. Jauch, *Are Quanta Real?* (Bloomington, Ill.: 1973); Alfred Lande, "The Case for Indeterminism," in Hook, ed., *op. cit.*, pp. 83-89; Henry Margenau, "The Philosophical Legacy of Contemporary Quantum Theory," in *Mind and Cosmos*, ed. Robert G. Colodny (Pittsburgh: 1966), p. 354. A typical example of the opposing view is Dennis W. Sciama, "Determinism and the Cosmos," in Hook, ed., *op. cit.*, pp. 90-91. Sciama bases his case against indeterminism on the possibility of hidden variables in subatomic physical systems apparently indeterministic in nature. But see Jauch, pp. 101-102, on the thus far negative results of scientific efforts to find evidence to support the hidden-variable thesis. To some extent, the dispute appears to be wholly philosophical; see, e.g., S. Körner, "On Philosophical Arguments in Physics," in *Observation and Interpretation*, ed. S. Körner (London: 1957), pp. 97-101; and Philipp Frank, "Einstein, Mach and Logical Positivism," in *Albert Einstein: Philosopher-Scientist*, ed. Paul Arthur Schilpp (Evanston, Ill.: 1949), pp. 271-286.

18. Felix Mainx, *Foundations of Biology* (Chicago: 1955), p. 74. J.J.C. Smart, *op. cit.*, p. 123, makes the same point.

19. See Sir John Eccles, "Science and Freedom," *Humanist*, 32 (1972), pp. 15-18, on the relatively rudimentary state of scientific theory about brain processes.

20. Karl Popper, *Of Clouds and Clocks* (St. Louis: 1966), pp. 13-14, advances the same objection against Compton's attempt to explain the relationship between quantum indeterminacy and human decisions.

21. Cf. Ernst Cassirer, *Determinism and Indeterminism in Modern Physics* (New Haven, London: 1956), pp. 207-213.

22. Erwin Schrödinger, *Science and Humanism* (Cambridge: 1951), pp. 60-61 (emphasis his). See also F. S. C. Northrup, *The Logic of the Sciences and the Humanities* (New York: 1959), ch. 11, for an analysis of statistical laws in quantum mechanics.

23. Frederick Ferré, "Self-Determinism," *American Philosophical Quarterly*, 10 (1973), p. 165, makes a complementary point. He argues that quantum indeterminacy leaves no room for "ambiguities" of outcome at any level.

24. Carl G. Hempel, "Scientific Explanation," in *Philosophy of Science Today*, ed. Sidney Morgenbesser (New York: 1967), pp. 79-88. We do not endorse the deductive-nomological model but only point out the role it—and similar philosophical interpretations of science—can play in making plausible a deterministic worldview.

25. Jacques Monod, *Chance and Necessity* (New York: 1971), p. 21. Another restriction is suggested by Egon Brunswik, *The Conceptual Framework of Psychology* (Chicago: 1952), pp. 10-11.

26. Werner Heisenberg, *The Physicist's Conception of Nature* (London: 1958), pp. 180-181 (emphasis his).

27. Michael Scriven, "Explanations, Predictions, and Laws," in *Readings in the Philosophy of Science*, ed. Baruch Brody (Englewood Cliffs, N.J.: 1970), p. 100.

28. See Thomas Hobbes, *The Questions concerning Liberty, Necessity, and Chance*, in Molesworth, ed., *op. cit.*, vol. 5, pp. 105 and 303.

29. Smart, *op. cit.*, p. 8.

30. *Ibid.*, p. 68.

31. *Ibid.*, p. 47 (emphasis his).

32. *Ibid.*, pp. 120-126.

33. We assume that this extrascientific inquiry is philosophy. Philosophy need not be regarded as a mixed bag, partly mysticism, partly logic, and partly legitimate inquiry, with all the latter part destined to be parceled out in due time to another type of inquiry—science.

34. Sidgwick, *op. cit.,* p. 64.

35. P. H. Nowell-Smith, "Free Will and Moral Responsibility," *Mind,* 57 (1948), p. 47.

36. John Hospers, *Human Conduct: Problems of Ethics* (shorter ed.; New York, Chicago, San Francisco, Atlanta: 1972), pp. 397-453; he refers the reader to other works of his developing the bearing of psychoanalysis upon responsibility.

37. Ernest Jones, *Essays in Applied Psychoanalysis* (New York: 1964), vol. 2, pp. 184-186.

38. Sigmund Freud, *Psychopathology of Everyday Life,* in *Basic Writings of Sigmund Freud,* ed. A. A. Brill (New York: 1938), pp. 161-162.

39. Sigmund Freud, *Introductory Lectures on Psychoanalysis,* ed. James Strachey and Anna Freud (London: 1963), p. 28.

40. St. Thomas Aquinas, *Summa theologiae,* 1-2, q. 13, a. 6, obj. 3. While the statement of the objection here is clear, the response in *Summa theologiae,* 1, q. 82, a. 2, ad 1, seems more precise.

41. W. D. Ross, *Foundations of Ethics* (Oxford: 1939), p. 230.

42. Joseph Priestley, *The Doctrine of Philosophical Necessity Illustrated* (London: 1782), pp. 56-57, provides a classic statement of the argument. Rem Blanchard Edwards, *Freedom, Responsibility and Obligation* (The Hague: 1969), provides (p. 2, note 2), additional bibliography and criticizes (pp. 2-17) this argument.

43. George E. Hughes, "Motive and Duty," *Mind,* 53 (1944), p. 317, makes this point clearly. See also Edwards, *op. cit.,* p. 12. Many authors who approach the point express their insight in a confusing way, suggesting that the act of choice somehow adds to the strength or attractiveness of one purpose.

44. Morton White, "Positive Freedom, Negative Freedom and Possibility," *Journal of Philosophy,* 70 (1973), pp. 315-316.

45. For discussion and bibliography, see K. W. Rankin, *Choice and Chance* (Oxford: 1961), pp. 4-12; Mortimer J. Adler, *The Idea of Freedom* (2 vols.; Garden City, N.Y.: 1958, 1961), vol. 2, pp. 294-302 and 488-525; J. R. Lucas, *op. cit.,* pp. 55-59; Lawrence D. Roberts, "Indeterminism, Chance, and Responsibility," *Ratio,* 13 (1971), pp. 195-199; James N. Jordan, "On Comprehending Free Will," *Southern Journal of Philosophy,* 11 (1973), pp. 193-195.

46. Philippa Foot, "Free Will as Involving Determinism," in *Free Will and Determinism,* ed. Bernard Berofsky (New York, London: 1966), pp. 95-108.

47. A. C. MacIntyre, *op. cit.,* p. 30.

48. A. J. Ayer, *The Concept of a Person and Other Essays* (London, New York: 1963), p. 255.

49. A. J. Ayer, *Philosophical Essays* (London, New York: 1954), p. 275.

50. Foot, *op. cit.,* pp. 106-107.

51. Lucas, *op. cit.,* p. 58 (emphasis his); see also Roberts, *loc. cit.,* who points out ambiguities in "chance" and shows their relevance to this argument.

52. See C. A. Campbell, *On Selfhood and Godhood* (London, New York: 1957), p. 255.

53. *Ibid.,* p. 176.

54. J. J. C. Smart, *Between Science and Philosophy* (New York: 1968), p. 300.

55. Campbell, *op. cit.,* pp. 177-178.

56. R. E. Hobart, "Free Will as Involving Determinism and Inconceivable without It," in Berofsky, ed., *op. cit.*, pp. 67-68.

57. David Hume, *A Treatise of Human Nature*, ed. L. A. Selby-Bigge (Oxford: 1888), p. 411.

58. Hobart, *op. cit.*, pp. 70-71 (emphasis his).

59. Foot, *op. cit.*, p. 105.

60. F. H. Bradley, *Ethical Studies* (2nd ed.; Oxford: 1927), p. 11 (emphasis his).

61. Hobart, *op. cit.*, p. 67.

62. R. L. Franklin, *Freewill and Determinism: A Study of Rival Conceptions of Man* (London, New York: 1968), pp. 216-220 and 285-301, esp. pp. 298-299, clearly sees the role of the principle of sufficient reason in the arguments of the *PNfc*.

63. This formulation of the principle is taken from the *Monadology*, sec. 32, trans. Robert Latta (London: 1898), p. 235. A critique and selection of relevant passages may be found in Bertrand Russell, *A Critical Exposition of the Philosophy of Leibniz* (Cambridge: 1900), pp. 25-39 and 209-212.

64. Taylor, *Metaphysics*, p. 104.

65. Laplace, *loc. cit.*

66. Taylor, *op. cit.*, p. 39.

67. Hobart, *op. cit.*, p. 80.

68. *Ibid.*, p. 83.

69. Roderick Chisholm, "Freedom and Action," in *Freedom and Determinism*, ed. Keith Lehrer (New York: 1966), p. 23.

70. Russell, *op. cit.*, pp. 54-63 and 219-222, quotes the relevant texts and shows the implications of the principle both for Leibniz's own thought and beyond the limits which Leibniz wished to set. We do not treat Leibniz's own views on freedom here, for we regard him as a compatibilist; see Adler, *op. cit.*, vol. 1, pp. 539-545, for an exposition of Leibniz's views.

71. J. J. C. Smart, "The Existence of God," in *New Essays in Philosophical Theology*, ed. Alasdair MacIntyre and Antony Flew (London: 1955), p. 46.

72. W. V. O. Quine, *From a Logical Point of View* (Cambridge, Mass.: 1953), p. 44.

73. John Dewey, *On Experience, Nature, and Freedom*, ed. Richard Bernstein (Indianapolis, New York: 1960), p. 284.

74. John Dewey, *Human Nature and Conduct* (New York: 1957), p. 309.

75. *Ibid.*, p. 305.

76. Dewey, *On Experience, Nature, and Freedom, loc. cit.*

77. Edward B. Tylor, "The Science of Culture," in *Readings in Anthropology*, ed. Morton H. Freid (New York: 1959), vol. 2, p. 4.

78. B. F. Skinner, *Beyond Freedom and Dignity* (New York: 1971), pp. 3-25.

79. B. F. Skinner, *Science and Human Behavior* (New York: 1953), p. 116.

80. William James, "The Dilemma of Determinism," in *The Will to Believe and Other Essays in Popular Philosophy* (New York: 1897), pp. 146-183.

81. See Skinner, *Science and Human Behavior*, pp. 426-436.

82. Karl Popper, *Conjectures and Refutations: The Growth of Scientific Knowledge* (London: 1963), p. 339.

83. *Ibid.*, pp. 342-343 (emphasis his).

84. Thomas Hobbes, in Molesworth, ed., *op. cit.*, vol. 5, pp. 428-429.

85. E.g., Lucas, *op. cit.*, pp. 75-76, seems to accept some limitation of God by himself in order to dissolve the traditional problem.

86. See Adler, *op. cit.*, vol. 2, pp. 467-473, for examples of theological compatibilism and a useful bibliography. See also *ibid.*, vol. 1, pp. 448-449, where Adler provides a reference to Molina and a brief discussion of *scientia media*. Molina's solution has two implications: that each individual's free acts are free only in the sense that they proceed from his individuality, and that even prior to God's practical knowledge an individual would do these acts. The first implication seems incompatible with *Sfc*; Molina seems to be a compatibilist like Leibniz. The second implication seems incompatible with the Christian teaching on grace which was clarified against Pelagius.

87. Cf. Campbell, *op. cit.*, pp. 171-172.

88. Henry L. Mansel, *Prolegomena Logica* (Oxford: 1851), pp. 304-305.

89. St. Thomas Aquinas, *Summa theologiae*, 1-2, q. 10, a. 4. The translation we provide is free; the text reads as follows: "Respondeo dicendum quod, sicut Dionysius dicit, 'ad providentiam divinam non pertinet naturam rerum corrumpere, sed servare' (*De divinis nominibus,* c. iv). Unde omnia movet secundum eorum conditionem: ita quod ex causis necessariis per motionem divinam consequuntur effectus ex necessitate; ex causis autem contingentibus sequuntur effectus contingenter. Quia igitur voluntas est activum principium non determinatum ad unum, sed indifferenter se habens ad multa, sic Deus ipsam movet, quod non ex necessitate ad unum determinat, sed remanet motus eius contingens et non necessarius, nisi in his ad quae naturaliter movetur."

90. For a more extended discussion, see Germain Grisez, *Beyond the New Theism: A Philosophy of Religion* (Notre Dame, London: 1975), pp. 241-272. This work grew out of an early draft of the present, brief section. The topic proved too large for adequate treatment as part of a work primarily devoted to freedom.

4. COMPATIBILISM

1. Michel du Bay, *De libero hominis arbitrio eiusque potestate* (Louvain: 1563), chapter 7, writing twenty-five years before the birth of Hobbes, gives a precise formulation of compatibilism: "What comes about voluntarily comes about freely even if it comes about necessarily."

2. Richard Taylor, "Determinism," *Encyclopedia of Philosophy,* vol. 2, p. 366.

3. Thus the reconciliationist attempt need not be based exclusively upon the compatibility with *Nfc* of physical freedom and freedom to do as one pleases. One also can focus upon creative or ideal freedom. Spinoza emphasizes ideal freedom; for an example of reconciliationism emphasizing creative freedom, see John Dewey, "Philosophies of Freedom," in *On Experience, Nature, and Freedom,* ed. Richard Bernstein (Indianapolis, New York: 1960), pp. 283-284.

4. This point does not modify our negative evaluation of this sort of argument; our present point concerns the meaning of "free choice," not the truth of *Sfc*.

5. J. R. Lucas, *The Freedom of the Will* (Oxford: 1970), pp. 22-26, makes several of the same points we make here and cites relevant literature. He expresses (p. 15) the same skepticism we do about the expectation that a philosophical dispute can be settled by stipulating a meaning for a key word.

6. Myles Brand, "Introduction: Ability, Possibility, and Power," in *The Nature of Human Action,* ed. Myles Brand (Glenview, Ill.: 1970), pp. 129-130, makes such a point in respect to Austin's arguments that not all *cans* are constitutionally *iffy.*

7. Lucas, *op. cit.*, p. 21, makes the same point and calls soft determinism a "salvage

operation, to enable the cornered determinist to continue using the everyday concepts of praise, blame, reward, and punishment, or something very like them, in spite of his disbelief in freedom."

8. G. N. A. Vesey, "Agent and Spectator: The Double-Aspect Theory," in *Royal Institute of Philosophy Lectures,* vol. 1, *The Human Agent* (London, New York: 1968), pp. 139-159, relates the position with which we are concerned here to a wider context; we adopt his felicitous name for the position but use it in a specific sense.

9. A. I. Melden, *Free Action* (London, New York: 1961), p. 184; cf. pp. 201-202, where Melden characterizes the supposed error he is dealing with as a "category mistake." He thinks that "the trouble is that the applicability in principle of the causal model is taken for granted." But Melden does not show that the determinist is making a category mistake rather than a false statement. It seems clear to us that many determinists either assert that the causal model is applicable in principle to human acts or assert a proposition which entails this, and that they regard such assertions precisely as what they hold. If such assertions are false, determinists are in error, not confused.

10. The literature is vast. A few treatments which are either seminal or recent and important are: C. I. Lewis, *Mind and the World Order: Outline of a Theory of Knowledge* (New York: 1956), pp. 139-143; *An Analysis of Knowledge and Valuation* (LaSalle, Ill.: 1946), pp. 3, 6, 16-17, and esp. 203-206 and 480-481; Arthur Edward Murphy, *The Theory of Practical Reason,* ed. A. I. Melden (LaSalle, Ill.: 1964), pp. 181-182; F. Waismann, "Language Strata," in *Logic and Language, Second Series,* ed. Antony Flew (New York: 1953), pp. 28-31; D. M. MacKay, "On the Logical Indeterminacy of a Free Choice," *Mind,* 69 (1960), pp. 31-40; Anthony Kenny, "Freedom, Spontaneity and Indifference," in *Essays on Freedom of Action,* ed. Ted Honderich (London, Boston: 1973), pp. 89-104.

11. Stuart Hampshire, *Freedom of the Individual* (London: 1965), p. 111, rejects the replacement of the language of action with a "neutral language of natural law," but leaves open the possibility that "some other thesis of determinism" might be applicable to human actions.

12. Wilfrid Sellars, *Science, Perception and Reality* (London, New York: 1963), seems to espouse a version of this possibility when he says (p. 40) that the conceptual framework of persons completes the scientific image "*not* with more ways of saying what is the case, but with the language of community and individual intentions. . ." (emphasis his).

13. Richard Rorty, "Mind-Body Identity, Privacy and Categories," *Review of Metaphysics,* 19 (1965), pp. 24-54, makes a plausible case for the elimination of ordinary language about sensations. We think a similarly plausible case could be made for the elimination of the language of action, provided that one is willing to accept all the implications of determinism.

14. Lucas, *op. cit.,* pp. 17-18, makes the same point.

15. All quotations from this work in the text are from: Immanuel Kant, *Critique of Pure Reason,* trans. Norman Kemp Smith (London, New York: 1929).

16. Lewis White Beck, *A Commentary on Kant's Critique of Practical Reason* (Chicago: 1960), p. 192. John R. Silber, "The Ethical Significance of Kant's *Religion,*" in Immanuel Kant, *Religion within the Limits of Reason Alone,* trans. T. M. Greene and Hoyt H. Hudson (New York: 1960), pp. xciv-ciii, provides an analysis which confirms ours of the problems raised by Kant's solution to the third antinomy.

17. Lucas, *op. cit.,* p. 18.

18. Lucas, *ibid.,* provides a similar example.

19. Hegel is perhaps the most important philosopher who holds a point-of-view theory of reconciling what would otherwise be contradictions. He thinks he can surmount all antinomies by moving to a higher viewpoint in the dialectic; his inconsistency appears in his inability in principle to reconcile the viewpoint of the Absolute with those of its moments, since there is no higher viewpoint from which one can regard both the Absolute and its moments.

20. We realize that many philosophers would reject what we say here about propositional knowledge, inasmuch as we deny conceptual relativism. This topic, if pursued, would open too wide an area of debate for adequate treatment in the present work. We think that a valid defense of the nonrelativity of propositional knowledge is presented by Roger Trigg, *Reason and Commitment* (Cambridge: 1973).

5. PRELIMINARIES TO THE ARGUMENT

1. Our notion of propositional acts is somewhat like J. L. Austin's notion of illocutionary acts and R. M. Hare's notion of the neustic component of a sentence. However, we are not prepared to commit ourselves to the view that propositional acts are exclusively linguistic.

2. See Plato, *Theatetus* 182D-183B; Aristotle, *Metaphysics* iv, 1005b6-1012b31.

3. C. K. Grant, "Pragmatic Implication," *Philosophy*, 33 (1958), p. 309.

4. Bertrand Russell and Alfred North Whitehead, *Principia Mathematica* (2nd ed.; Cambridge: 1927), vol. 1, pp. 37-38 and 60-65.

5. *Ibid.*, p. 38.

6. J. R. Lucas, *The Freedom of the Will* (Oxford: 1970), pp. 116-120, cites this point as one of the reasons why philosophers remain skeptical about the effectiveness of the argument that determinism is self-refuting.

7. See Frederic Fitch, "Self-Reference and Philosophy," *Mind*, 55 (1946), pp. 64-73; Jørgen Jørgensen, "Some Reflexions on Reflexivity," *Mind*, 62 (1953), pp. 289-290; and R. L. Martin, "Towards a Solution of the Liar Paradox," *Philosophical Review*, 76 (1967), pp. 279-311.

8. See Robert J. Richman, "On the Self-Reference of a Meaning Theory," *Philosophical Studies*, 4 (1953), pp. 69-72.

9. See W. V. O. Quine, *The Ways of Paradox* (New York: 1966), pp. 4 and 13-14.

10. *Ibid.*, pp. 8-12.

11. See Jørgensen, *op. cit.*, pp. 290-291; Alf Ross, "On Self-Reference and a Puzzle in Constitutional Law," *Mind*, 78 (1969), pp. 7-12; Gilbert Ryle, "Heterologicality," *Analysis*, 11 (1950-1951), pp. 67-68.

12. W. D. Hart, "On Self-Reference," *Philosophical Review*, 79 (1970), pp. 523-528, points out that there are logical peculiarities in certain of the statements we call "performatively self-referential." In those performatively self-referential statements where the reference is to the sentence as a sentence in a particular language, translation can become problematical. But this difficulty is not as troublesome as Hart suggests, since translation does not preserve the statement, but only the proposition. Obviously, the proposition in a performatively self-referential statement—as distinct from a performatively self-referential proposition—in which the reference is to the sentence as an instance of a particular language will not be self-referential when translated into some other language.

13. Jaakko Hintikka, *Knowledge and Belief* (Ithaca, N.Y.: 1962), pp. 64-78, provides a discussion of Moore's paradox of saying and disbelieving. Hintikka's notion of doxastic indefensibility is somewhat similar to our notion of self-defeat.

14. James N. Jordan, "Determinism's Dilemma," *Review of Metaphysics,* 23 (1969), pp. 50, 64, and 66.

15. David Wiggins, "Freedom, Knowledge, Belief and Causality," in *Royal Institute of Philosophy Lectures,* vol. 3, *Knowledge and Necessity* (London: 1970), p. 134 (emphasis his).

16. See Jaakko Hintikka, "*Cogito ergo Sum*: Performance or Inference?" *Philosophical Review,* 71 (1962), pp. 3-32.

17. See Richard Rorty, "The Limits of Reductionism," in *Experience, Existence and the Good,* ed. I. Lieb (Carbondale, Ill.: 1961), pp. 104-107.

18. Lionel Kenner, "Causality, Determinism and the Will," *Philosophy,* 39 (1964), p. 234, points out that it may be less easy than one might suppose to utter a deterministic hypothesis simply as a heuristic principle: "Now, it is customary these days to treat 'Every event has a cause' as a heuristic maxim. It is certainly true that the proposition can neither be proved nor disproved, but it would be a joke in very bad taste for an elderly scientist to tell his apprentices that they must always go on looking for a cause unless the elderly scientist believed that there, in fact, always *was* a cause. 'Always look for a cause' is only honest advice if it is believed that there always is a cause. When the determinist formulates his position in terms of causality the proposition 'Every event must have a cause' must be taken as a statement of fact. It is quite another matter that this key proposition in the formulation of the determinist position can neither be proved nor disproved" (emphasis his).

19. John R. Searle, *Speech Acts: An Essay in the Philosophy of Language* (Cambridge: 1969), pp. 54-71.

20. Wilfrid Sellars, "Language as Thought and as Communication," *Philosophy and Phenomenological Research,* 29 (1969), p. 511 (emphasis his).

21. Wilfrid Sellars, *Science and Metaphysics: Variations on Kantian Themes* (London, New York: 1968), p. 175.

22. Roderick M. Chisholm, *Perceiving: A Philosophical Study* (Ithaca, N.Y.: 1957), pp. 3-39 and 96-112; *Theory of Knowledge* (Englewood Cliffs, N.J.: 1966), pp. 38-55; "On the Nature of Empirical Evidence," in *Empirical Knowledge: Readings from Contemporary Sources,* ed. Roderick M. Chisholm and Robert J. Schwartz (Englewood Cliffs, N.J.: 1973), pp. 224-249; *The Problem of the Criterion* (Milwaukee: 1973), pp. 33-37.

23. W. V. O. Quine, *The Roots of Reference* (LaSalle, Ill.: 1973), p. 138.

24. Arthur Edward Murphy, *The Theory of Practical Reason,* ed. A. I. Melden (LaSalle, Ill.: 1964), p. 182.

25. Max Black, *Margins of Precision* (Ithaca, London: 1970), pp. 86-89.

26. See Jonathan Glover, *Responsibility* (New York: 1970), p. 23, note 1: The hypothesis that a machine is governed by causal laws ". . . is only verified, strictly speaking, when it is the *simplest* hypothesis to give the greatest power of successful prediction. It is notoriously true that logically incompatible theories can generate identical predictions. Although the notion of simplicity must be invoked here to explain how determinism is verifiable, I shall not attempt the difficult task of analysing the concept" (emphasis his).

27. Richard Taylor, *Metaphysics* (2nd ed.; Englewood Cliffs, N.J.: 1974), p. 105.

28. Wilfrid Sellars, *Science, Perception and Reality* (New York, London: 1963), p. 355.

29. Chisholm, "On the Nature of Empirical Evidence," p. 241.

6. FREE CHOICE ESTABLISHED

1. Immanuel Kant, *Critique of Practical Reason,* in *Kant's Critique of Practical Reason and Other Works on the Theory of Ethics,* trans. T. K. Abbott (4th ed., rev.; London: 1889), pp. 116-117 and 131-133.

2. Michael Slote, *Reason and Scepticism* (London, New York: 1970), pp. 99-100.

3. For a more extensive discussion of rationality norms as the ethics of inquiry and a comparison of them with Kant's notion of regulative principles, see Germain Grisez, *Beyond the New Theism: A Philosophy of Religion* (Notre Dame, London: 1975), pp. 76-81 and 168-172.

Index